MARVEL UNIVERSE AVENGERS ASSEMBLE VOL. 2. Contains material originally published in magazine form as MARVEL UNIVERSE AVENGERS ASSEMBLE #5-8. First printing 2014. ISBN# 978-0-7851-8880-3. Published by MARVEL WORLDWIDE, INC., a subsidiary of MARVEL ENTERTAINMENT, LLC. OFFICE OF PUBLICATION: 135 West 50th Street, New York, NY 10020. Copyright © 2014 Marvel Characters, Inc. All rights reserved. All characters featured in this issue and the distinctive names and likenesses thereof, and all related indicia are trademarks of Marvel Characters, Inc. No similarity between any of the names, characters, persons, and/or institutions in this magazine with those of any living or dead person or institution is intended, and any such similarity which may exist is purely coincidental. **Printed in the U.S.A.** ALAN FINE, EVP - Office of the President, Marvel Worldwide, Inc. and EVP & CMO Marvel Characters B.V.; DAN BUCKLEY, Publisher & President - Print, Animation & Digital Divisions; JOE QUESADA, Chief Creative Officer; TOM BREVOORT, SVP of Publishing; DAVID BOGART, SVP of Operations & Procurement, Publishing; C.B. CEBULSKI, SVP of Creator & Content Development; DAVID GABRIEL, SVP Print, Sales & Marketing; JIM O'KEEFE, VP of Operations & Logistics; DAN CARR, Executive Director of Publishing Technology; SUSAN CRESPI, Editorial Operations Manager; ALEX MORALES, Publishing Operations Manager; STAN LEE, Chairman Emeritus. For information regarding advertising in Marvel Comics or on Marvel.com, please contact Niza Disla, Director of Marvel Partnerships, at ndisla@marvel.com. For Marvel subscription inquiries, please call 800-217-9158. **Manufactured between 6/6/2014 and 7/14/2014 by SHERIDAN BOOKS, INC., CHELSEA, MI, USA.**

10 9 8 7 6 5 4 3 2 1

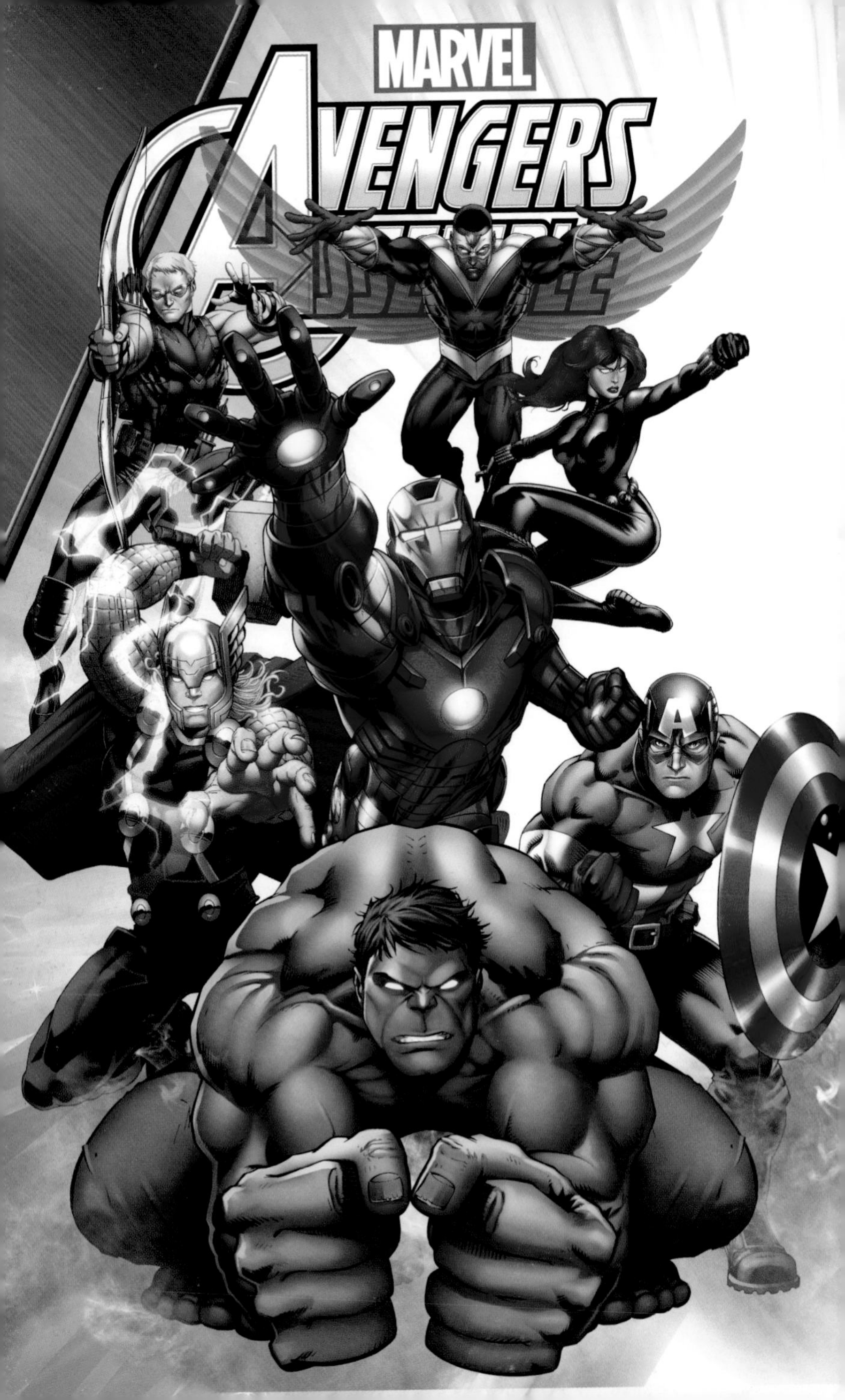
MARVEL
AVENGERS

Based on the TV series episodes by
**MAN OF ACTION, KEVIN BURKE,
CHRIS "DOC" WYATT,
ED VALENTINE, JACOB SEMAHN
& DANIELLE WOLFF**

Adapted by
JOE CARAMAGNA

Editor
SEBASTIAN GIRNER

Consulting Editor
JON MOISAN

Senior Editor
MARK PANICCIA

Collection Editor
ALEX STARBUCK

Assistant Editor
SARAH BRUNSTAD

Editors, Special Projects
**JENNIFER GRÜNWALD
& MARK D. BEAZLEY**

Senior Editor, Special Projects
JEFF YOUNGQUIST

SVP Print, Sales & Marketing
DAVID GABRIEL

Editor In Chief
AXEL ALONSO

Chief Creative Officer
JOE QUESADA

Publisher
DAN BUCKLEY

Executive Producer
ALAN FINE

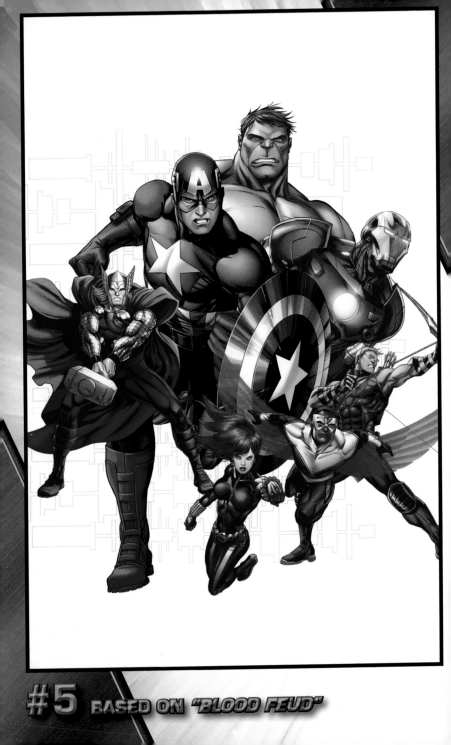

#5 BASED ON *"BLOOD FEUD"*

MARVEL
AVENGERS ASSEMBLE

IRON MAN

CAPTAIN AMERICA

THOR

BLACK WIDOW

HAWKEYE

HULK

FALCON

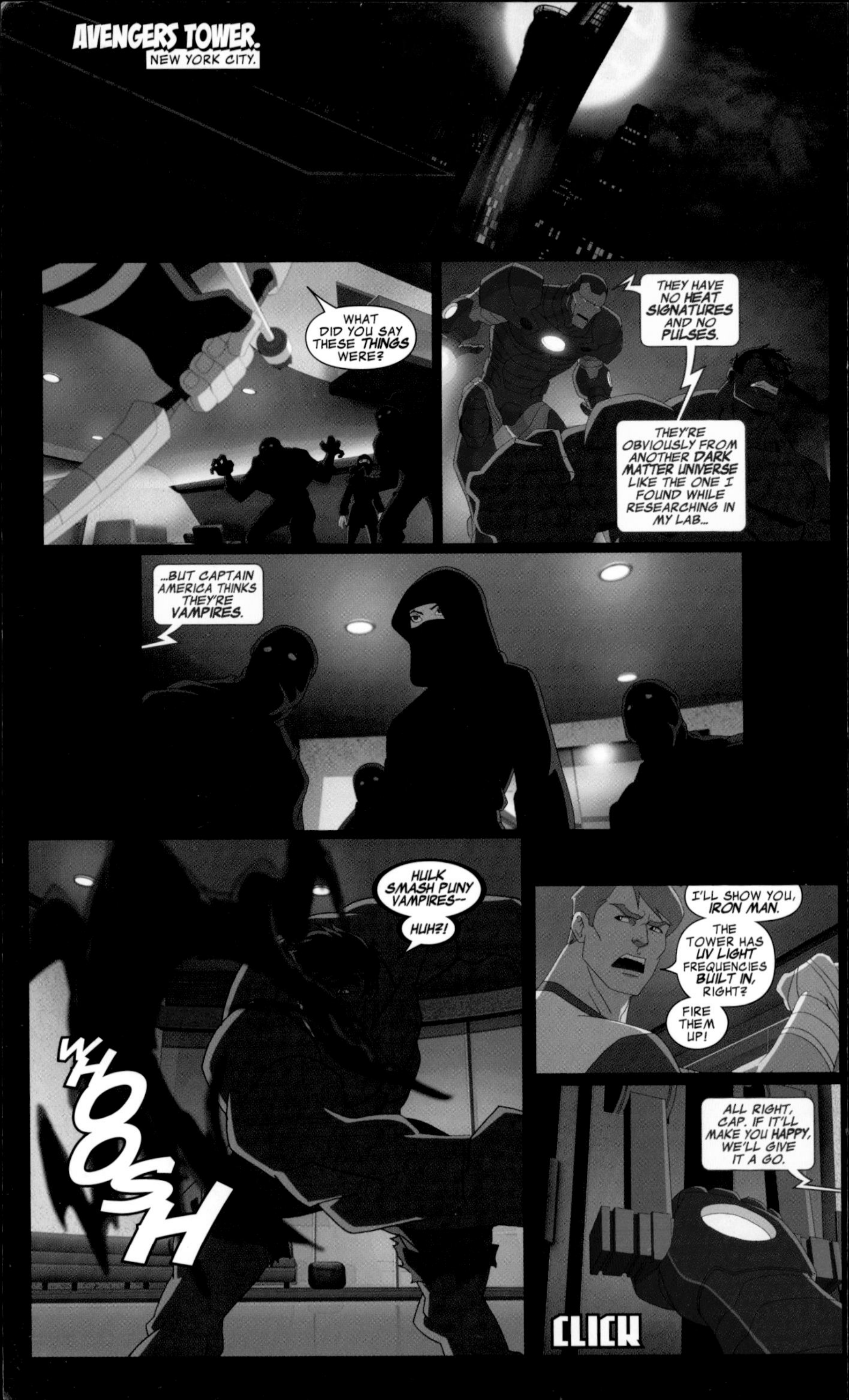
AVENGERS TOWER.
NEW YORK CITY.
WHAT DID YOU SAY THESE THINGS WERE?
THEY HAVE NO HEAT SIGNATURES AND NO PULSES.
THEY'RE OBVIOUSLY FROM ANOTHER DARK MATTER UNIVERSE LIKE THE ONE I FOUND WHILE RESEARCHING IN MY LAB...
...BUT CAPTAIN AMERICA THINKS THEY'RE VAMPIRES.
HULK SMASH PUNY VAMPIRES--
HUH?!
WHOOSH
I'LL SHOW YOU, IRON MAN.
THE TOWER HAS UV LIGHT FREQUENCIES BUILT IN, RIGHT?
FIRE THEM UP!
ALL RIGHT, CAP. IF IT'LL MAKE YOU HAPPY, WE'LL GIVE IT A GO.
CLICK

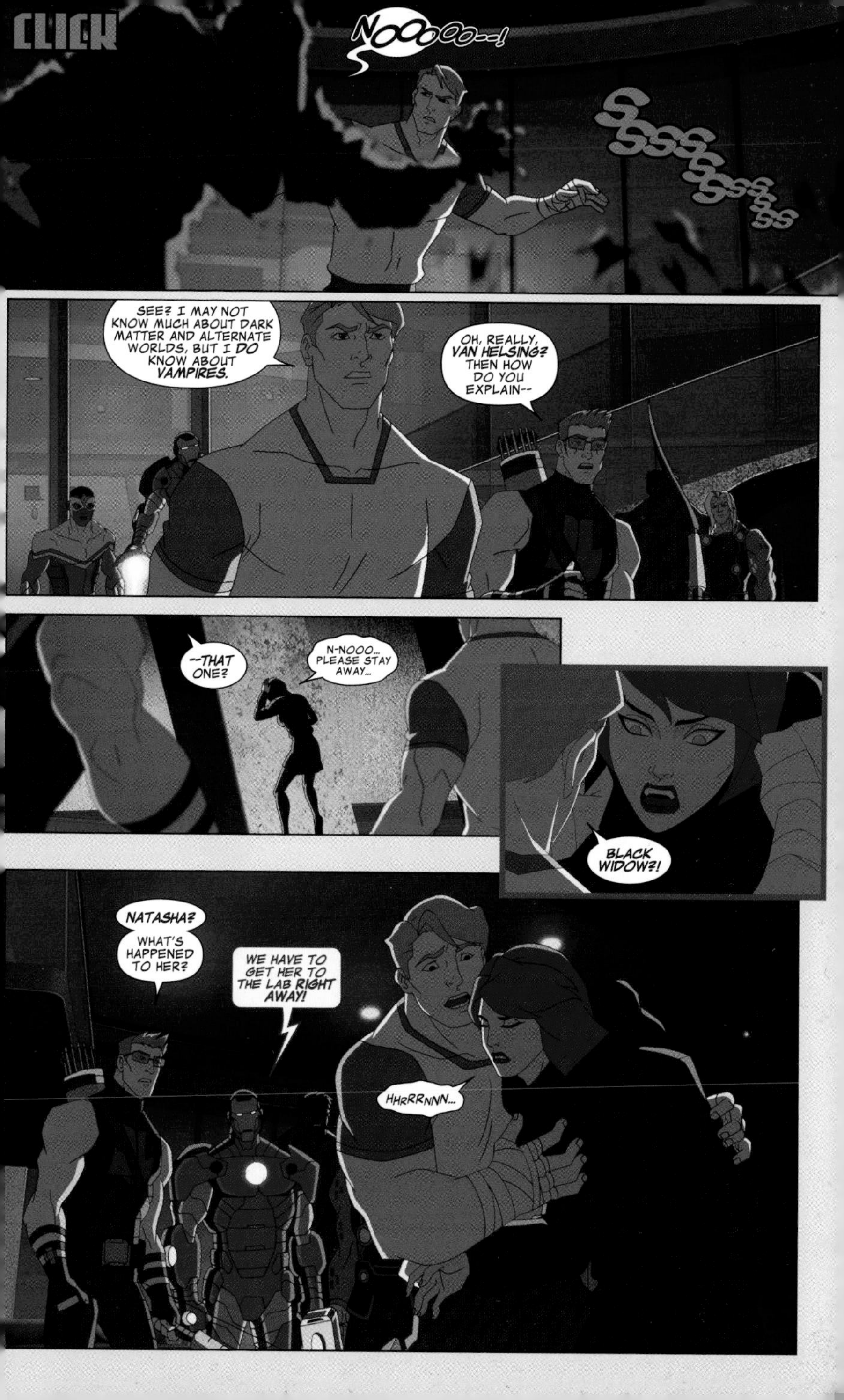
CLICK
NOOOOOO--!
SSSSSSSSSS
SEE? I MAY NOT KNOW MUCH ABOUT DARK MATTER AND ALTERNATE WORLDS, BUT I DO KNOW ABOUT VAMPIRES.
OH, REALLY, VAN HELSING? THEN HOW DO YOU EXPLAIN--
--THAT ONE?
N-NOOO... PLEASE STAY AWAY...
BLACK WIDOW?!
NATASHA? WHAT'S HAPPENED TO HER?
WE HAVE TO GET HER TO THE LAB RIGHT AWAY!
HHRRNNN...

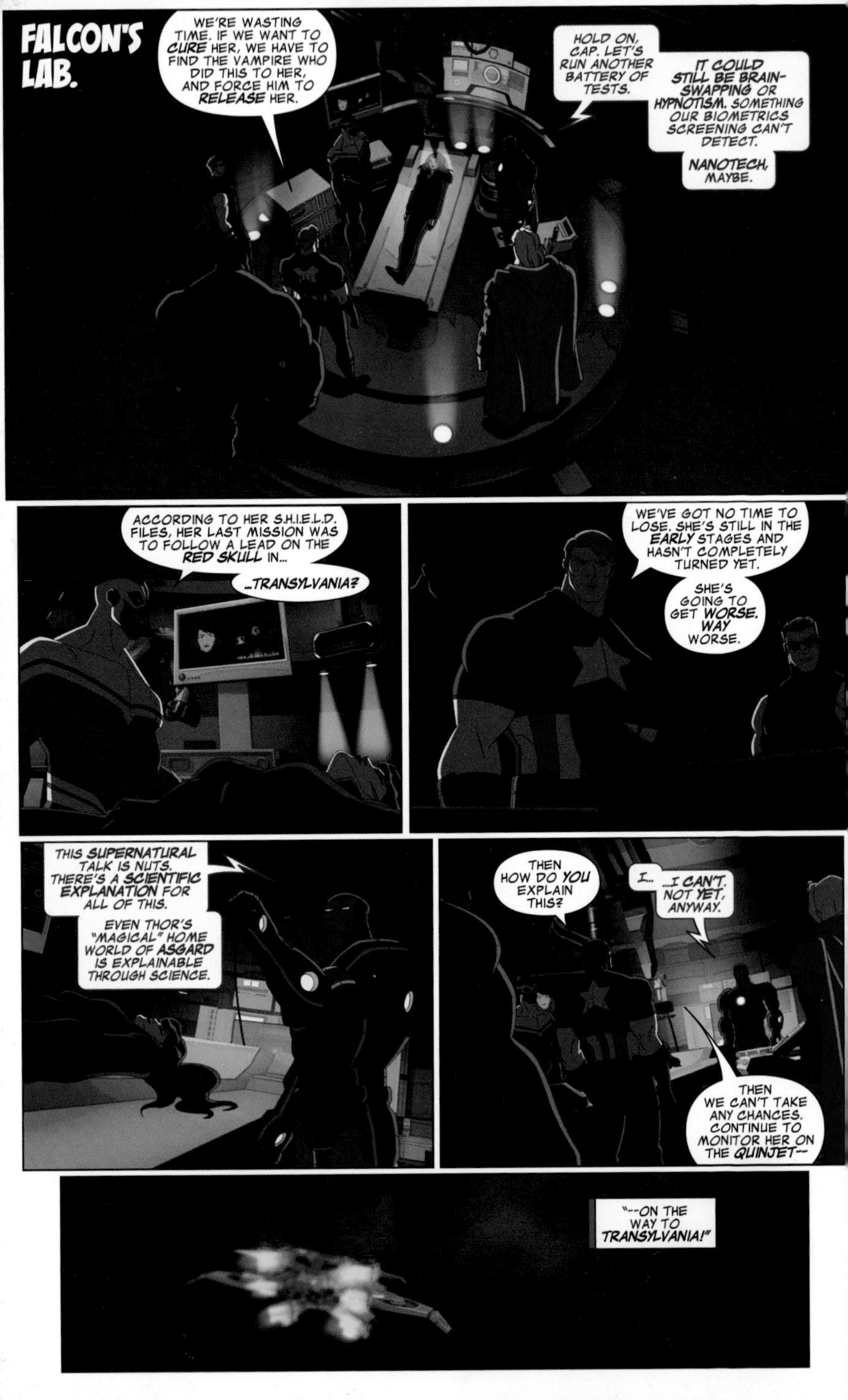
FALCON'S LAB.
WE'RE WASTING TIME. IF WE WANT TO CURE HER, WE HAVE TO FIND THE VAMPIRE WHO DID THIS TO HER, AND FORCE HIM TO RELEASE HER.
HOLD ON, CAP. LET'S RUN ANOTHER BATTERY OF TESTS.
IT COULD STILL BE BRAIN-SWAPPING OR HYPNOTISM. SOMETHING OUR BIOMETRICS SCREENING CAN'T DETECT.
NANOTECH, MAYBE.
ACCORDING TO HER S.H.I.E.L.D. FILES, HER LAST MISSION WAS TO FOLLOW A LEAD ON THE RED SKULL IN...
...TRANSYLVANIA?
WE'VE GOT NO TIME TO LOSE. SHE'S STILL IN THE EARLY STAGES AND HASN'T COMPLETELY TURNED YET.
SHE'S GOING TO GET WORSE. WAY WORSE.
THIS SUPERNATURAL TALK IS NUTS. THERE'S A SCIENTIFIC EXPLANATION FOR ALL OF THIS.
EVEN THOR'S "MAGICAL" HOME WORLD OF ASGARD IS EXPLAINABLE THROUGH SCIENCE.
THEN HOW DO YOU EXPLAIN THIS?
I... ...I CAN'T. NOT YET, ANYWAY.
THEN WE CAN'T TAKE ANY CHANCES. CONTINUE TO MONITOR HER ON THE QUINJET--
"--ON THE WAY TO TRANSYLVANIA!"

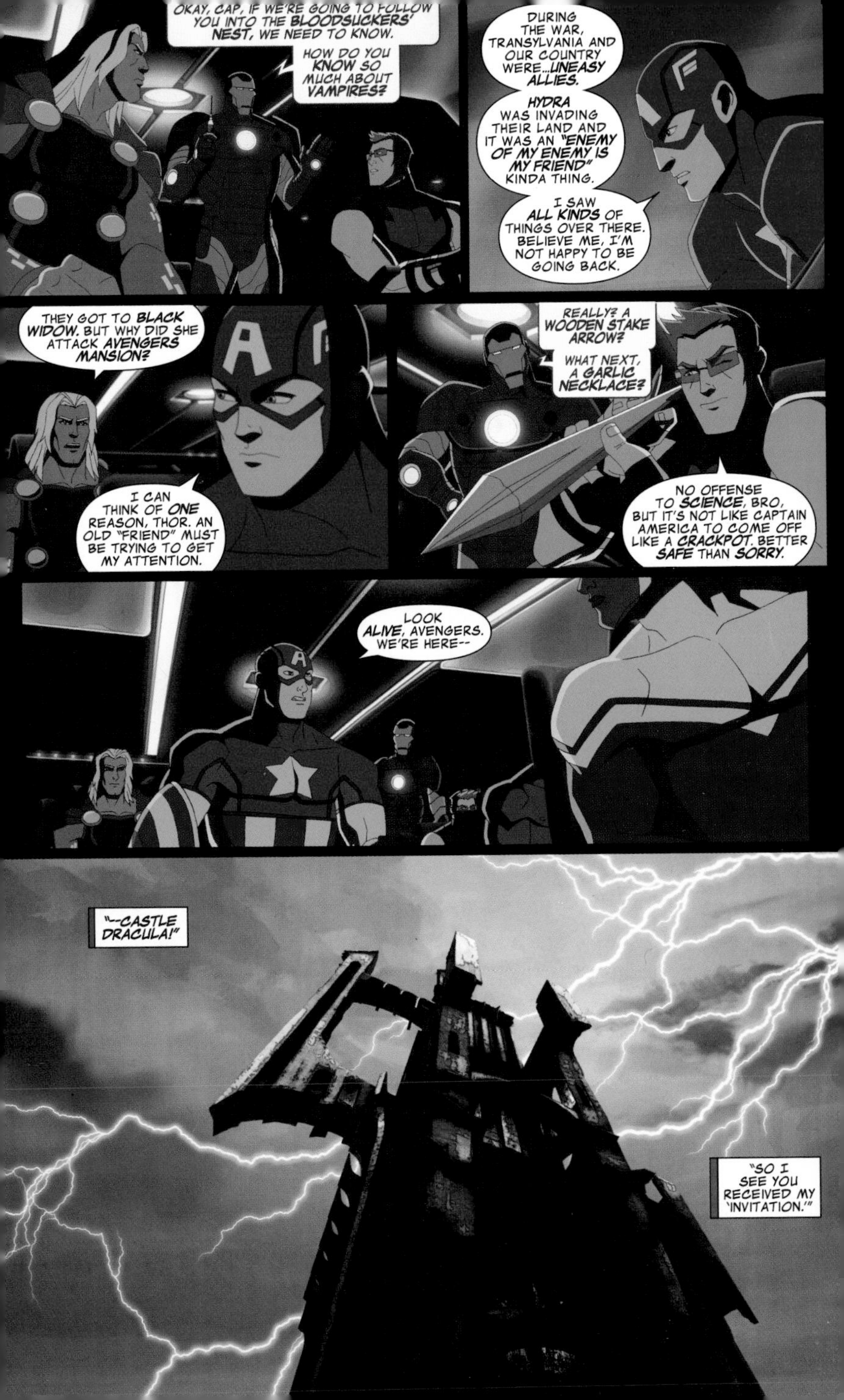
OKAY, CAP, IF WE'RE GOING TO FOLLOW YOU INTO THE BLOODSUCKERS' NEST, WE NEED TO KNOW.
HOW DO YOU KNOW SO MUCH ABOUT VAMPIRES?
DURING THE WAR, TRANSYLVANIA AND OUR COUNTRY WERE...UNEASY ALLIES.
HYDRA WAS INVADING THEIR LAND AND IT WAS AN "ENEMY OF MY ENEMY IS MY FRIEND" KINDA THING.
I SAW ALL KINDS OF THINGS OVER THERE. BELIEVE ME, I'M NOT HAPPY TO BE GOING BACK.
THEY GOT TO BLACK WIDOW. BUT WHY DID SHE ATTACK AVENGERS MANSION?
I CAN THINK OF ONE REASON, THOR. AN OLD "FRIEND" MUST BE TRYING TO GET MY ATTENTION.
REALLY? A WOODEN STAKE ARROW?
WHAT NEXT, A GARLIC NECKLACE?
NO OFFENSE TO SCIENCE, BRO, BUT IT'S NOT LIKE CAPTAIN AMERICA TO COME OFF LIKE A CRACKPOT. BETTER SAFE THAN SORRY.
LOOK ALIVE, AVENGERS. WE'RE HERE--
"--CASTLE DRACULA!"
"SO I SEE YOU RECEIVED MY 'INVITATION.'"

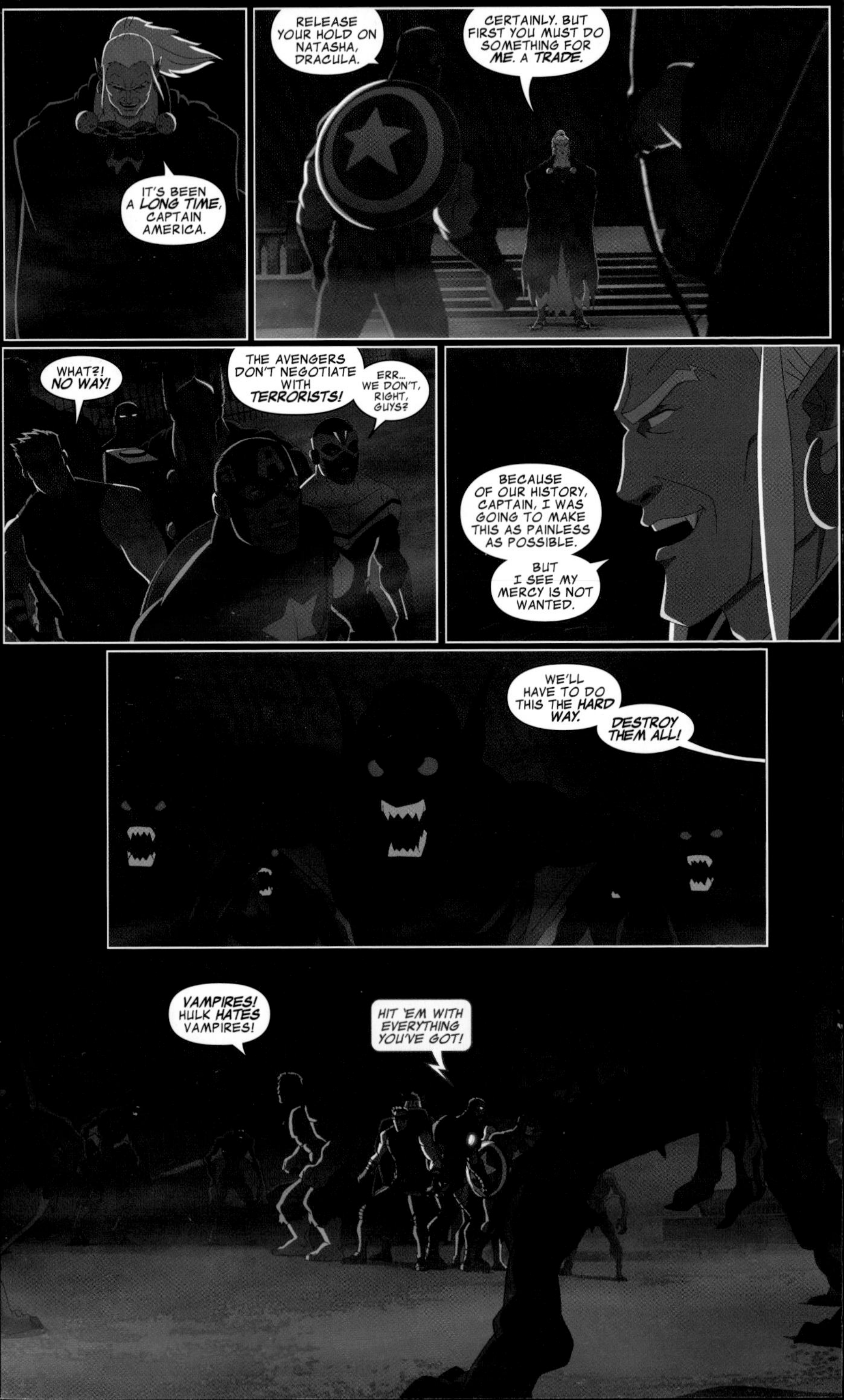

IT'S BEEN A LONG TIME, CAPTAIN AMERICA.
RELEASE YOUR HOLD ON NATASHA, DRACULA.
CERTAINLY. BUT FIRST YOU MUST DO SOMETHING FOR ME. A TRADE.
WHAT?! NO WAY!
THE AVENGERS DON'T NEGOTIATE WITH TERRORISTS!
ERR... WE DON'T, RIGHT, GUYS?
BECAUSE OF OUR HISTORY, CAPTAIN, I WAS GOING TO MAKE THIS AS PAINLESS AS POSSIBLE.
BUT I SEE MY MERCY IS NOT WANTED.
WE'LL HAVE TO DO THIS THE HARD WAY.
DESTROY THEM ALL!
VAMPIRES! HULK HATES VAMPIRES!
HIT 'EM WITH EVERYTHING YOU'VE GOT!

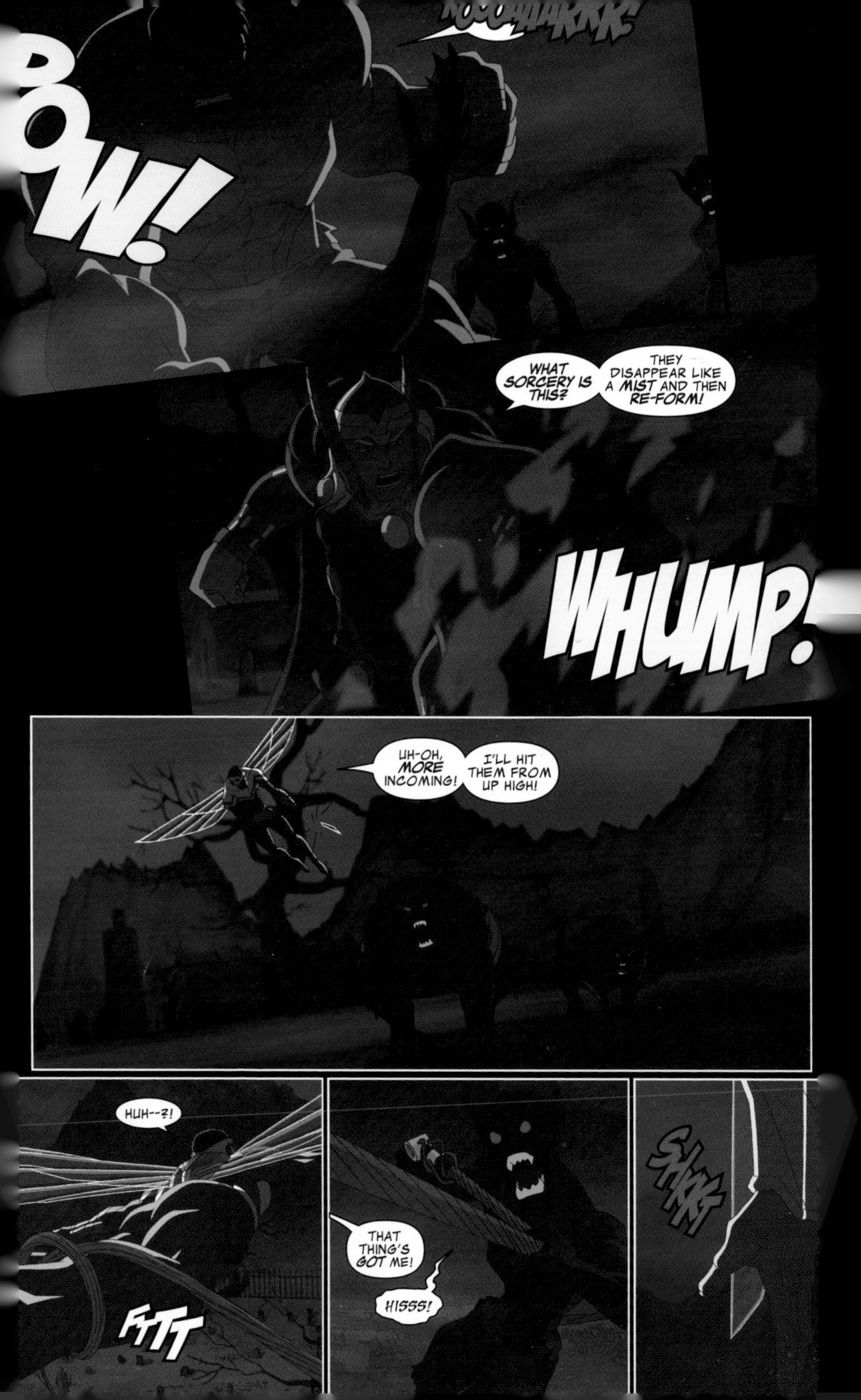
RRRAAARRRRR!
BOOW!
WHAT SORCERY IS THIS?
THEY DISAPPEAR LIKE A MIST AND THEN RE-FORM!
WHUMP!
UH-OH, MORE INCOMING!
I'LL HIT THEM FROM UP HIGH!
HUH--?!
FTTT
THAT THING'S GOT ME!
HISSS!
SHKKT

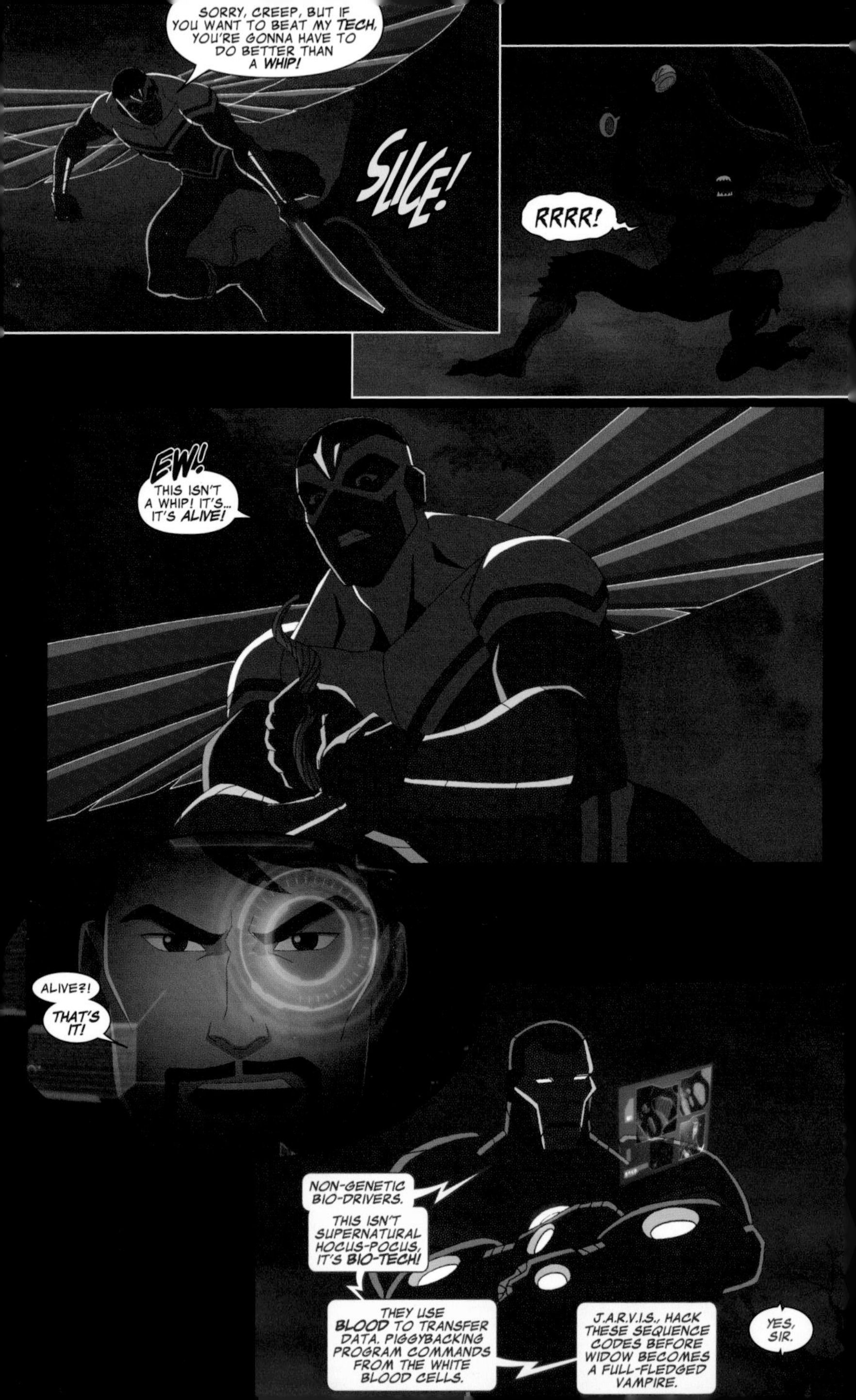

SORRY, CREEP, BUT IF YOU WANT TO BEAT MY TECH, YOU'RE GONNA HAVE TO DO BETTER THAN A WHIP!
SLICE!
RRRR!
EW! THIS ISN'T A WHIP! IT'S... IT'S ALIVE!
ALIVE?!
THAT'S IT!
NON-GENETIC BIO-DRIVERS.
THIS ISN'T SUPERNATURAL HOCUS-POCUS, IT'S BIO-TECH!
THEY USE BLOOD TO TRANSFER DATA. PIGGYBACKING PROGRAM COMMANDS FROM THE WHITE BLOOD CELLS.
J.A.R.V.I.S., HACK THESE SEQUENCE CODES BEFORE WIDOW BECOMES A FULL-FLEDGED VAMPIRE.
YES, SIR.

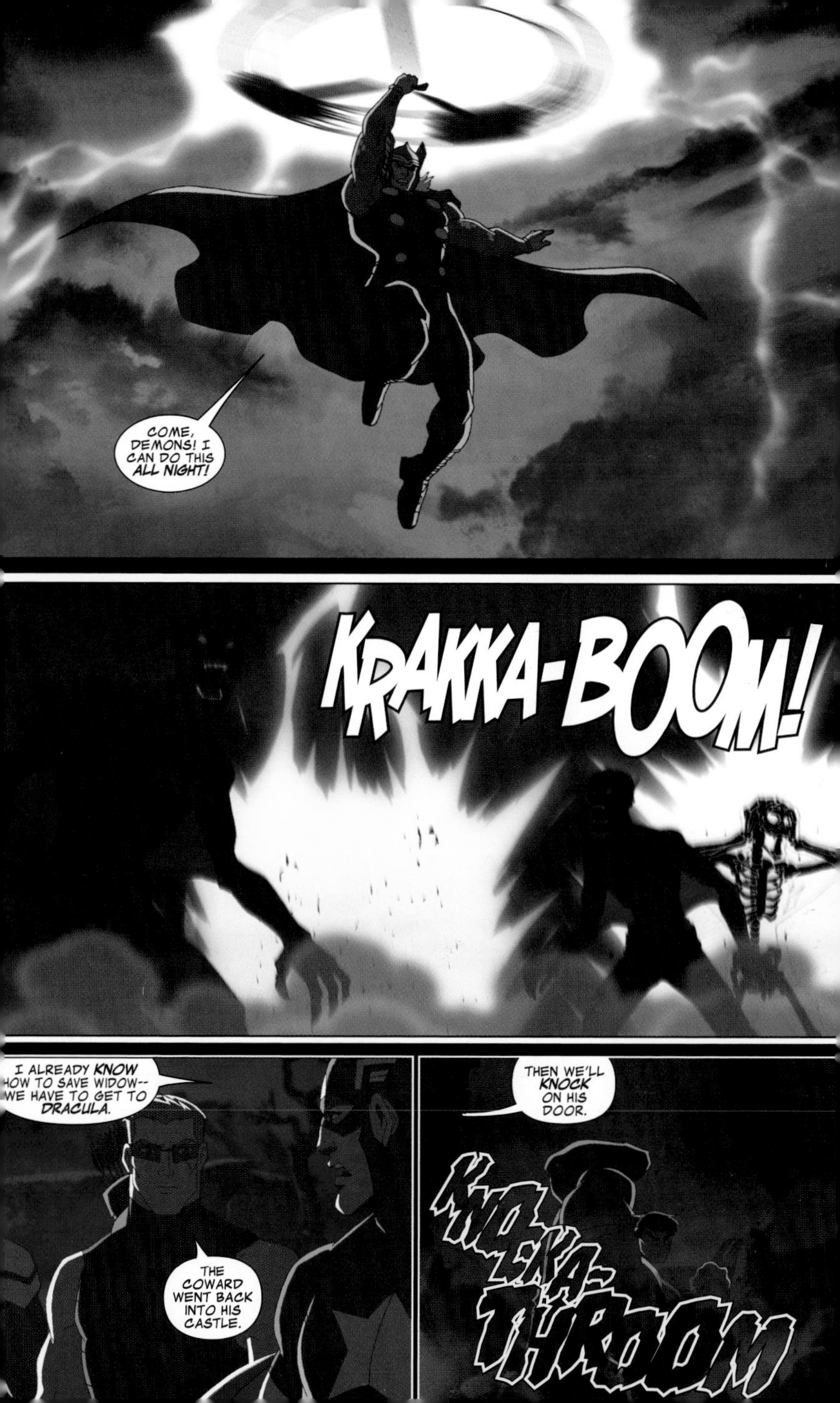
COME, DEMONS! I CAN DO THIS ALL NIGHT!
KRAKKA-BOOM!
I ALREADY KNOW HOW TO SAVE WIDOW-- WE HAVE TO GET TO DRACULA.
THE COWARD WENT BACK INTO HIS CASTLE.
THEN WE'LL KNOCK ON HIS DOOR.
KRA-KA-THROOM

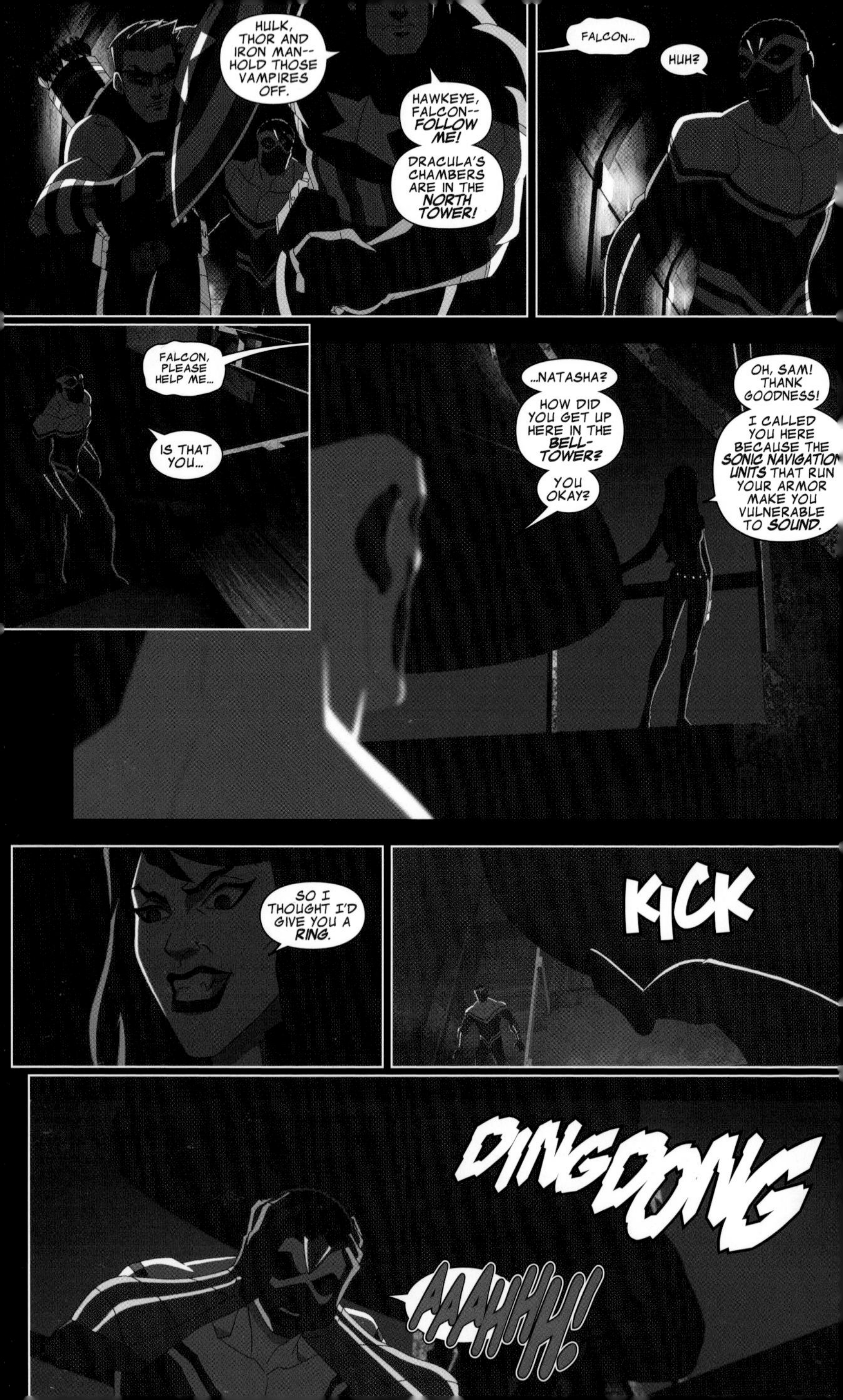
HULK, THOR AND IRON MAN--HOLD THOSE VAMPIRES OFF.
HAWKEYE, FALCON--FOLLOW ME!
DRACULA'S CHAMBERS ARE IN THE NORTH TOWER!
FALCON...
HUH?
FALCON, PLEASE HELP ME...
IS THAT YOU...
...NATASHA?
HOW DID YOU GET UP HERE IN THE BELL-TOWER?
YOU OKAY?
OH, SAM! THANK GOODNESS!
I CALLED YOU HERE BECAUSE THE SONIC NAVIGATION UNITS THAT RUN YOUR ARMOR MAKE YOU VULNERABLE TO SOUND.
SO I THOUGHT I'D GIVE YOU A RING.
KICK
DING DONG
AAAHHH!!

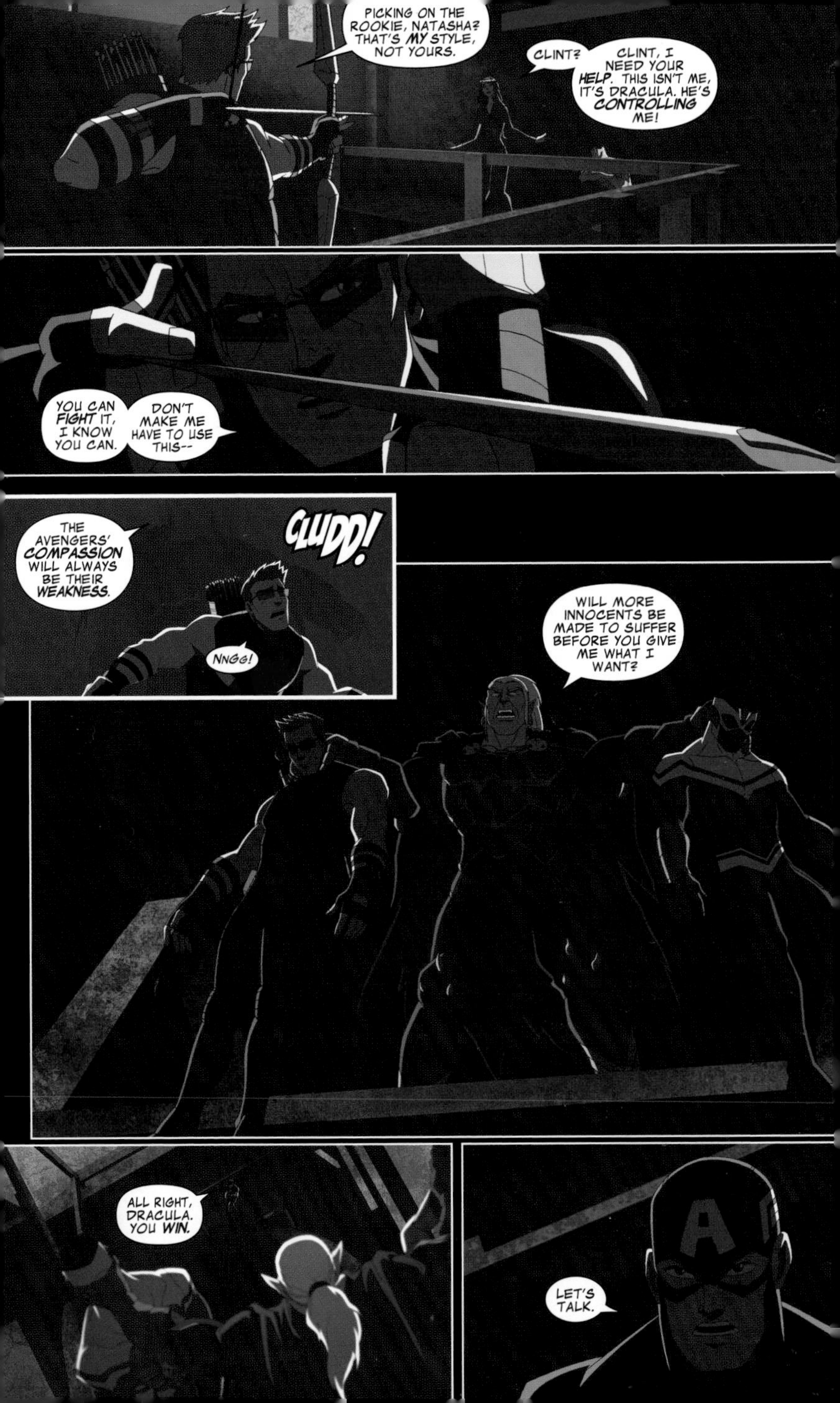
PICKING ON THE ROOKIE, NATASHA? THAT'S MY STYLE, NOT YOURS.
CLINT?
CLINT, I NEED YOUR HELP. THIS ISN'T ME, IT'S DRACULA. HE'S CONTROLLING ME!
YOU CAN FIGHT IT, I KNOW YOU CAN.
DON'T MAKE ME HAVE TO USE THIS--
THE AVENGERS' COMPASSION WILL ALWAYS BE THEIR WEAKNESS.
CLUDD!
NNGG!
WILL MORE INNOCENTS BE MADE TO SUFFER BEFORE YOU GIVE ME WHAT I WANT?
ALL RIGHT, DRACULA. YOU WIN.
LET'S TALK.

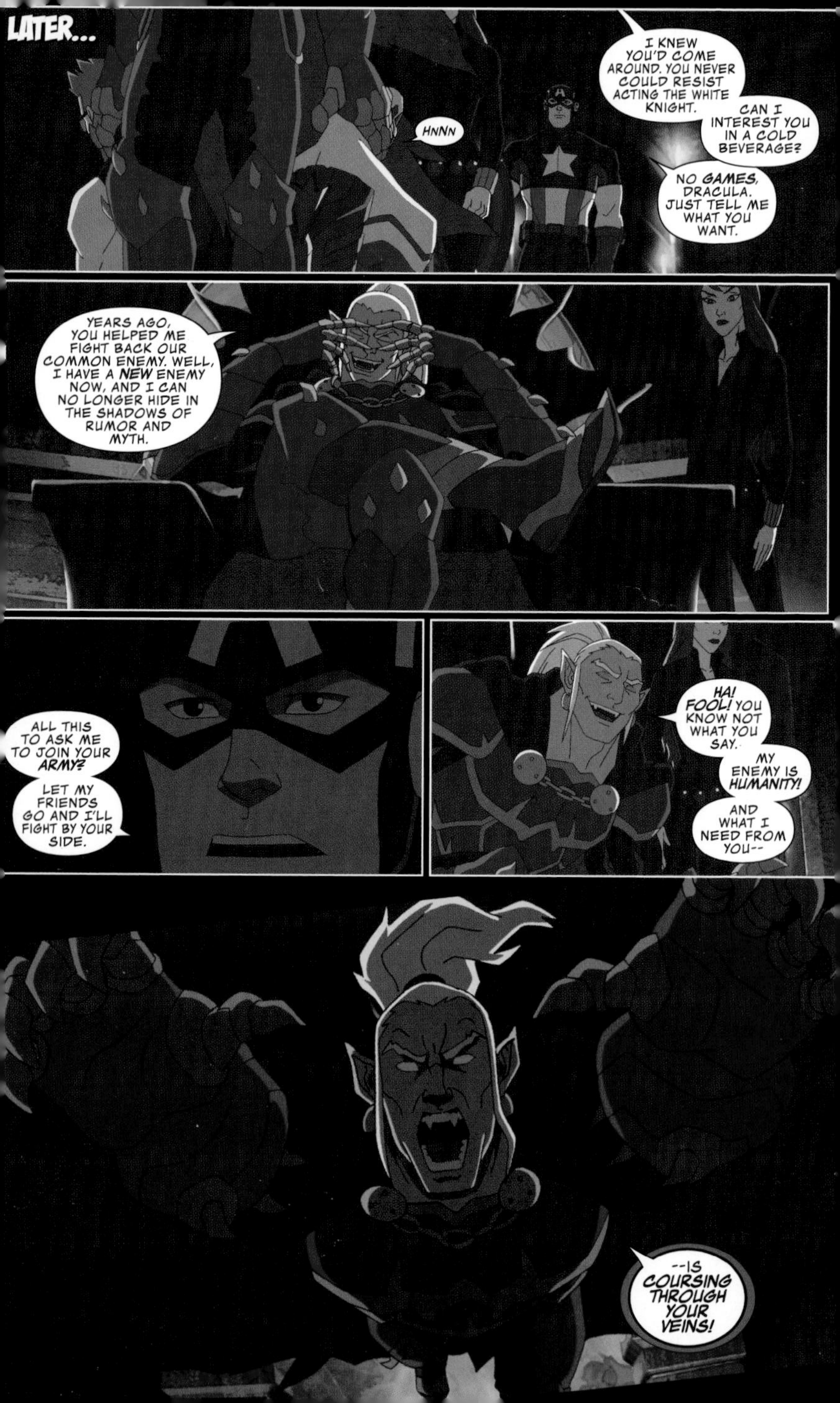
LATER...
I KNEW YOU'D COME AROUND. YOU NEVER COULD RESIST ACTING THE WHITE KNIGHT.
HNNN
CAN I INTEREST YOU IN A COLD BEVERAGE?
NO GAMES, DRACULA. JUST TELL ME WHAT YOU WANT.
YEARS AGO, YOU HELPED ME FIGHT BACK OUR COMMON ENEMY. WELL, I HAVE A NEW ENEMY NOW, AND I CAN NO LONGER HIDE IN THE SHADOWS OF RUMOR AND MYTH.
ALL THIS TO ASK ME TO JOIN YOUR ARMY?
LET MY FRIENDS GO AND I'LL FIGHT BY YOUR SIDE.
HA! FOOL! YOU KNOW NOT WHAT YOU SAY.
MY ENEMY IS HUMANITY!
AND WHAT I NEED FROM YOU--
--IS COURSING THROUGH YOUR VEINS!

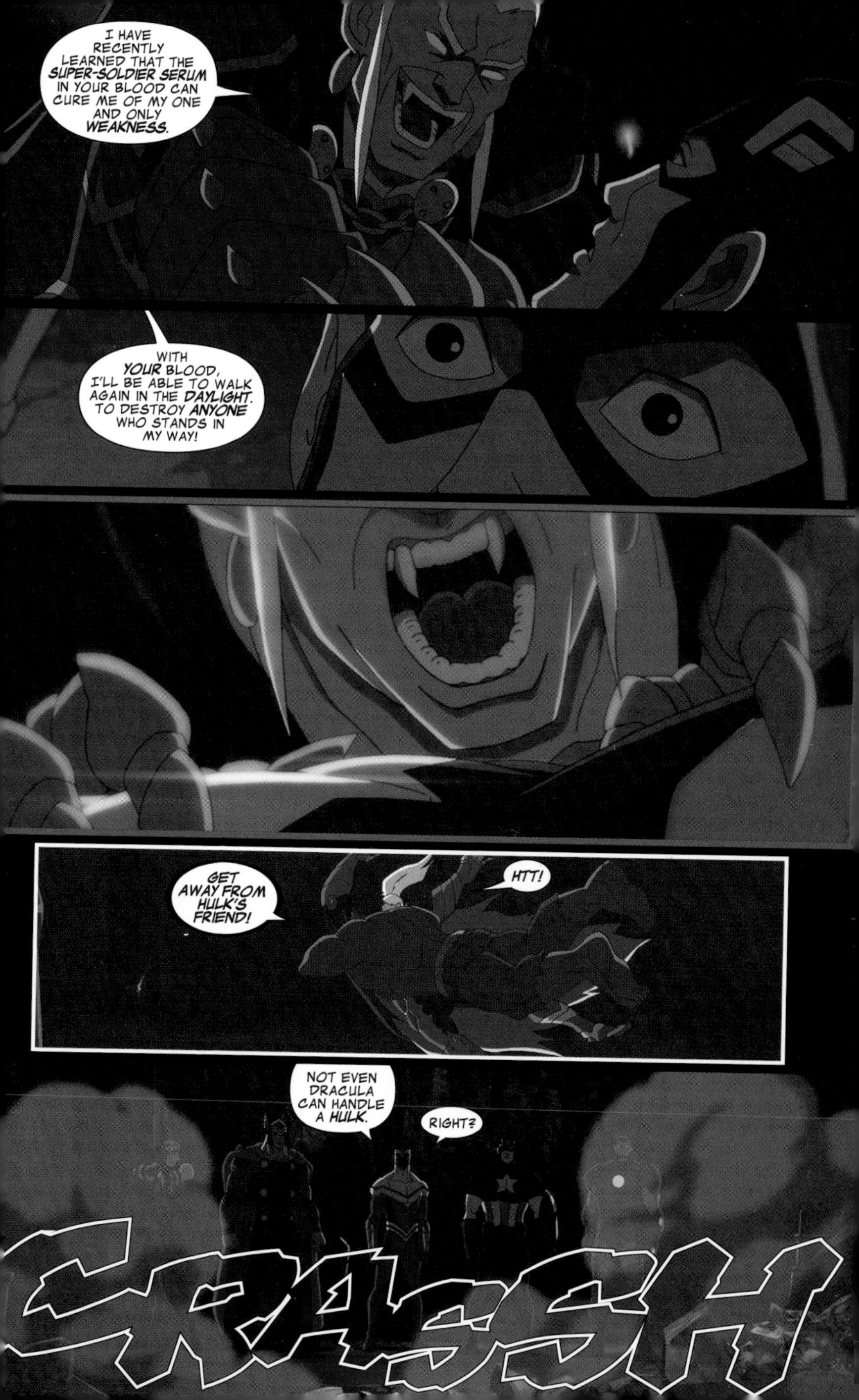
I HAVE RECENTLY LEARNED THAT THE SUPER-SOLDIER SERUM IN YOUR BLOOD CAN CURE ME OF MY ONE AND ONLY WEAKNESS.
WITH YOUR BLOOD, I'LL BE ABLE TO WALK AGAIN IN THE DAYLIGHT. TO DESTROY ANYONE WHO STANDS IN MY WAY!
GET AWAY FROM HULK'S FRIEND!
HTT!
NOT EVEN DRACULA CAN HANDLE A HULK.
RIGHT?
CRASH

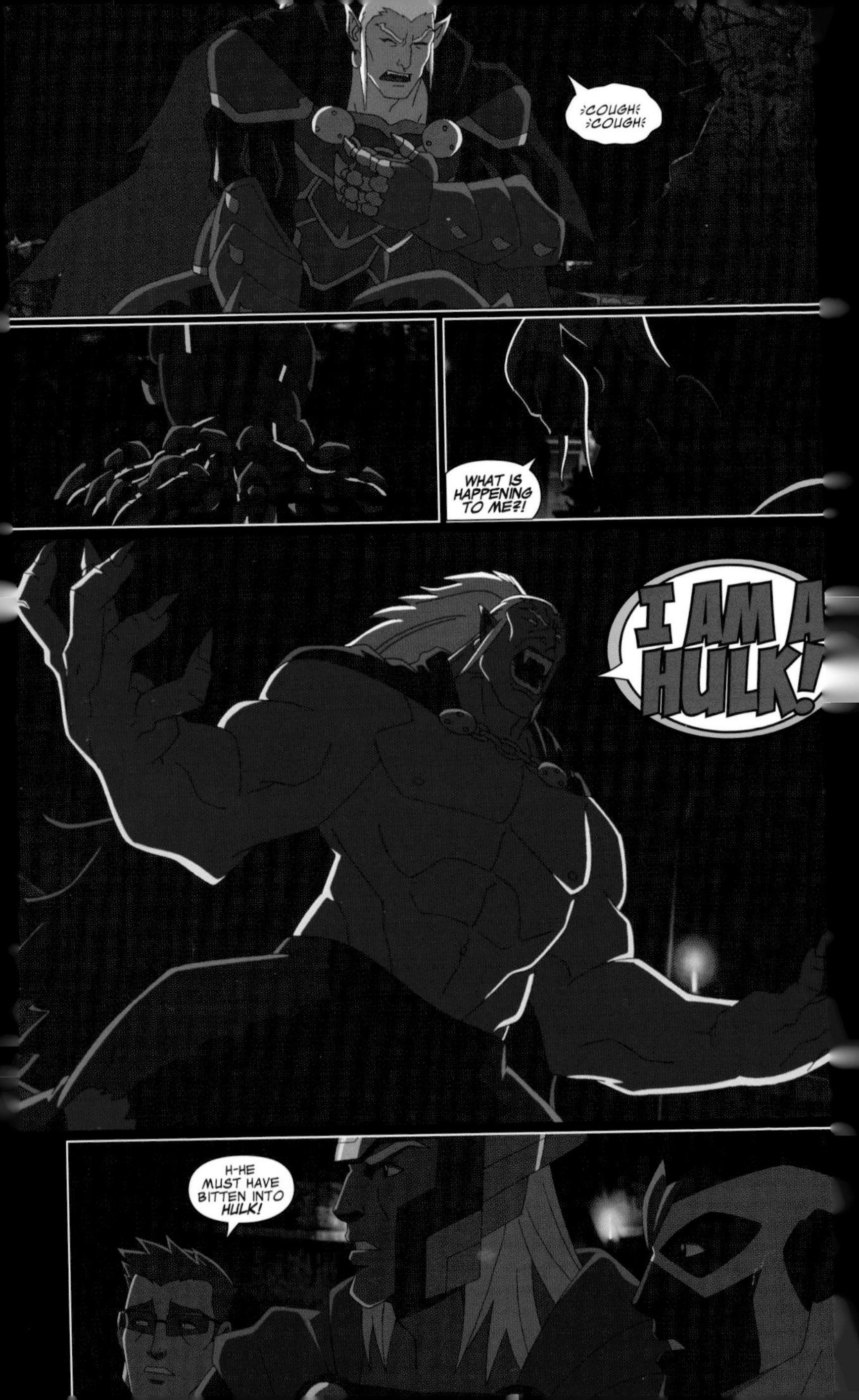
COUGH
COUGH
WHAT IS HAPPENING TO ME?!
I AM A HULK!
H-HE MUST HAVE BITTEN INTO HULK!

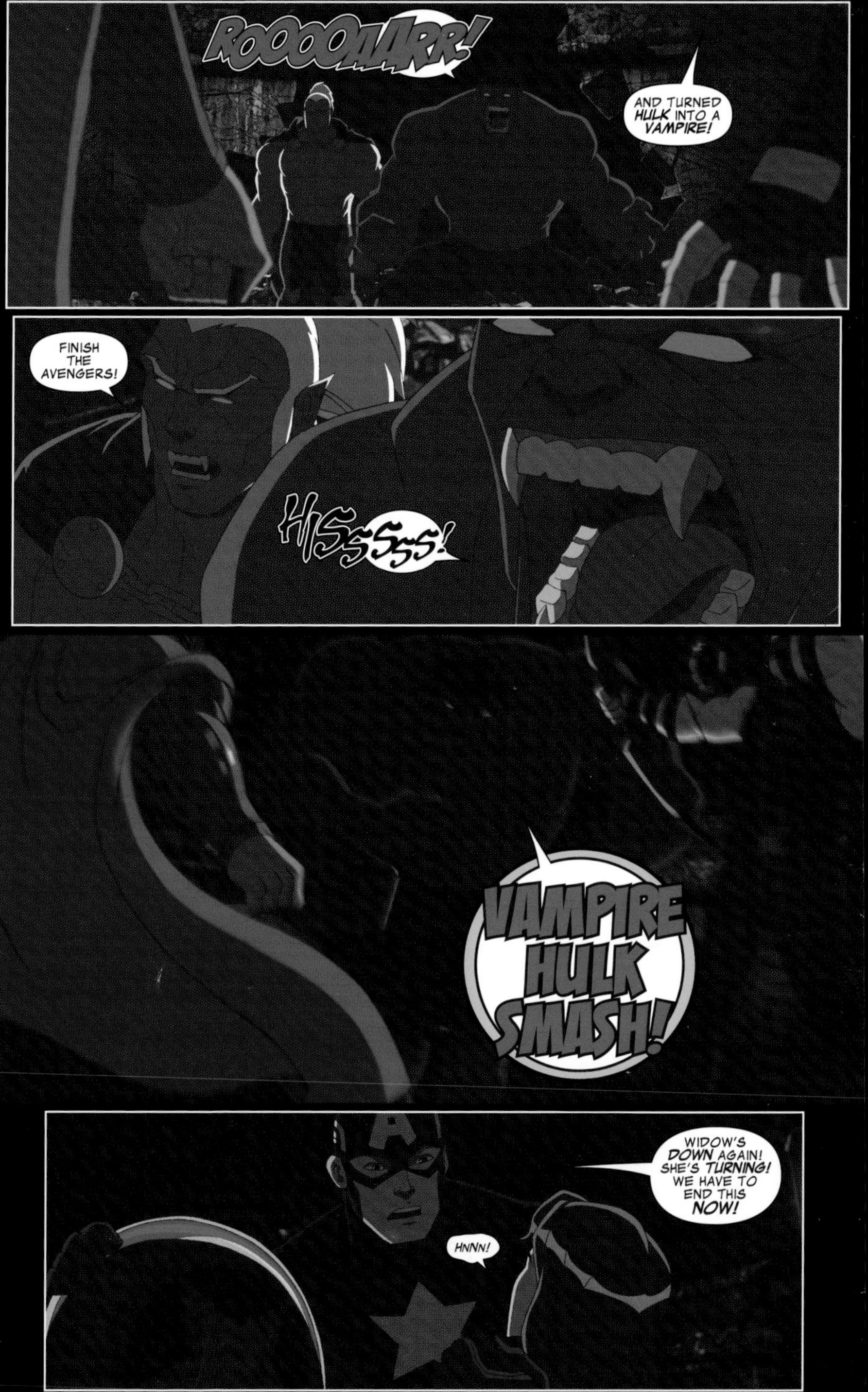
ROOOOAARR!
AND TURNED HULK INTO A VAMPIRE!
FINISH THE AVENGERS!
HISSSSS!
VAMPIRE HULK SMASH!
WIDOW'S DOWN AGAIN! SHE'S TURNING! WE HAVE TO END THIS NOW!
HNNN!

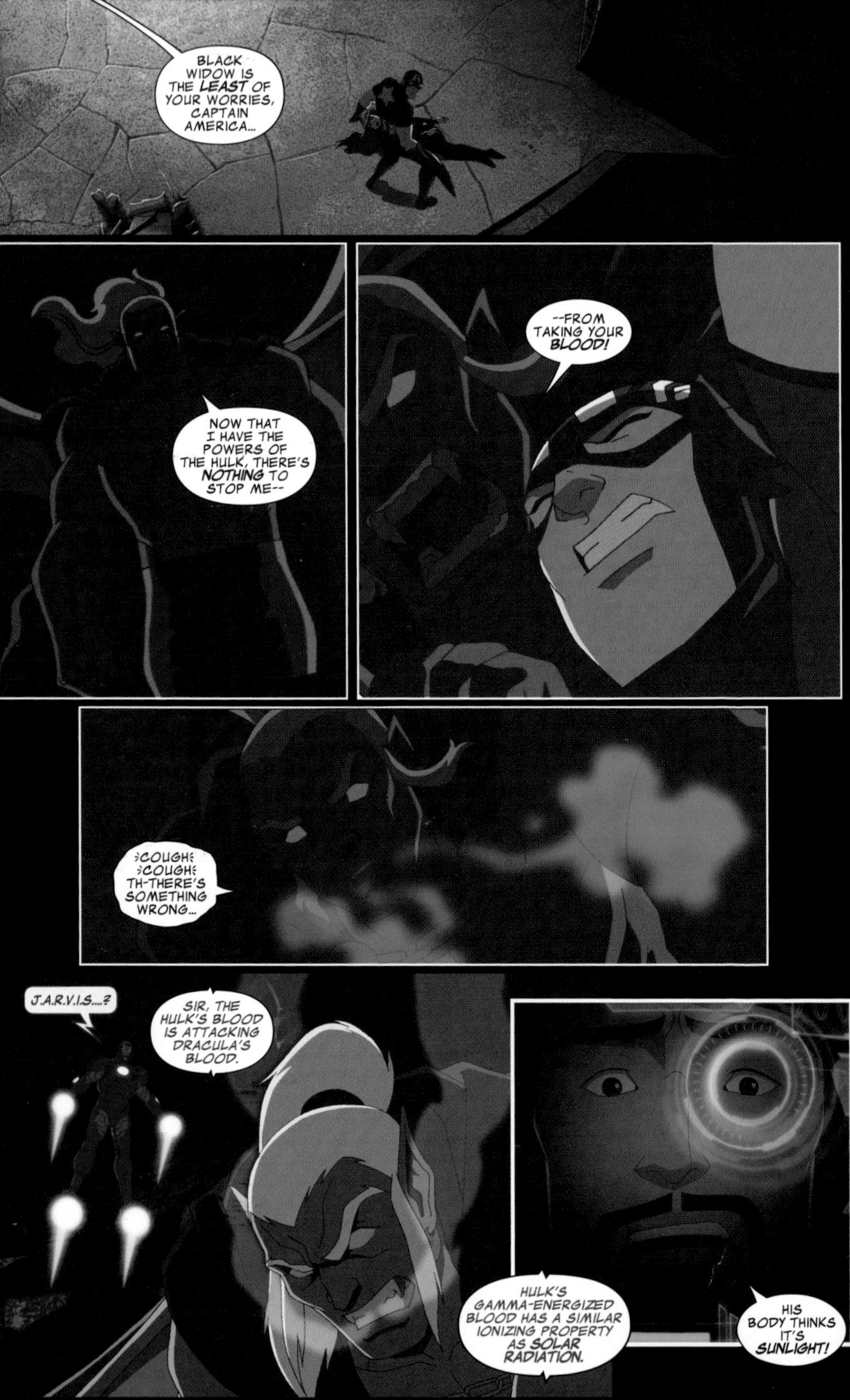
BLACK WIDOW IS THE LEAST OF YOUR WORRIES, CAPTAIN AMERICA...
NOW THAT I HAVE THE POWERS OF THE HULK, THERE'S NOTHING TO STOP ME--
--FROM TAKING YOUR BLOOD!
COUGH *COUGH* TH-THERE'S SOMETHING WRONG...
J.A.R.V.I.S....?
SIR, THE HULK'S BLOOD IS ATTACKING DRACULA'S BLOOD.
HULK'S GAMMA-ENERGIZED BLOOD HAS A SIMILAR IONIZING PROPERTY AS SOLAR RADIATION.
HIS BODY THINKS IT'S SUNLIGHT!

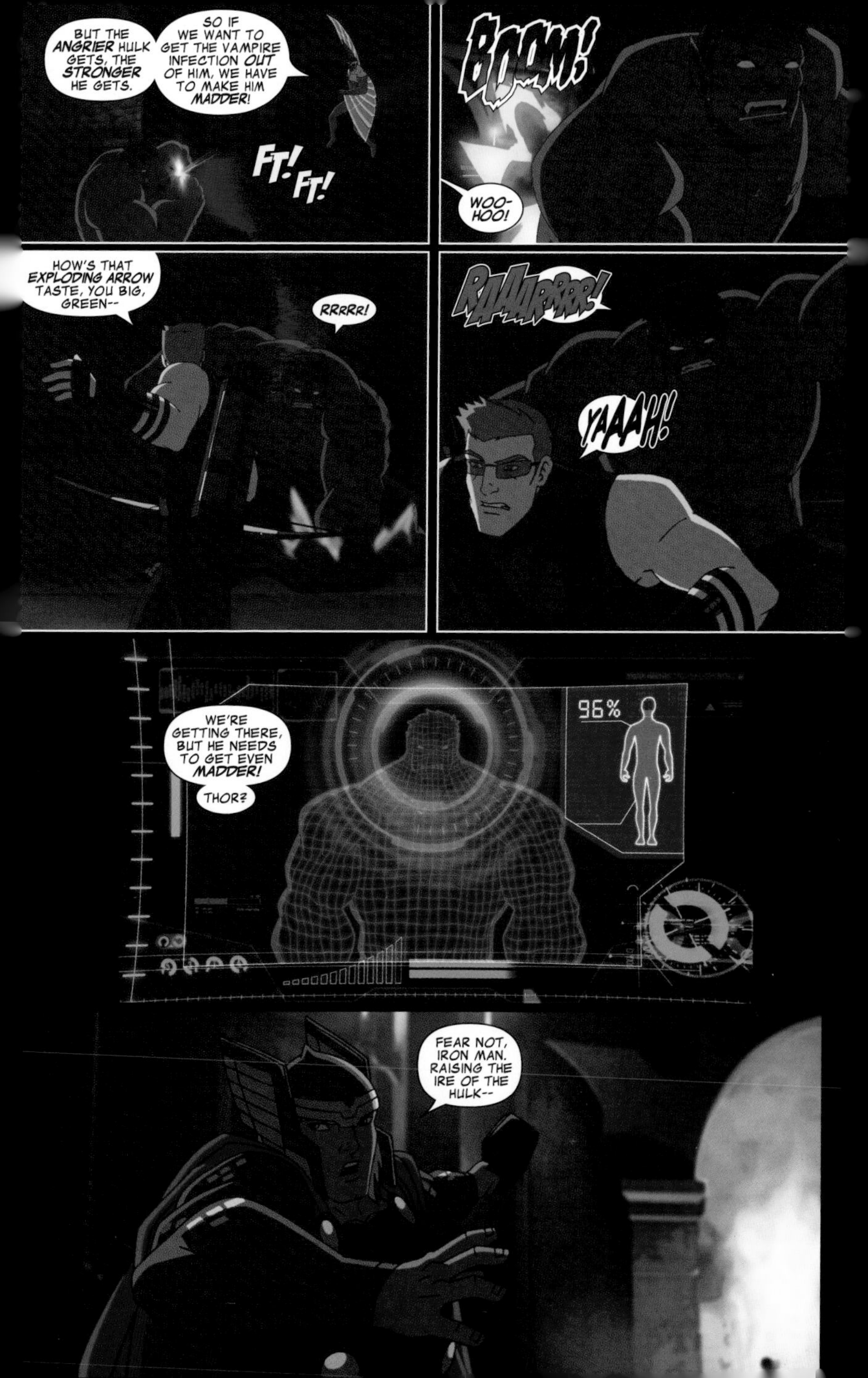
BUT THE ANGRIER HULK GETS, THE STRONGER HE GETS.
SO IF WE WANT TO GET THE VAMPIRE INFECTION OUT OF HIM, WE HAVE TO MAKE HIM MADDER!
FT! FT!
BOOM!
WOO-HOO!
HOW'S THAT EXPLODING ARROW TASTE, YOU BIG, GREEN--
RRRRR!
RAAARRRR!
YAAAH!
WE'RE GETTING THERE, BUT HE NEEDS TO GET EVEN MADDER!
THOR?
96%
FEAR NOT, IRON MAN. RAISING THE IRE OF THE HULK--

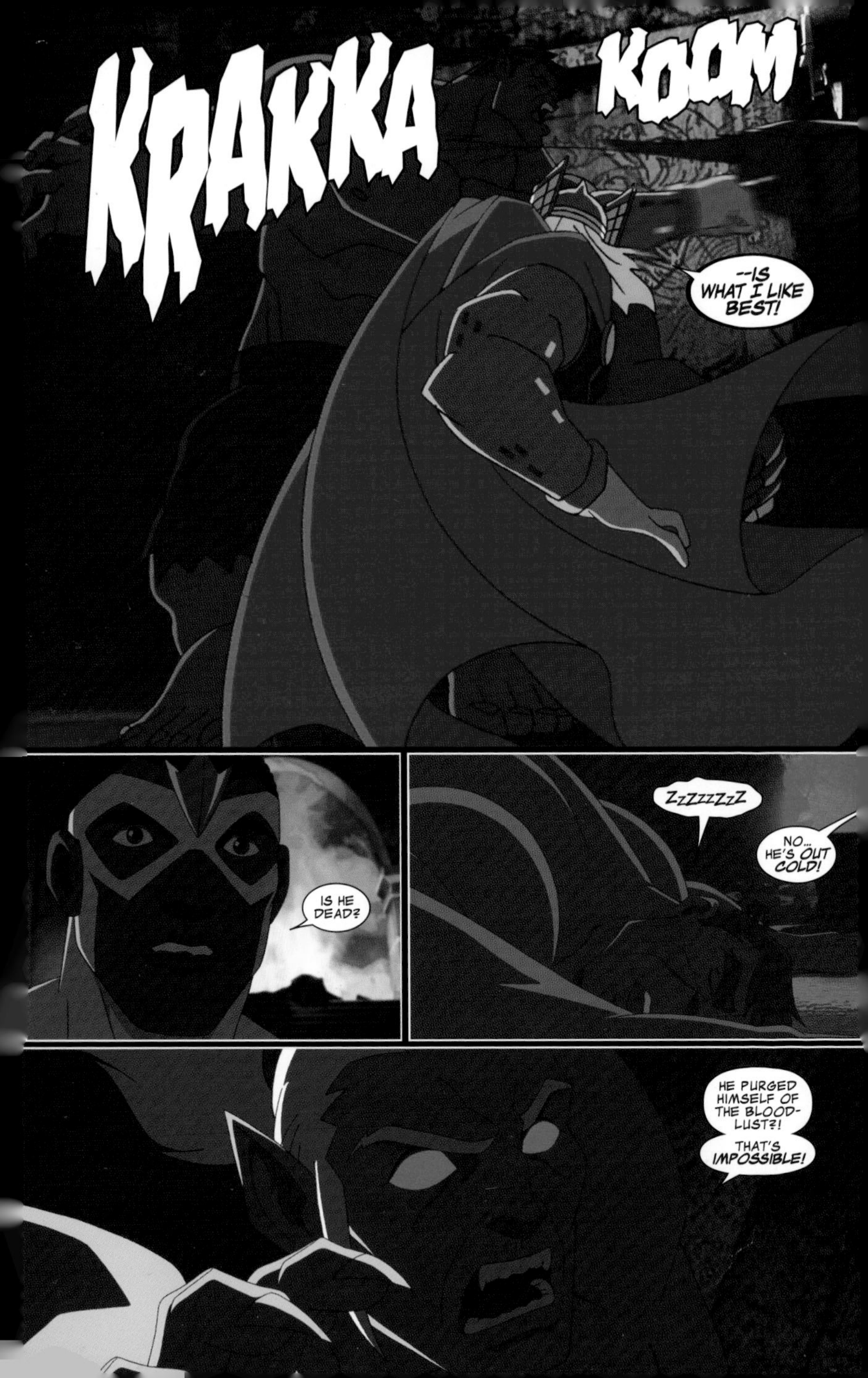
KRAKKA
KOOM
--IS WHAT I LIKE BEST!
IS HE DEAD?
ZzZZZZzZ
NO... HE'S OUT COLD!
HE PURGED HIMSELF OF THE BLOOD-LUST?!
THAT'S IMPOSSIBLE!

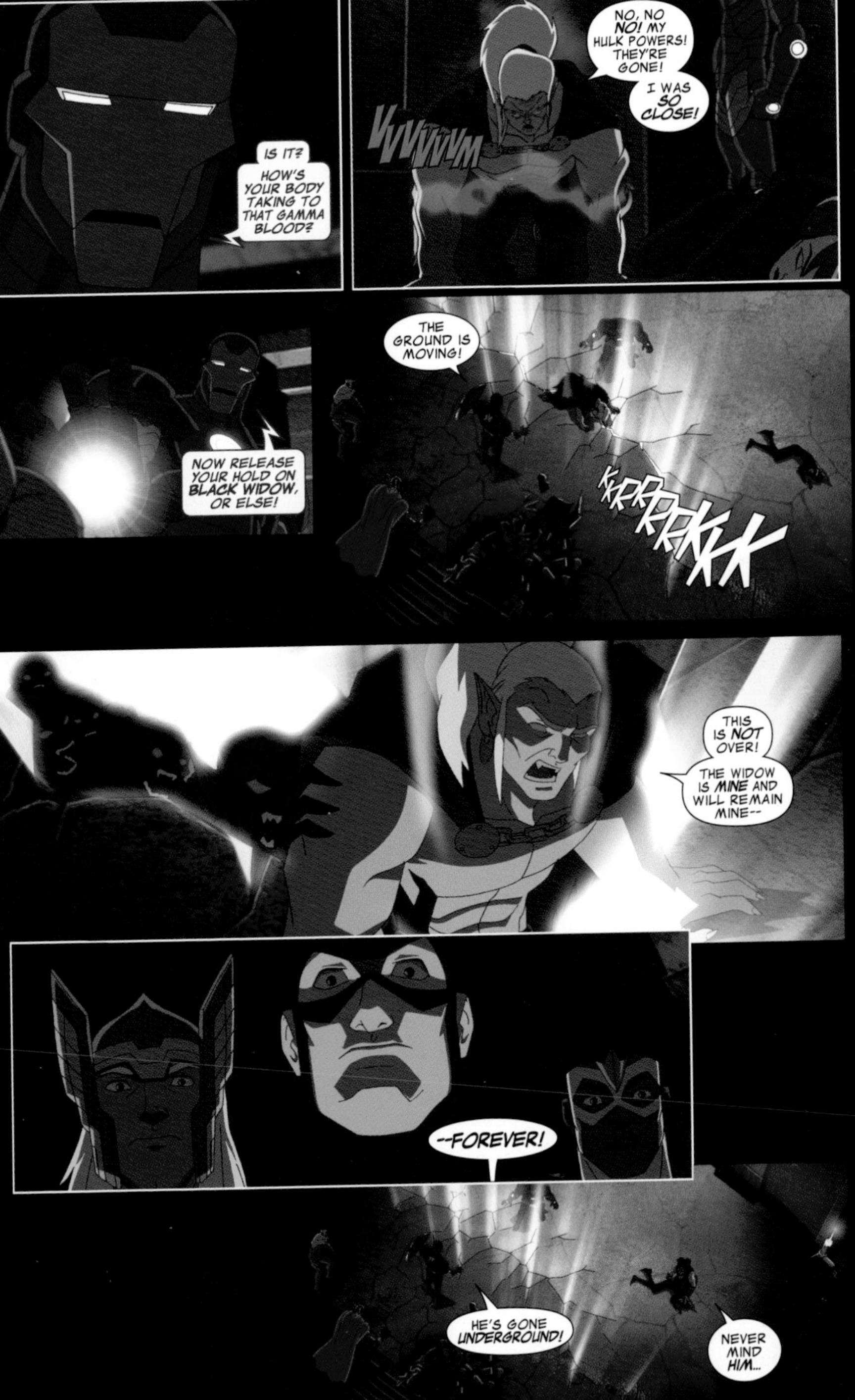
IS IT?
HOW'S YOUR BODY TAKING TO THAT GAMMA BLOOD?
VVVVVVVM
NO, NO NO! MY HULK POWERS! THEY'RE GONE!
I WAS SO CLOSE!
NOW RELEASE YOUR HOLD ON BLACK WIDOW, OR ELSE!
THE GROUND IS MOVING!
KKRRRRRKKK
THIS IS NOT OVER!
THE WIDOW IS MINE AND WILL REMAIN MINE--
--FOREVER!
HE'S GONE UNDERGROUND!
NEVER MIND HIM...

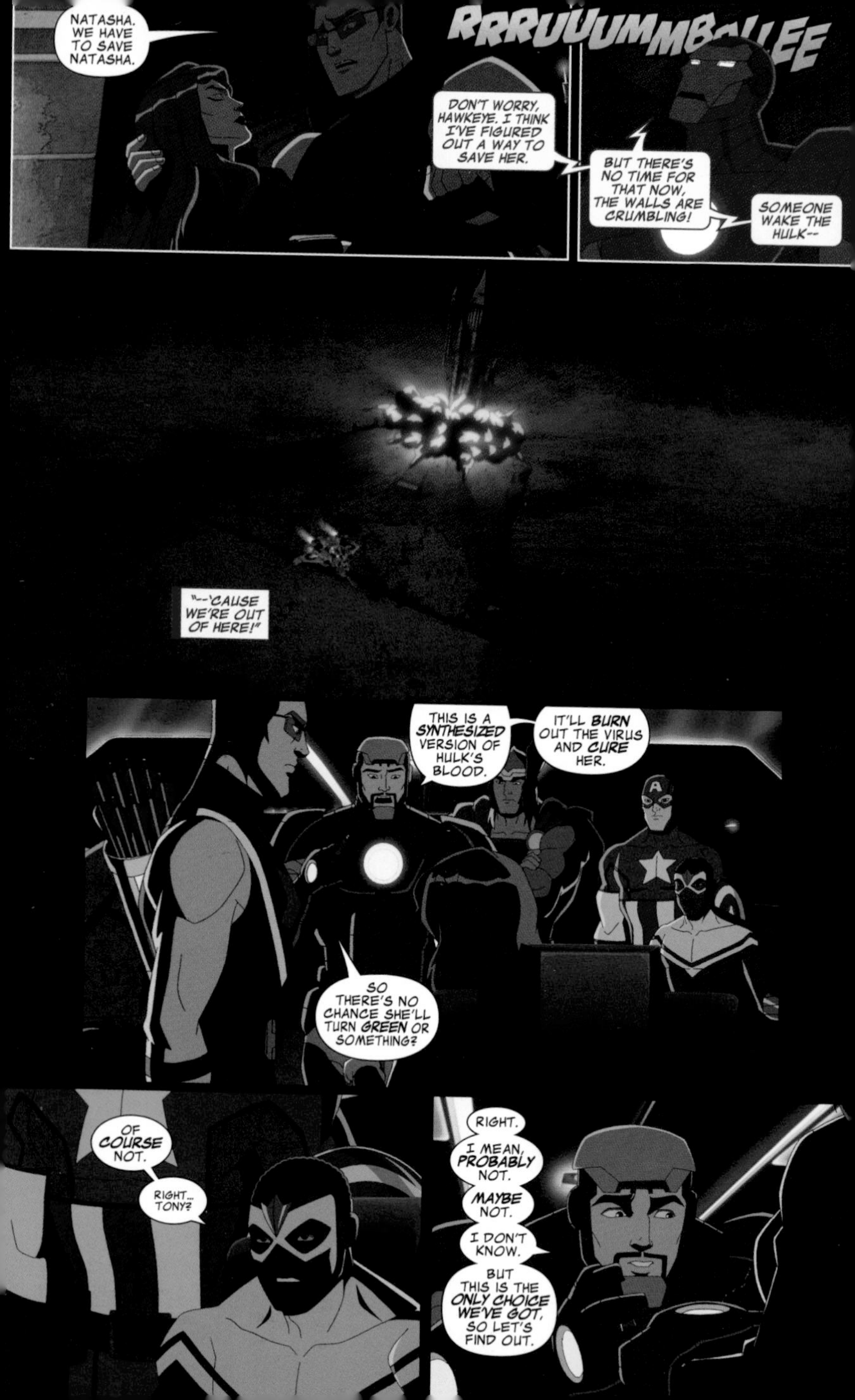
NATASHA. WE HAVE TO SAVE NATASHA.
RRRUUUMMBBLLEE
DON'T WORRY, HAWKEYE. I THINK I'VE FIGURED OUT A WAY TO SAVE HER.
BUT THERE'S NO TIME FOR THAT NOW. THE WALLS ARE CRUMBLING!
SOMEONE WAKE THE HULK--
"--'CAUSE WE'RE OUT OF HERE!"
THIS IS A SYNTHESIZED VERSION OF HULK'S BLOOD.
IT'LL BURN OUT THE VIRUS AND CURE HER.
SO THERE'S NO CHANCE SHE'LL TURN GREEN OR SOMETHING?
OF COURSE NOT.
RIGHT... TONY?
RIGHT.
I MEAN, PROBABLY NOT.
MAYBE NOT.
I DON'T KNOW.
BUT THIS IS THE ONLY CHOICE WE'VE GOT, SO LET'S FIND OUT.

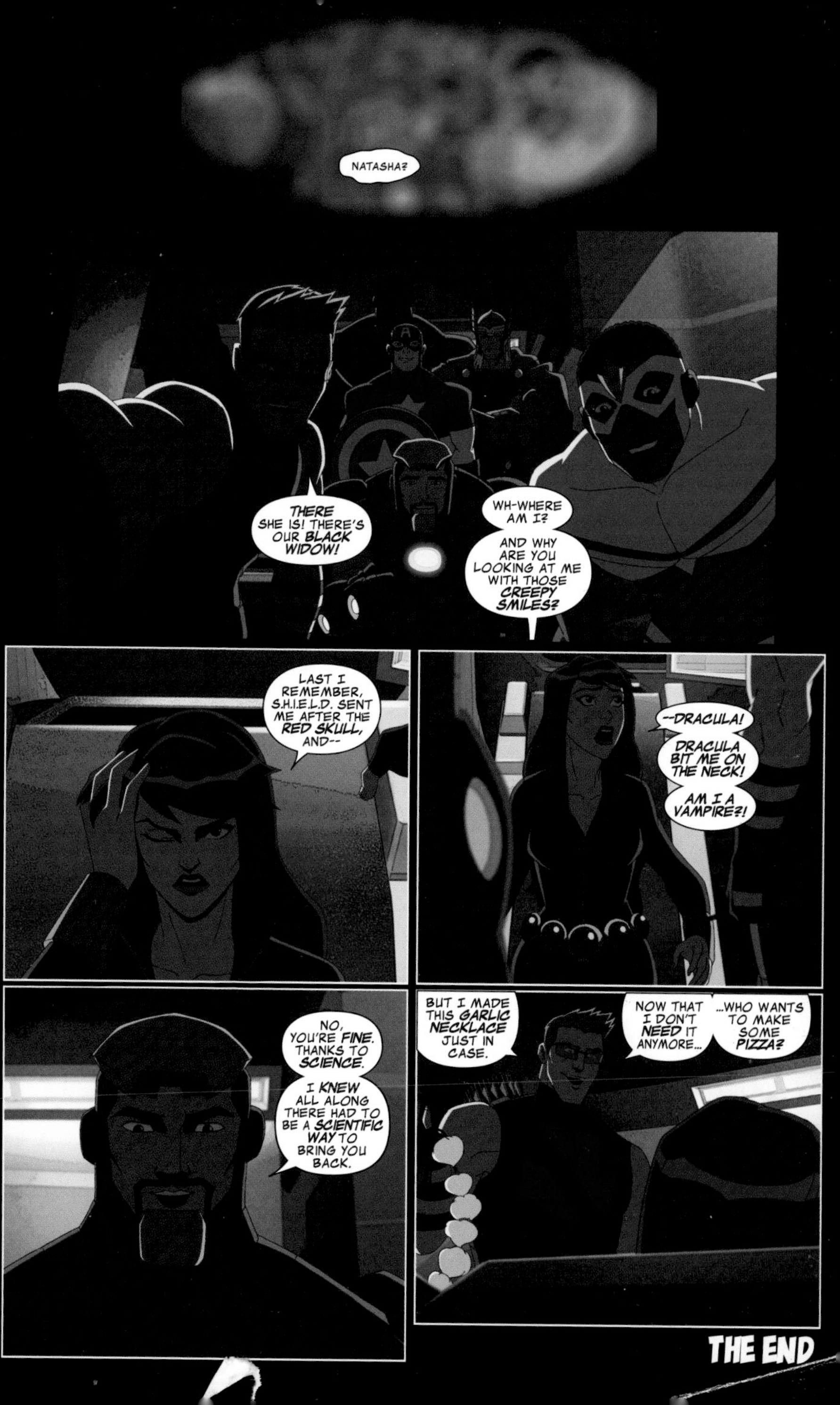
NATASHA?
THERE SHE IS! THERE'S OUR BLACK WIDOW!
WH-WHERE AM I?
AND WHY ARE YOU LOOKING AT ME WITH THOSE CREEPY SMILES?
LAST I REMEMBER, S.H.I.E.L.D. SENT ME AFTER THE RED SKULL, AND--
--DRACULA!
DRACULA BIT ME ON THE NECK!
AM I A VAMPIRE?!
NO, YOU'RE FINE. THANKS TO SCIENCE.
I KNEW ALL ALONG THERE HAD TO BE A SCIENTIFIC WAY TO BRING YOU BACK.
BUT I MADE THIS GARLIC NECKLACE JUST IN CASE.
NOW THAT I DON'T NEED IT ANYMORE...
...WHO WANTS TO MAKE SOME PIZZA?
THE END

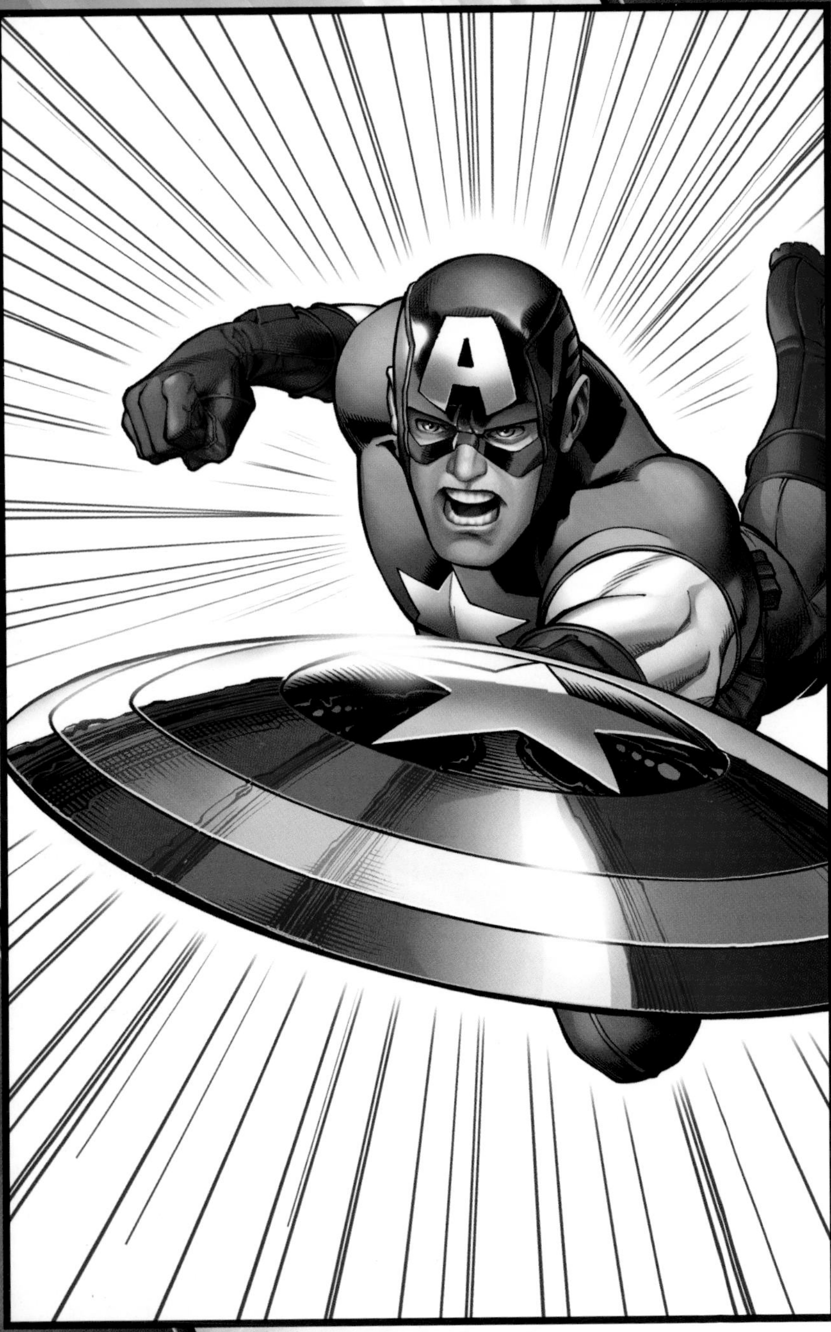

#6 BASED ON "SUPER-ADAPTOID"

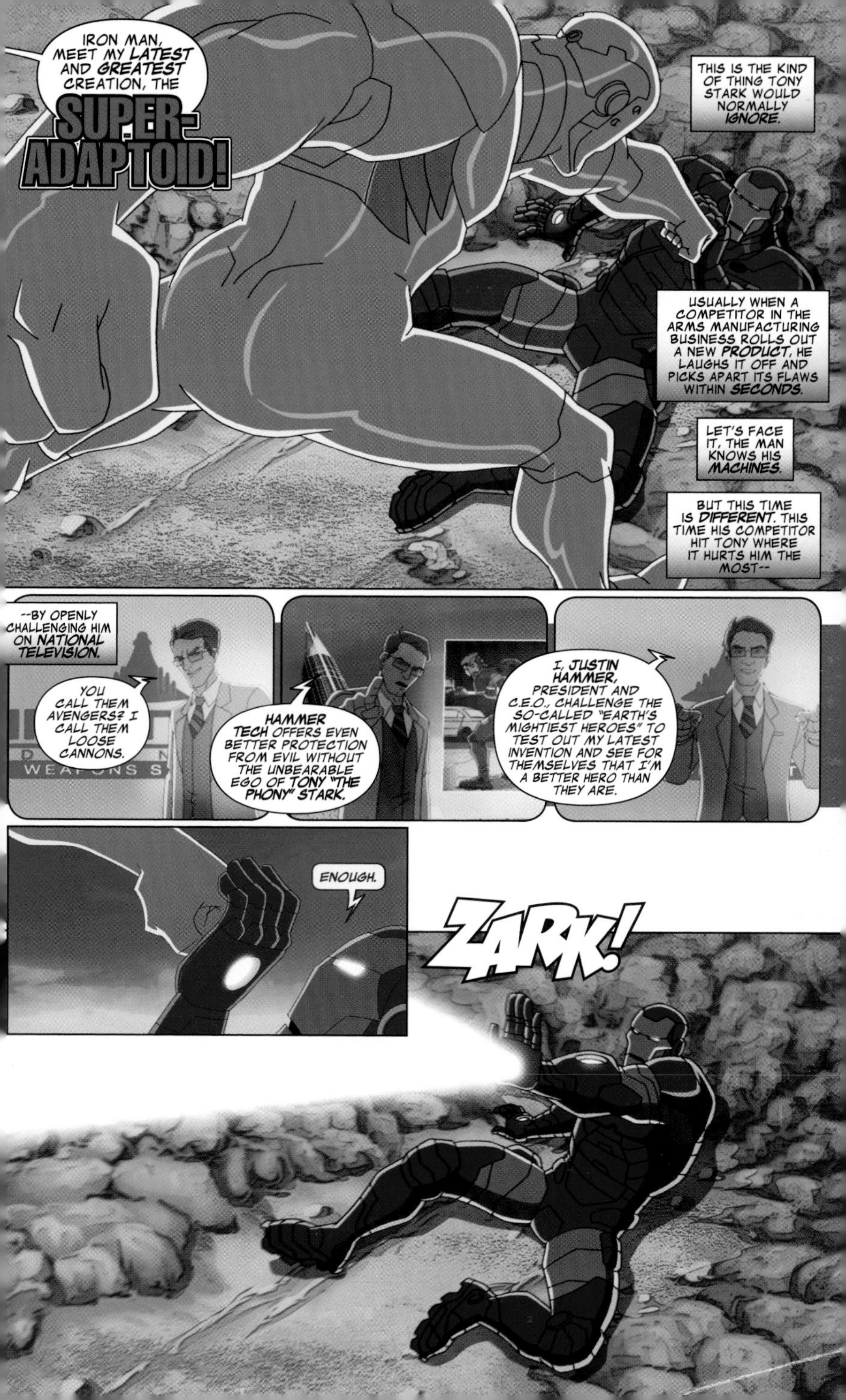
IRON MAN, MEET MY LATEST AND GREATEST CREATION, THE
SUPER-ADAPTOID!
THIS IS THE KIND OF THING TONY STARK WOULD NORMALLY IGNORE.
USUALLY WHEN A COMPETITOR IN THE ARMS MANUFACTURING BUSINESS ROLLS OUT A NEW PRODUCT, HE LAUGHS IT OFF AND PICKS APART ITS FLAWS WITHIN SECONDS.
LET'S FACE IT, THE MAN KNOWS HIS MACHINES.
BUT THIS TIME IS DIFFERENT. THIS TIME HIS COMPETITOR HIT TONY WHERE IT HURTS HIM THE MOST--
--BY OPENLY CHALLENGING HIM ON NATIONAL TELEVISION.
YOU CALL THEM AVENGERS? I CALL THEM LOOSE CANNONS.
HAMMER TECH OFFERS EVEN BETTER PROTECTION FROM EVIL WITHOUT THE UNBEARABLE EGO OF TONY "THE PHONY" STARK.
I, JUSTIN HAMMER, PRESIDENT AND C.E.O., CHALLENGE THE SO-CALLED "EARTH'S MIGHTIEST HEROES" TO TEST OUT MY LATEST INVENTION AND SEE FOR THEMSELVES THAT I'M A BETTER HERO THAN THEY ARE.
ENOUGH.
ZARK!

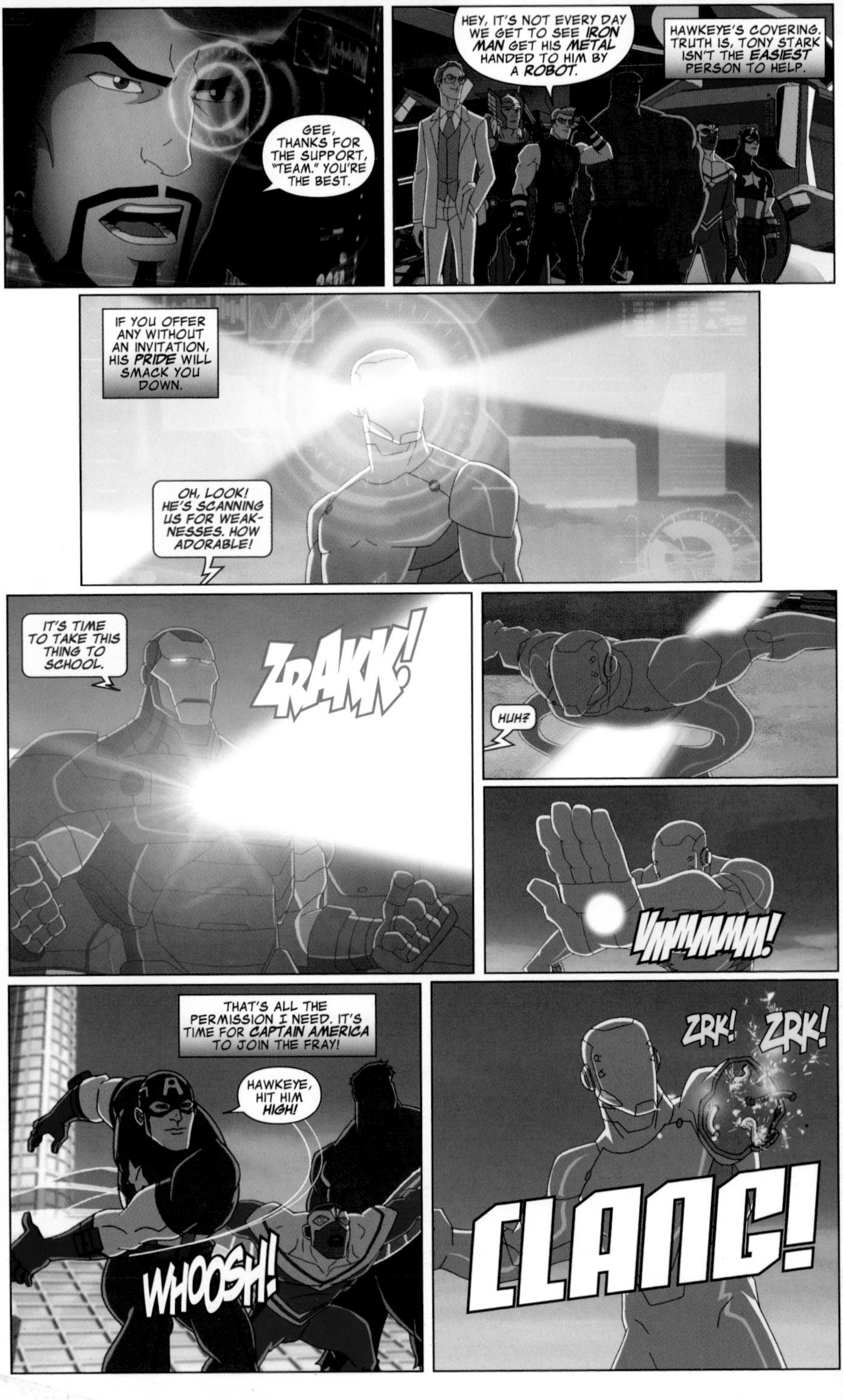
GEE, THANKS FOR THE SUPPORT, "TEAM." YOU'RE THE BEST.
HEY, IT'S NOT EVERY DAY WE GET TO SEE IRON MAN GET HIS METAL HANDED TO HIM BY A ROBOT.
HAWKEYE'S COVERING. TRUTH IS, TONY STARK ISN'T THE EASIEST PERSON TO HELP.
IF YOU OFFER ANY WITHOUT AN INVITATION, HIS PRIDE WILL SMACK YOU DOWN.
OH, LOOK! HE'S SCANNING US FOR WEAK-NESSES. HOW ADORABLE!
IT'S TIME TO TAKE THIS THING TO SCHOOL.
ZRAKK!
HUH?
VMMMMM!
THAT'S ALL THE PERMISSION I NEED. IT'S TIME FOR CAPTAIN AMERICA TO JOIN THE FRAY!
HAWKEYE, HIT HIM HIGH!
WHOOSH!
ZRK! ZRK!
CLANG!

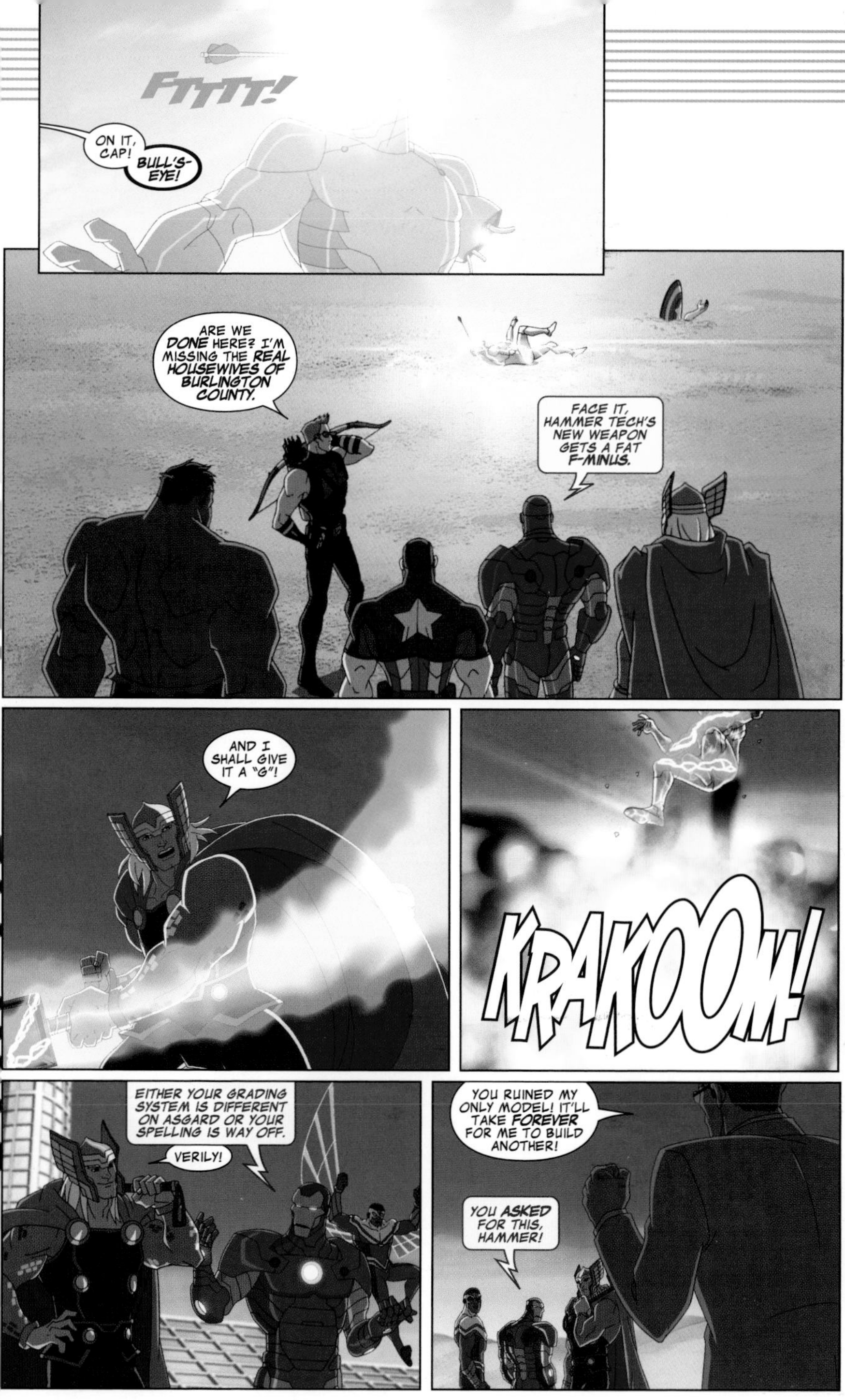
FTTTT!
ON IT, CAP!
BULL'S-EYE!
ARE WE DONE HERE? I'M MISSING THE REAL HOUSEWIVES OF BURLINGTON COUNTY.
FACE IT, HAMMER TECH'S NEW WEAPON GETS A FAT F-MINUS.
AND I SHALL GIVE IT A "G"!
KRAKOOOM!
EITHER YOUR GRADING SYSTEM IS DIFFERENT ON ASGARD OR YOUR SPELLING IS WAY OFF.
VERILY!
YOU RUINED MY ONLY MODEL! IT'LL TAKE FOREVER FOR ME TO BUILD ANOTHER!
YOU ASKED FOR THIS, HAMMER!

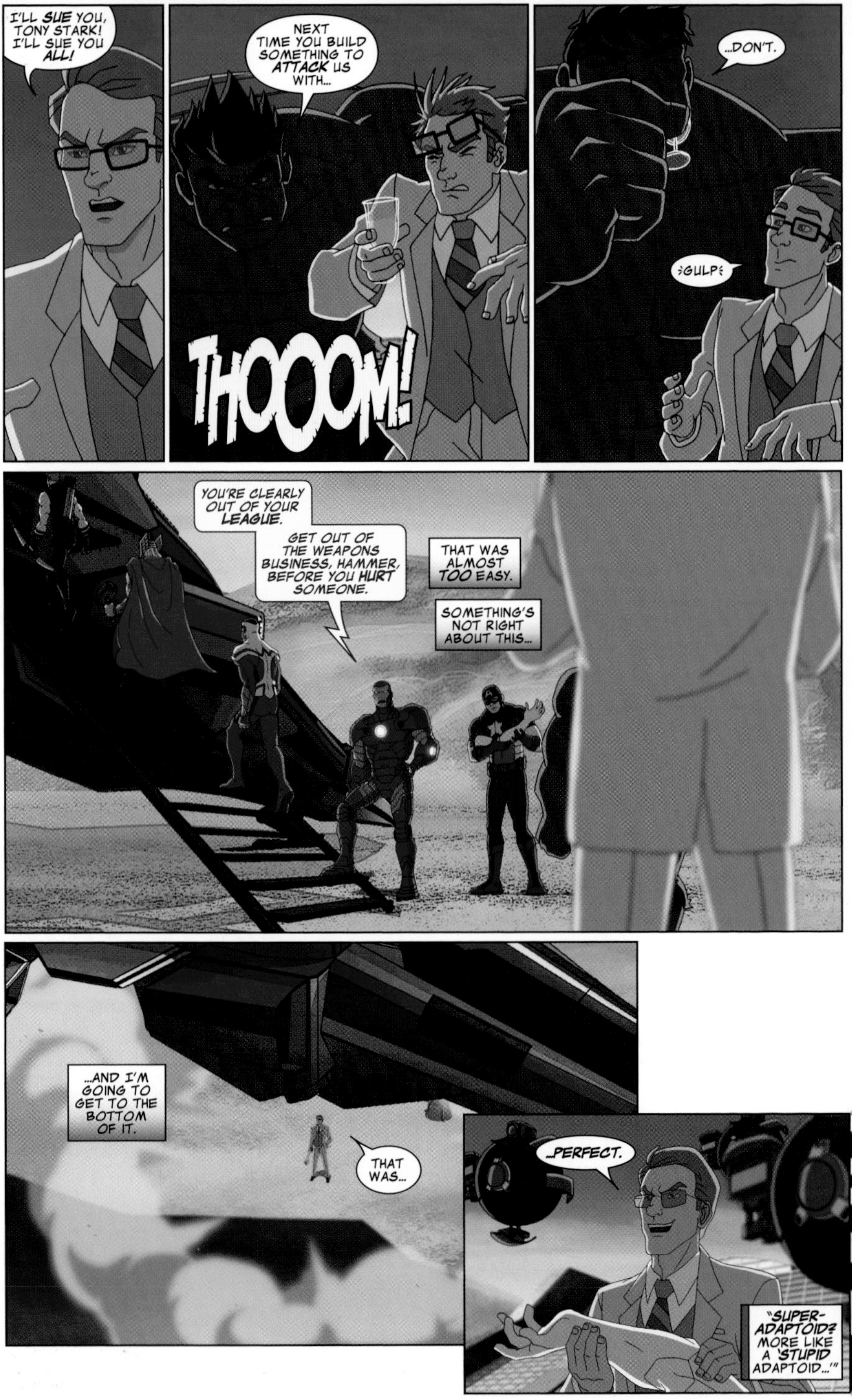

I'LL SUE YOU, TONY STARK! I'LL SUE YOU ALL!
NEXT TIME YOU BUILD SOMETHING TO ATTACK US WITH...
THOOOM!
...DON'T.
GULP
YOU'RE CLEARLY OUT OF YOUR LEAGUE.
GET OUT OF THE WEAPONS BUSINESS, HAMMER, BEFORE YOU HURT SOMEONE.
THAT WAS ALMOST TOO EASY.
SOMETHING'S NOT RIGHT ABOUT THIS...
...AND I'M GOING TO GET TO THE BOTTOM OF IT.
THAT WAS...
...PERFECT.
"SUPER-ADAPTOID? MORE LIKE A 'STUPID ADAPTOID...'"

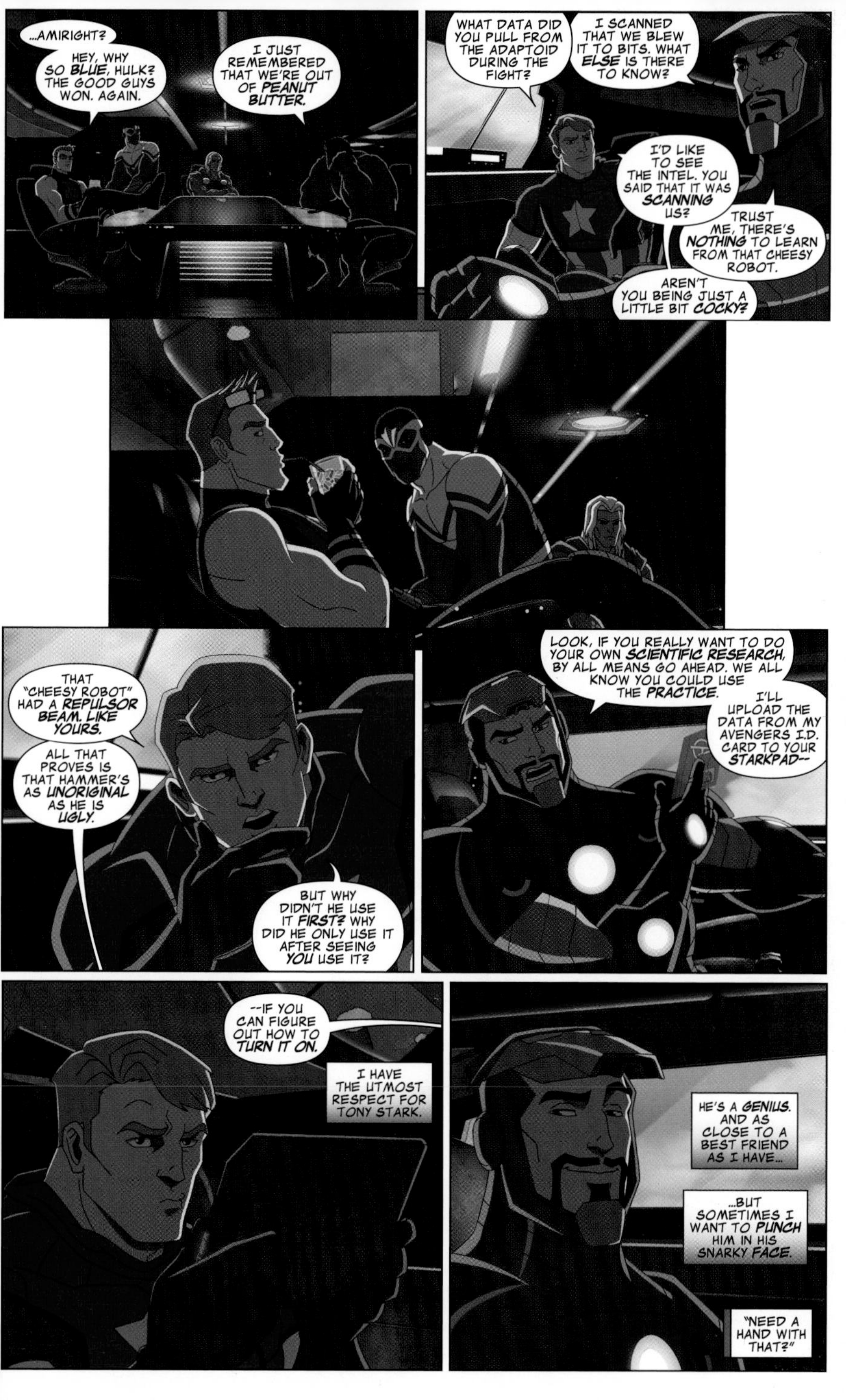
...AMIRIGHT?
HEY, WHY SO BLUE, HULK? THE GOOD GUYS WON. AGAIN.
I JUST REMEMBERED THAT WE'RE OUT OF PEANUT BUTTER.
WHAT DATA DID YOU PULL FROM THE ADAPTOID DURING THE FIGHT?
I SCANNED THAT WE BLEW IT TO BITS. WHAT ELSE IS THERE TO KNOW?
I'D LIKE TO SEE THE INTEL. YOU SAID THAT IT WAS SCANNING US?
TRUST ME, THERE'S NOTHING TO LEARN FROM THAT CHEESY ROBOT.
AREN'T YOU BEING JUST A LITTLE BIT COCKY?
THAT "CHEESY ROBOT" HAD A REPULSOR BEAM. LIKE YOURS.
ALL THAT PROVES IS THAT HAMMER'S AS UNORIGINAL AS HE IS UGLY.
BUT WHY DIDN'T HE USE IT FIRST? WHY DID HE ONLY USE IT AFTER SEEING YOU USE IT?
LOOK, IF YOU REALLY WANT TO DO YOUR OWN SCIENTIFIC RESEARCH, BY ALL MEANS GO AHEAD. WE ALL KNOW YOU COULD USE THE PRACTICE.
I'LL UPLOAD THE DATA FROM MY AVENGERS I.D. CARD TO YOUR STARKPAD--
--IF YOU CAN FIGURE OUT HOW TO TURN IT ON.
I HAVE THE UTMOST RESPECT FOR TONY STARK.
HE'S A GENIUS. AND AS CLOSE TO A BEST FRIEND AS I HAVE...
...BUT SOMETIMES I WANT TO PUNCH HIM IN HIS SNARKY FACE.
"NEED A HAND WITH THAT?"

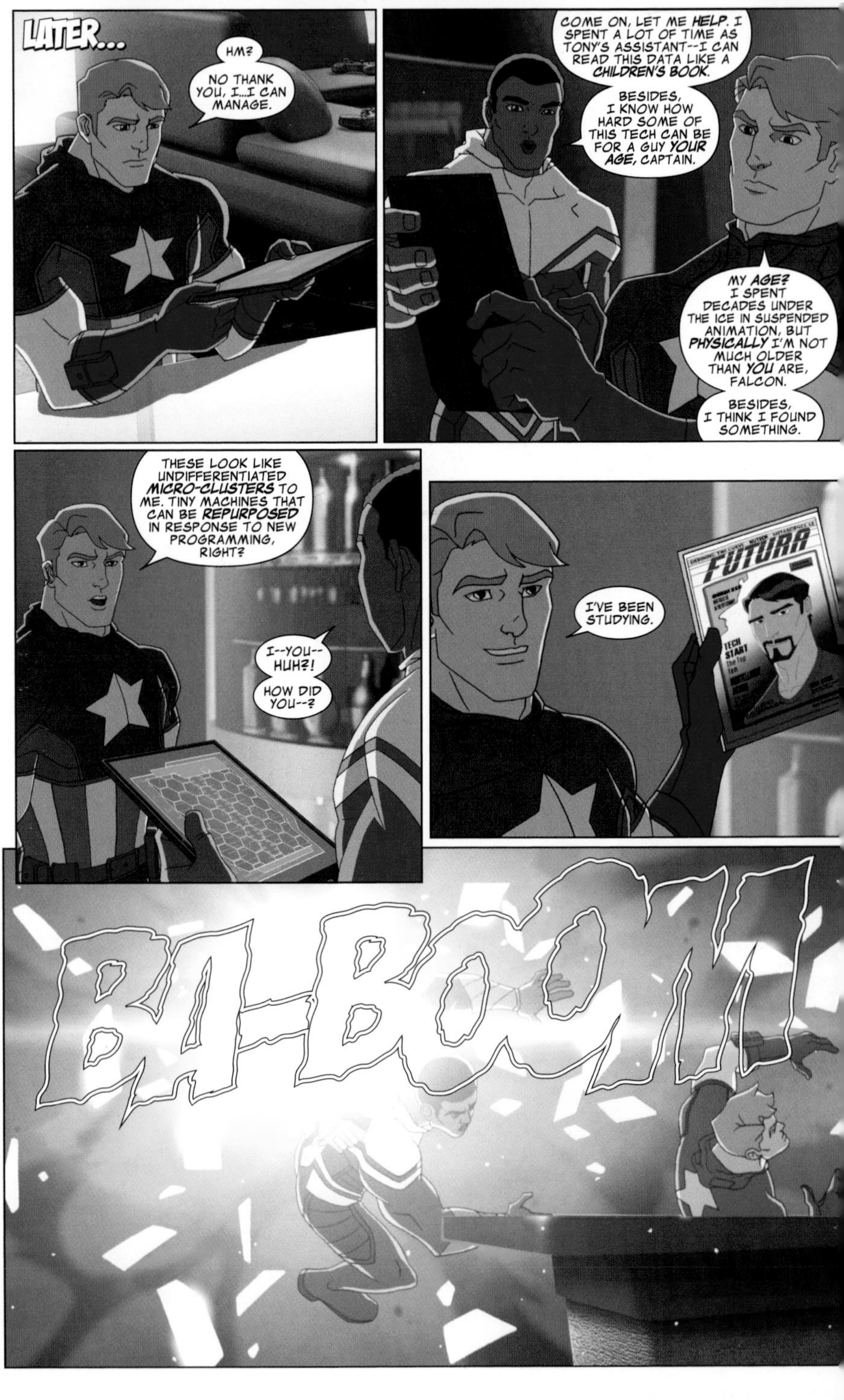
LATER...
HM?
NO THANK YOU, I...I CAN MANAGE.
COME ON, LET ME HELP. I SPENT A LOT OF TIME AS TONY'S ASSISTANT--I CAN READ THIS DATA LIKE A CHILDREN'S BOOK.
BESIDES, I KNOW HOW HARD SOME OF THIS TECH CAN BE FOR A GUY YOUR AGE, CAPTAIN.
MY AGE? I SPENT DECADES UNDER THE ICE IN SUSPENDED ANIMATION, BUT PHYSICALLY I'M NOT MUCH OLDER THAN YOU ARE, FALCON.
BESIDES, I THINK I FOUND SOMETHING.
THESE LOOK LIKE UNDIFFERENTIATED MICRO-CLUSTERS TO ME. TINY MACHINES THAT CAN BE REPURPOSED IN RESPONSE TO NEW PROGRAMMING, RIGHT?
I--YOU-- HUH?!
HOW DID YOU--?
I'VE BEEN STUDYING.
FUTURA
TECH START
The Top Ten
BA-BOOM!

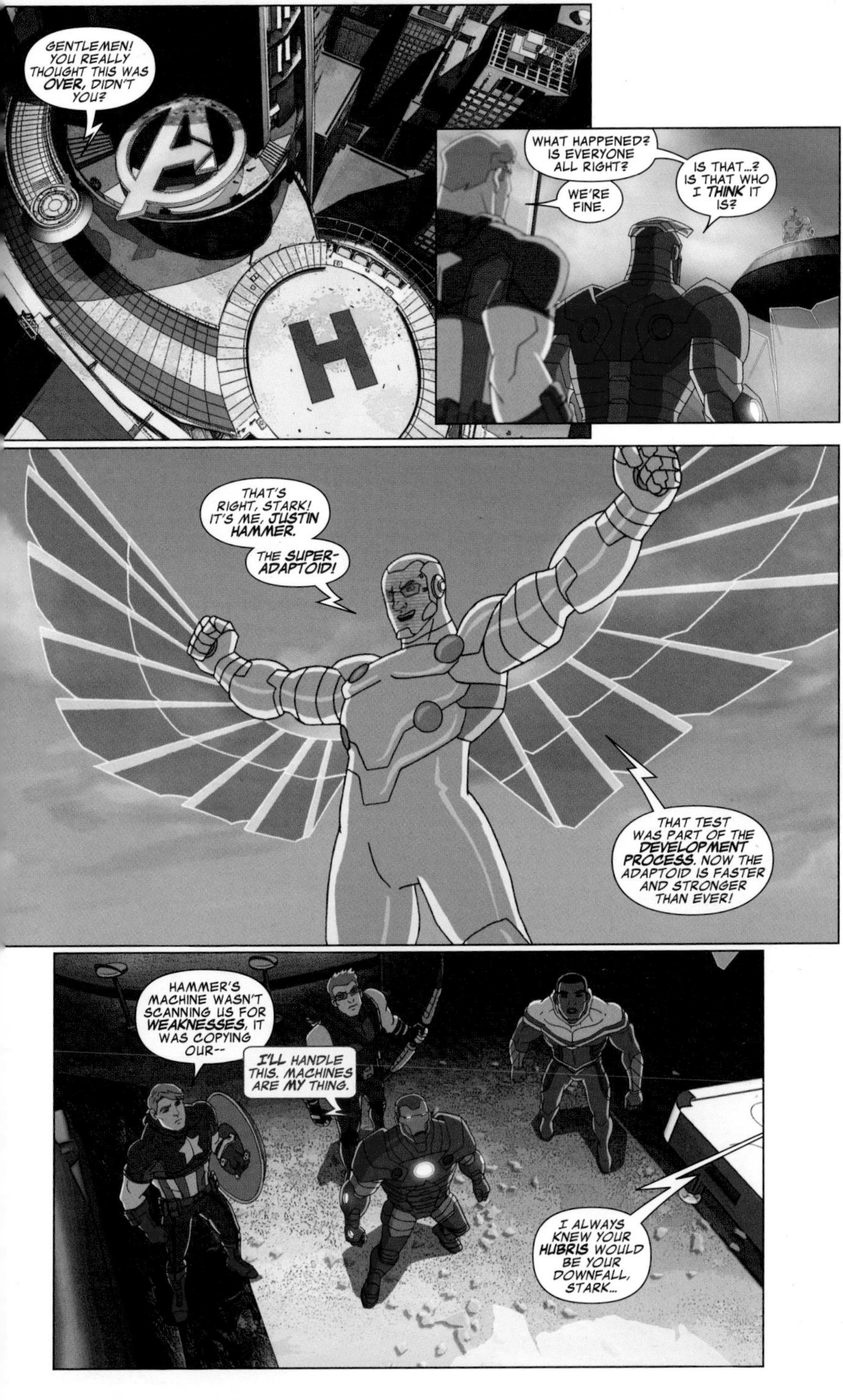
GENTLEMEN! YOU REALLY THOUGHT THIS WAS OVER, DIDN'T YOU?
WHAT HAPPENED? IS EVERYONE ALL RIGHT?
WE'RE FINE.
IS THAT...? IS THAT WHO I THINK IT IS?
THAT'S RIGHT, STARK! IT'S ME, JUSTIN HAMMER.
THE SUPER-ADAPTOID!
THAT TEST WAS PART OF THE DEVELOPMENT PROCESS. NOW THE ADAPTOID IS FASTER AND STRONGER THAN EVER!
HAMMER'S MACHINE WASN'T SCANNING US FOR WEAKNESSES, IT WAS COPYING OUR--
I'LL HANDLE THIS. MACHINES ARE MY THING.
I ALWAYS KNEW YOUR HUBRIS WOULD BE YOUR DOWNFALL, STARK...

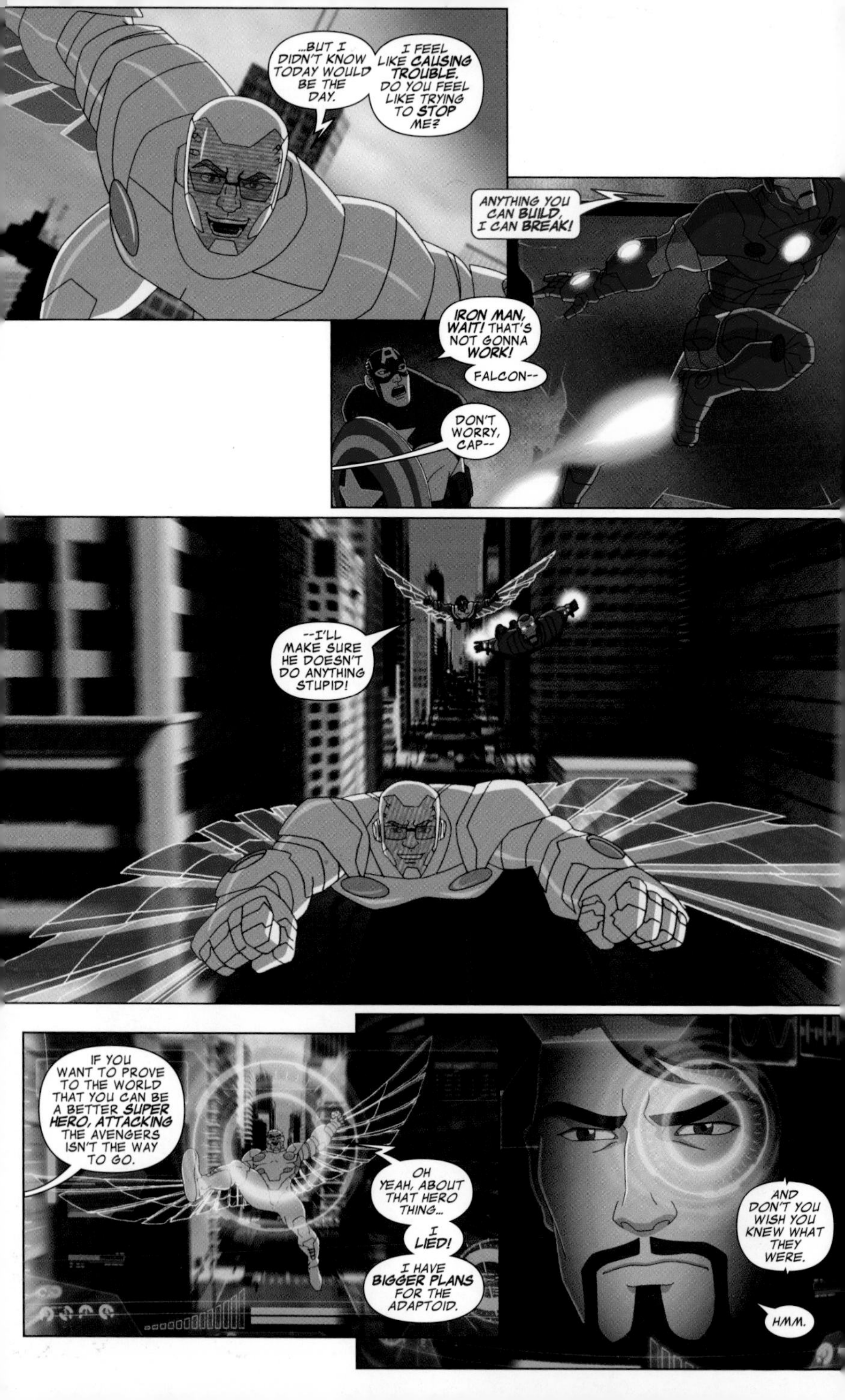
...BUT I DIDN'T KNOW TODAY WOULD BE THE DAY.
I FEEL LIKE CAUSING TROUBLE. DO YOU FEEL LIKE TRYING TO STOP ME?
ANYTHING YOU CAN BUILD, I CAN BREAK!
IRON MAN, WAIT! THAT'S NOT GONNA WORK!
FALCON--
DON'T WORRY, CAP--
--I'LL MAKE SURE HE DOESN'T DO ANYTHING STUPID!
IF YOU WANT TO PROVE TO THE WORLD THAT YOU CAN BE A BETTER SUPER HERO, ATTACKING THE AVENGERS ISN'T THE WAY TO GO.
OH YEAH, ABOUT THAT HERO THING...
I LIED!
I HAVE BIGGER PLANS FOR THE ADAPTOID.
AND DON'T YOU WISH YOU KNEW WHAT THEY WERE.
HMM.

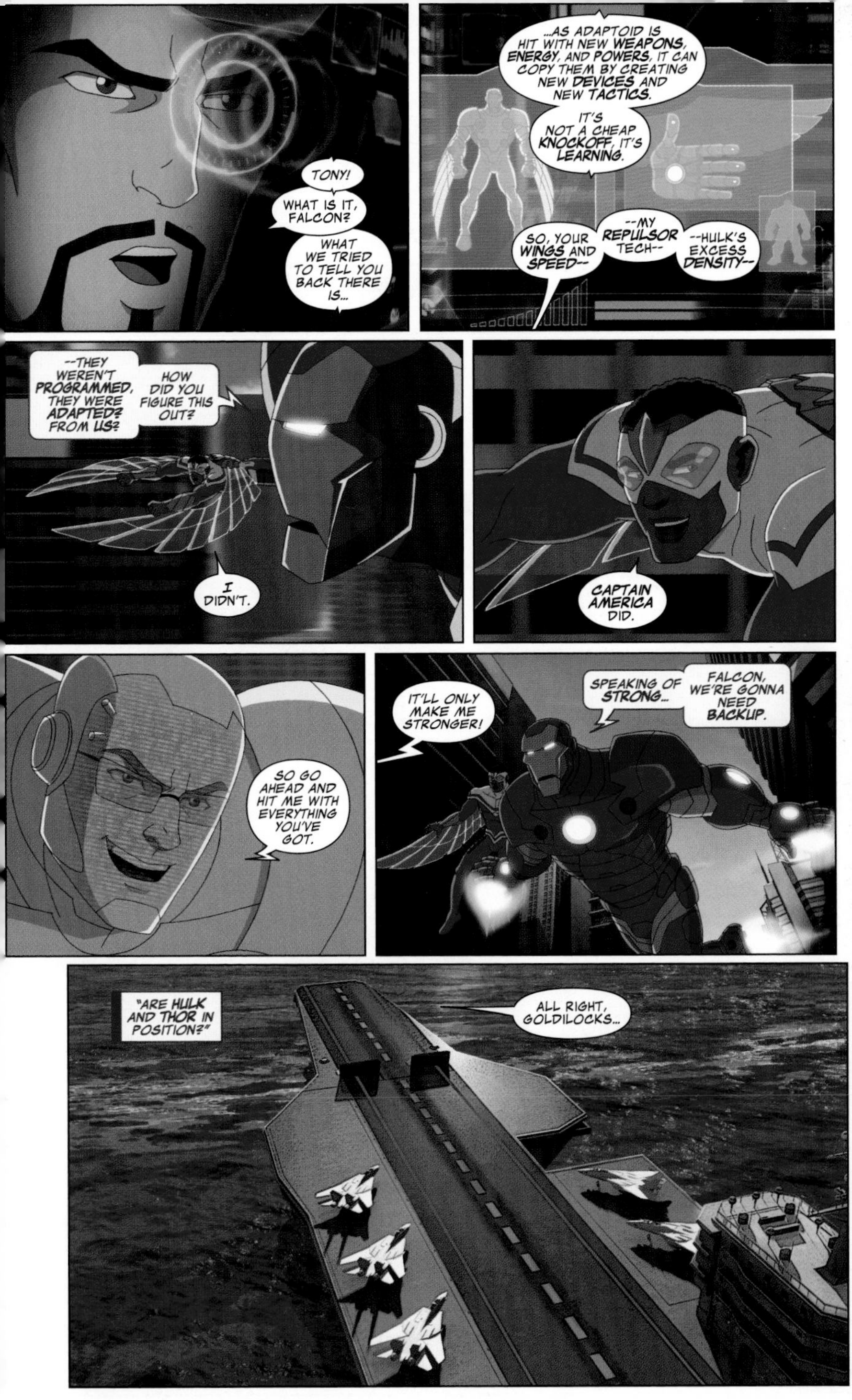
TONY!
WHAT IS IT, FALCON?
WHAT WE TRIED TO TELL YOU BACK THERE IS...
...AS ADAPTOID IS HIT WITH NEW WEAPONS, ENERGY, AND POWERS, IT CAN COPY THEM BY CREATING NEW DEVICES AND NEW TACTICS.
IT'S NOT A CHEAP KNOCKOFF, IT'S LEARNING.
SO, YOUR WINGS AND SPEED--
--MY REPULSOR TECH--
--HULK'S EXCESS DENSITY--
--THEY WEREN'T PROGRAMMED, THEY WERE ADAPTED? FROM US?
HOW DID YOU FIGURE THIS OUT?
I DIDN'T.
CAPTAIN AMERICA DID.
SO GO AHEAD AND HIT ME WITH EVERYTHING YOU'VE GOT.
IT'LL ONLY MAKE ME STRONGER!
SPEAKING OF STRONG...
FALCON, WE'RE GONNA NEED BACKUP.
"ARE HULK AND THOR IN POSITION?"
ALL RIGHT, GOLDILOCKS...

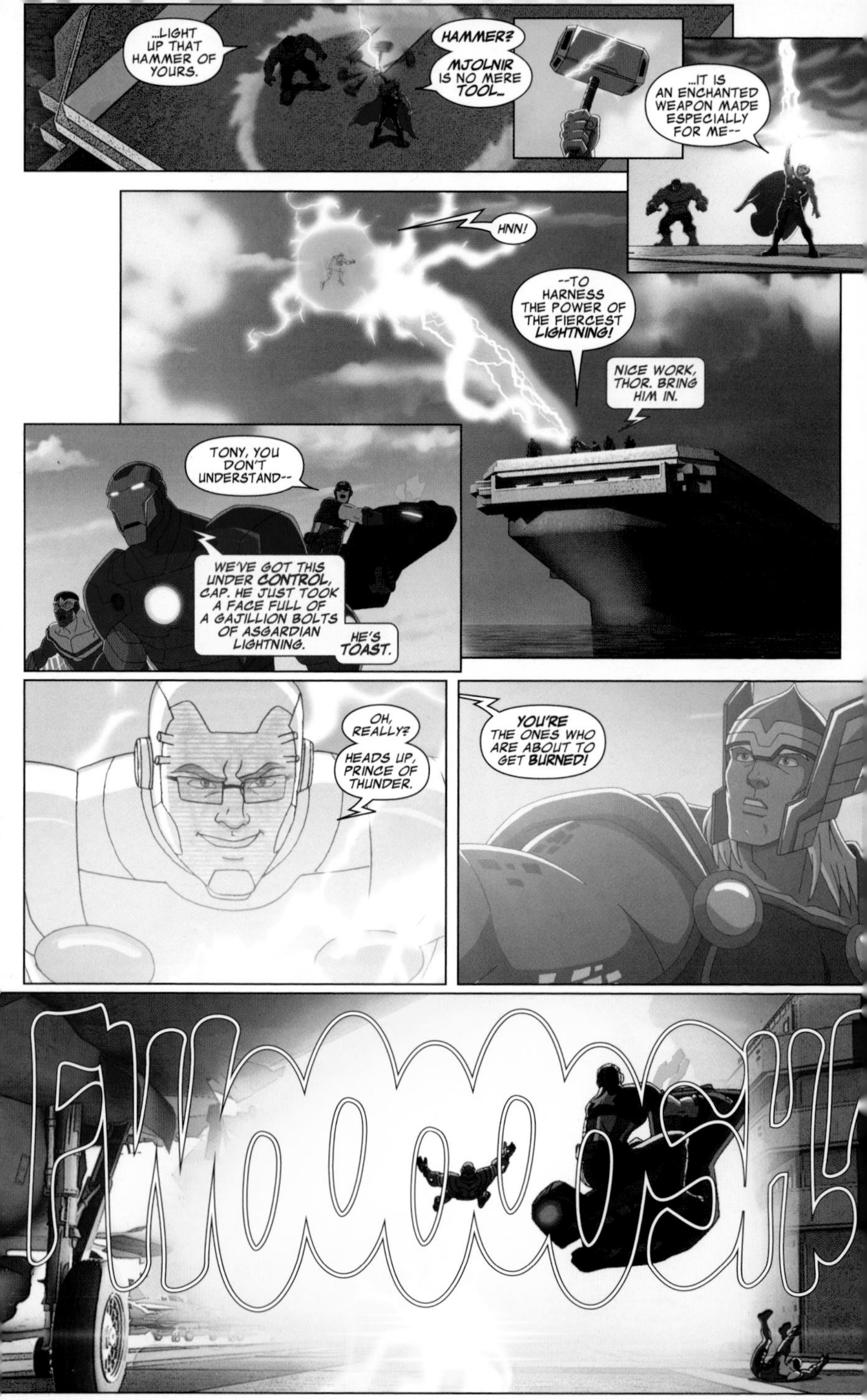
...LIGHT UP THAT HAMMER OF YOURS.
HAMMER?
MJOLNIR IS NO MERE TOOL...
...IT IS AN ENCHANTED WEAPON MADE ESPECIALLY FOR ME--
HNN!
--TO HARNESS THE POWER OF THE FIERCEST LIGHTNING!
NICE WORK, THOR. BRING HIM IN.
TONY, YOU DON'T UNDERSTAND--
WE'VE GOT THIS UNDER CONTROL, CAP. HE JUST TOOK A FACE FULL OF A GAJILLION BOLTS OF ASGARDIAN LIGHTNING.
HE'S TOAST.
OH, REALLY?
HEADS UP, PRINCE OF THUNDER.
YOU'RE THE ONES WHO ARE ABOUT TO GET BURNED!
FWOOOOOSH!

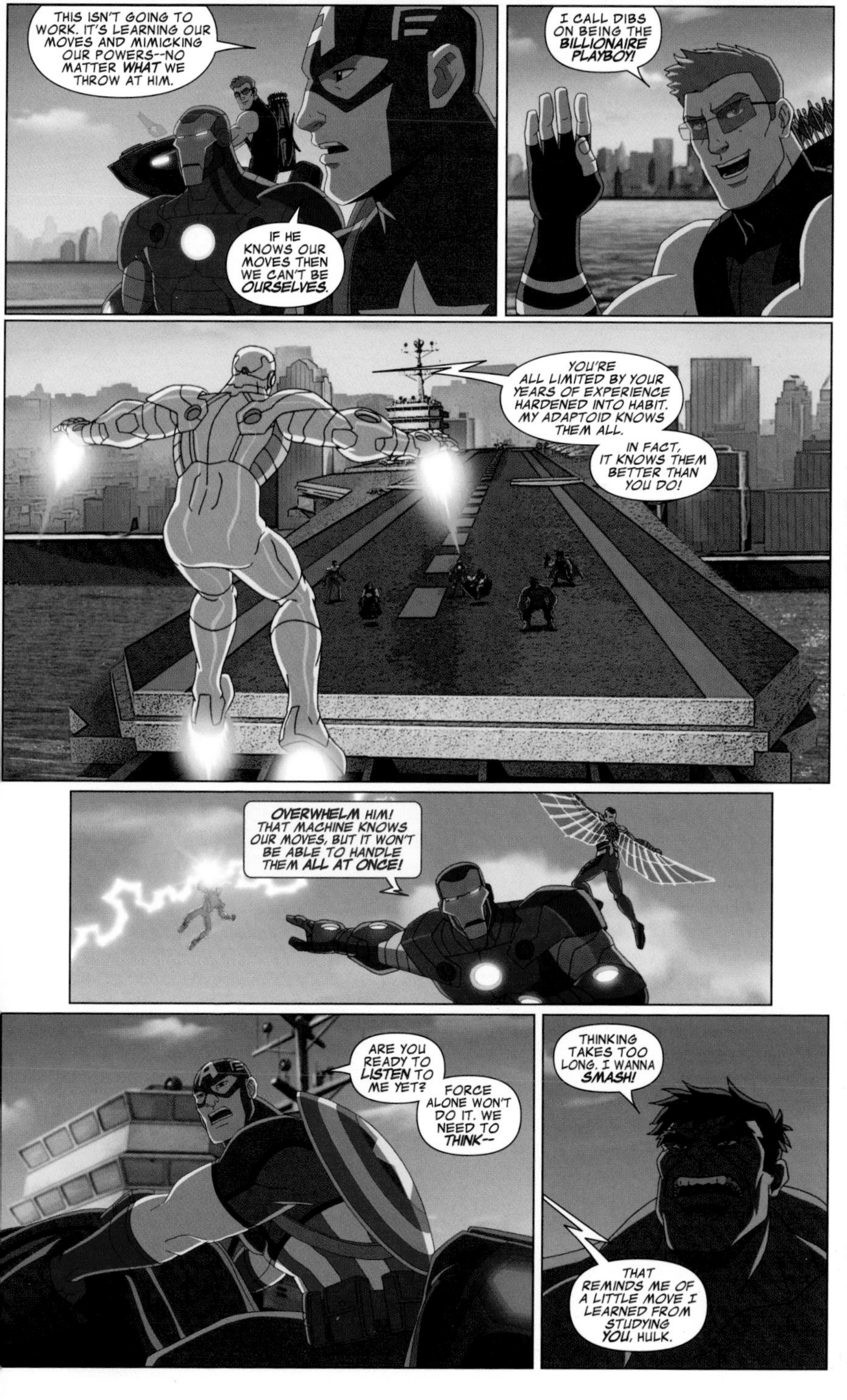

THIS ISN'T GOING TO WORK. IT'S LEARNING OUR MOVES AND MIMICKING OUR POWERS--NO MATTER WHAT WE THROW AT HIM.
IF HE KNOWS OUR MOVES THEN WE CAN'T BE OURSELVES.
I CALL DIBS ON BEING THE BILLIONAIRE PLAYBOY!
YOU'RE ALL LIMITED BY YOUR YEARS OF EXPERIENCE HARDENED INTO HABIT. MY ADAPTOID KNOWS THEM ALL.
IN FACT, IT KNOWS THEM BETTER THAN YOU DO!
OVERWHELM HIM! THAT MACHINE KNOWS OUR MOVES, BUT IT WON'T BE ABLE TO HANDLE THEM ALL AT ONCE!
ARE YOU READY TO LISTEN TO ME YET?
FORCE ALONE WON'T DO IT. WE NEED TO THINK--
THINKING TAKES TOO LONG. I WANNA SMASH!
THAT REMINDS ME OF A LITTLE MOVE I LEARNED FROM STUDYING YOU, HULK.

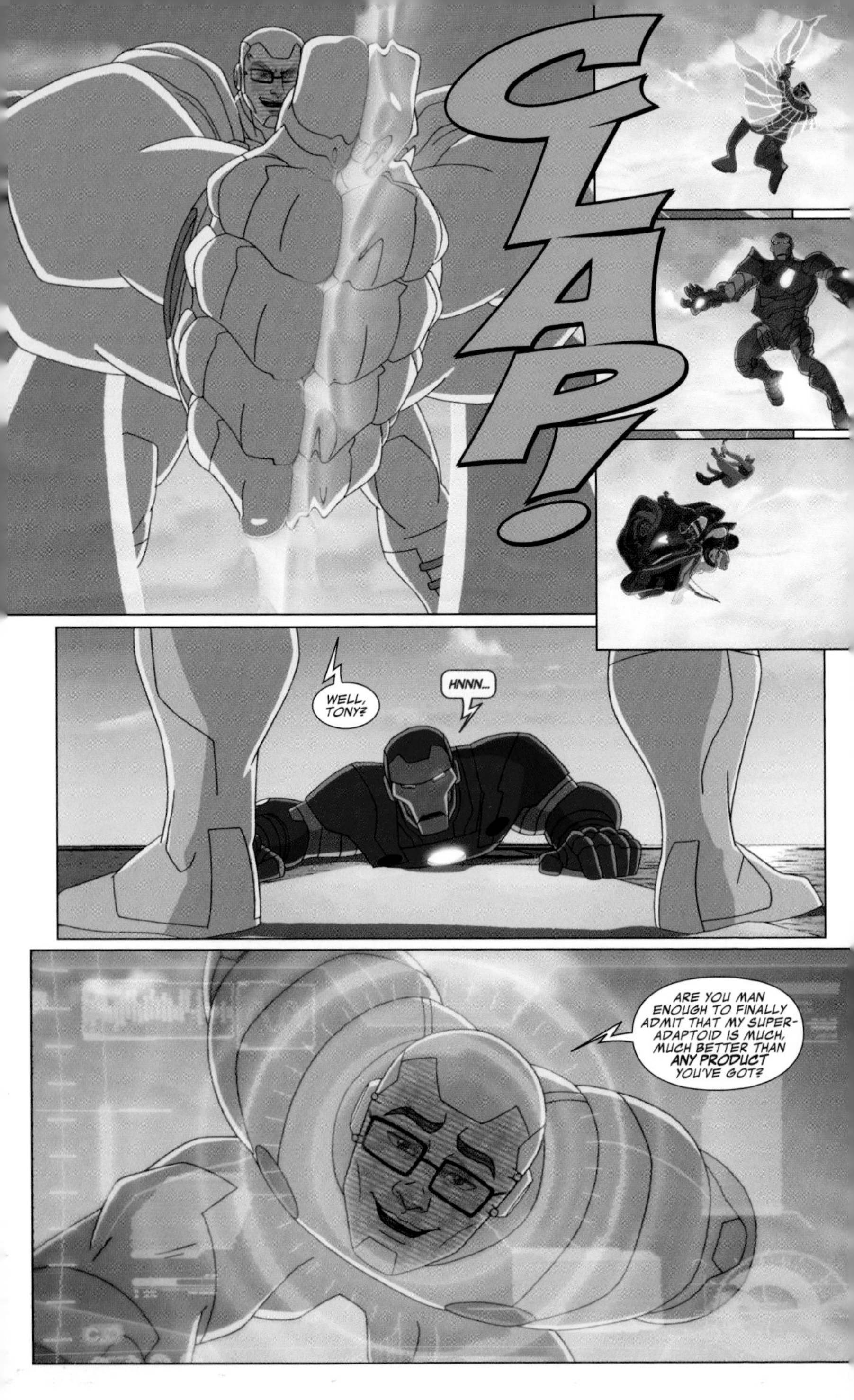
CLAP!
WELL, TONY?
HNNN...
ARE YOU MAN ENOUGH TO FINALLY ADMIT THAT MY SUPER-ADAPTOID IS MUCH, MUCH BETTER THAN ANY PRODUCT YOU'VE GOT?

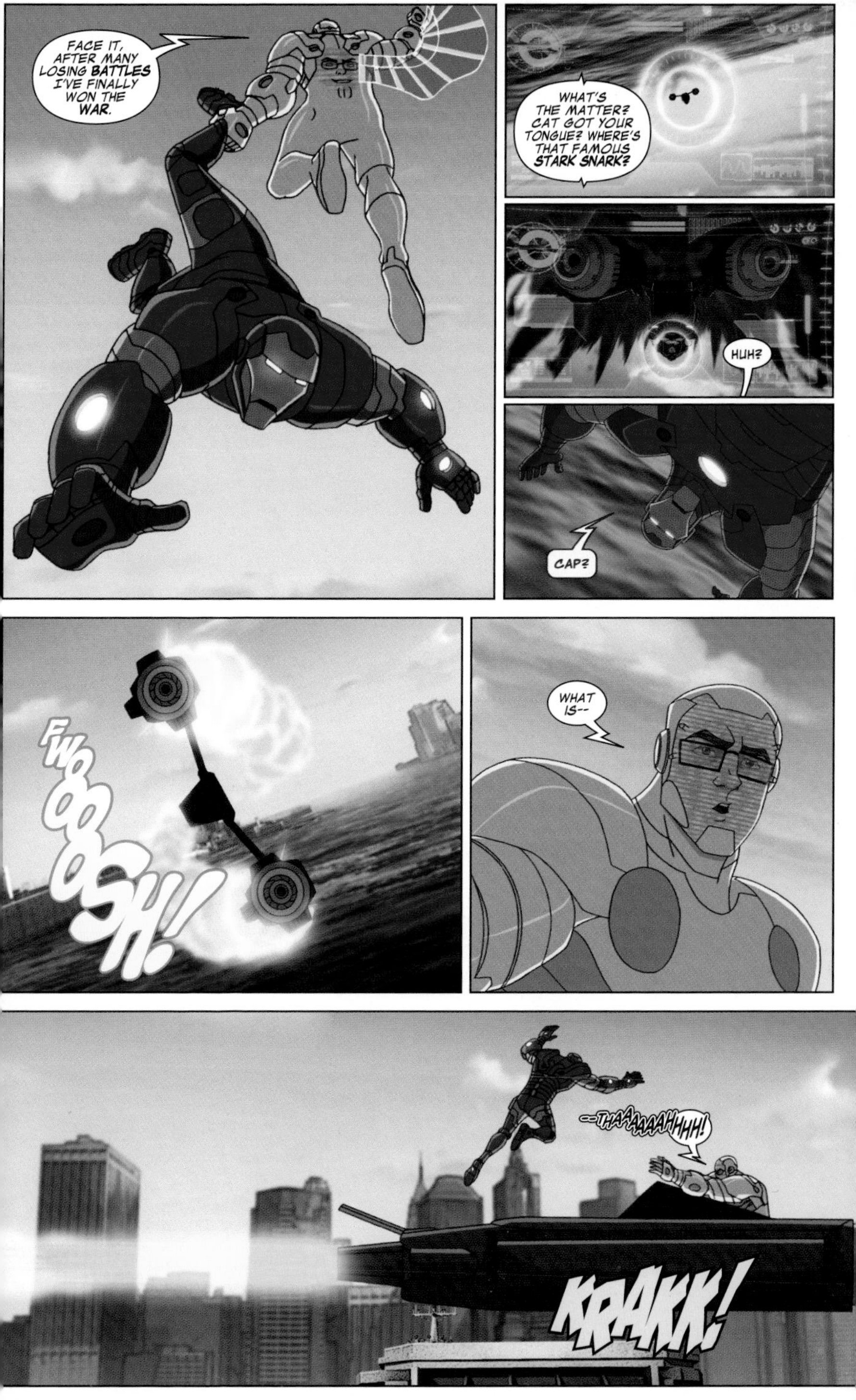
FACE IT, AFTER MANY LOSING BATTLES I'VE FINALLY WON THE WAR.
WHAT'S THE MATTER? CAT GOT YOUR TONGUE? WHERE'S THAT FAMOUS STARK SNARK?
HUH?
CAP?
FWOOOSH!!
WHAT IS--
--THAAAAAAHHHH!
KRAKK!

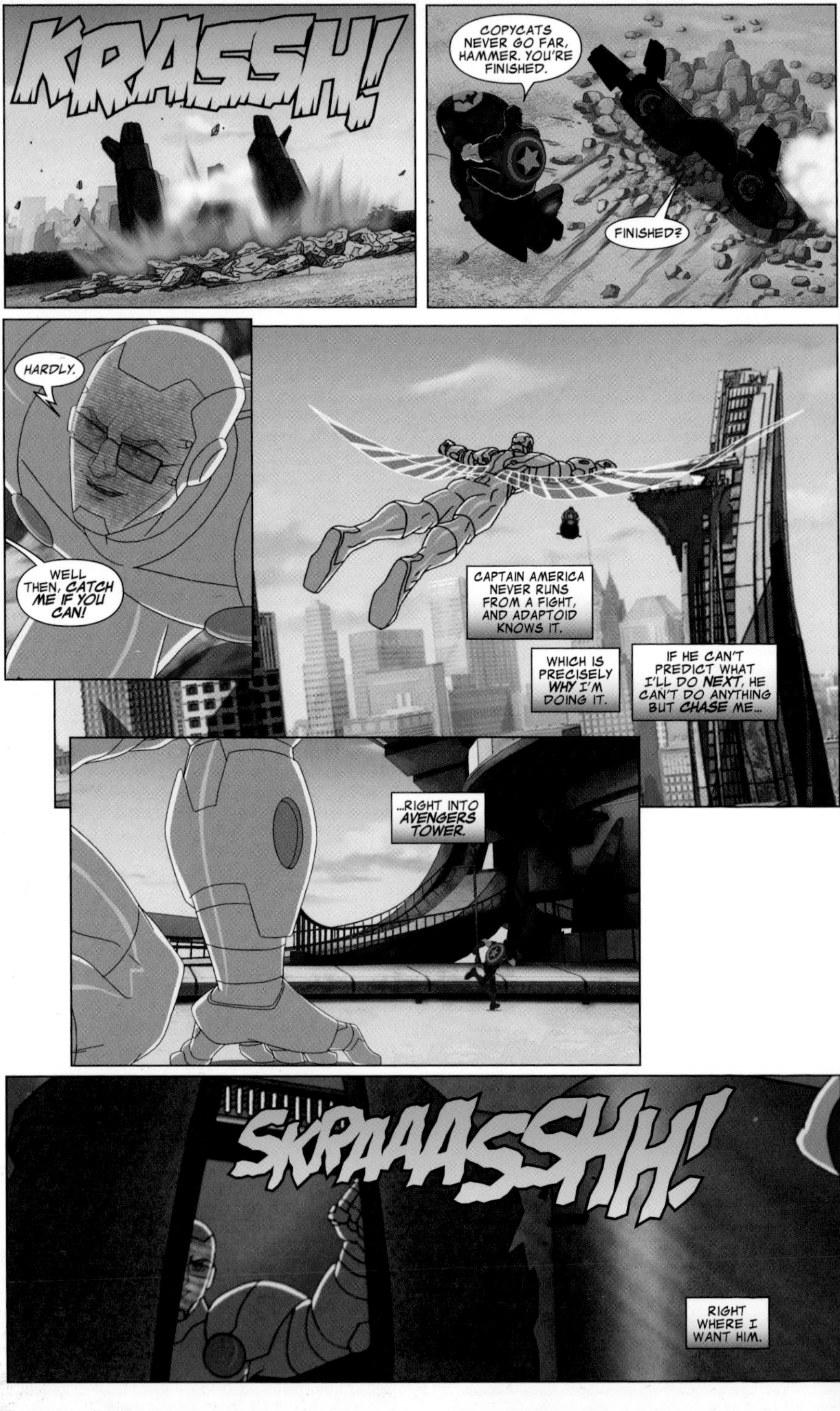
KRASSH!
COPYCATS NEVER GO FAR, HAMMER. YOU'RE FINISHED.
FINISHED?
HARDLY.
WELL THEN, CATCH ME IF YOU CAN!
CAPTAIN AMERICA NEVER RUNS FROM A FIGHT, AND ADAPTOID KNOWS IT.
WHICH IS PRECISELY WHY I'M DOING IT.
IF HE CAN'T PREDICT WHAT I'LL DO NEXT, HE CAN'T DO ANYTHING BUT CHASE ME...
...RIGHT INTO AVENGERS TOWER.
SKRAAASSHH!
RIGHT WHERE I WANT HIM.

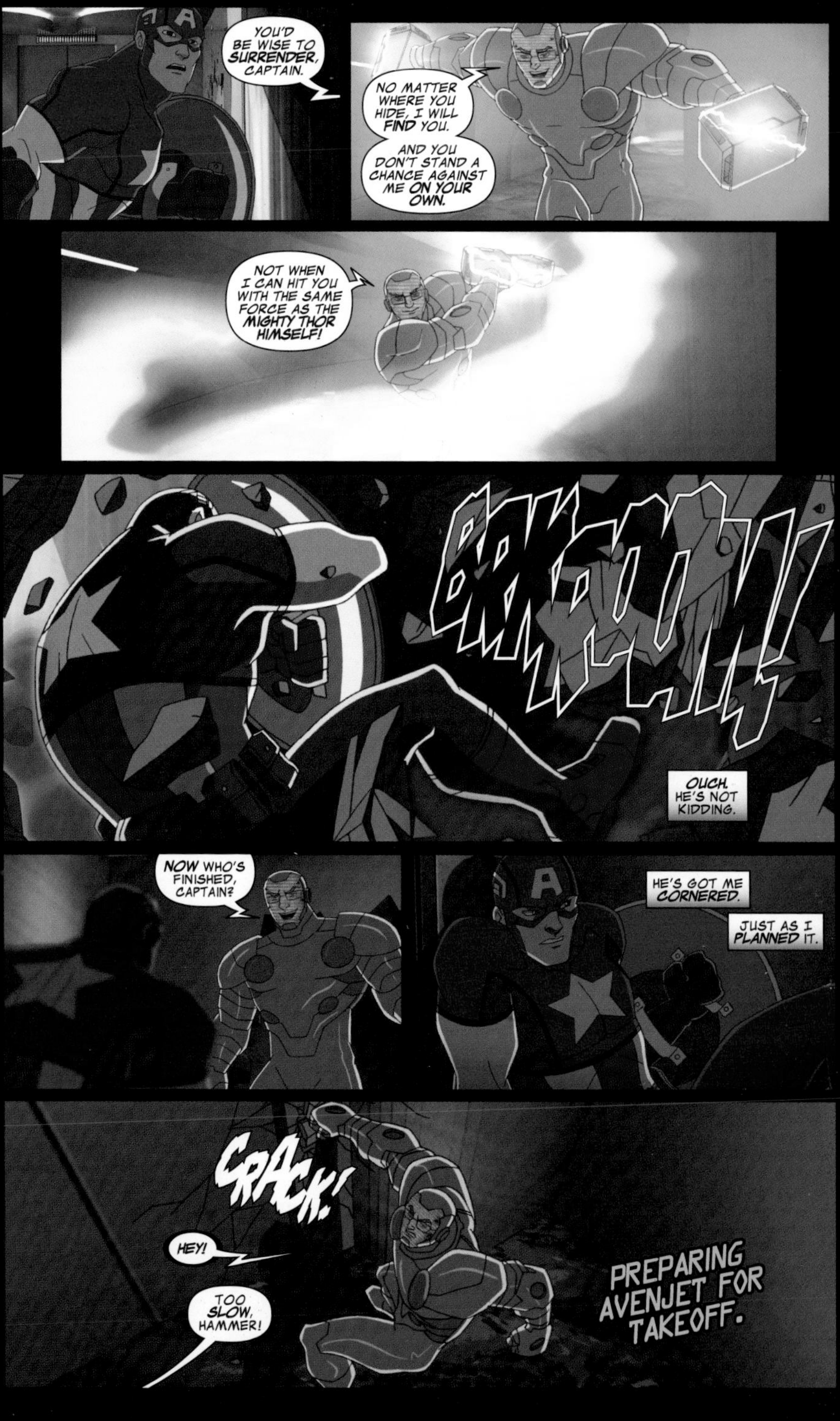
YOU'D BE WISE TO SURRENDER, CAPTAIN.
NO MATTER WHERE YOU HIDE, I WILL FIND YOU.
AND YOU DON'T STAND A CHANCE AGAINST ME ON YOUR OWN.
NOT WHEN I CAN HIT YOU WITH THE SAME FORCE AS THE MIGHTY THOR HIMSELF!
BRAKOOOM!
OUCH. HE'S NOT KIDDING.
NOW WHO'S FINISHED, CAPTAIN?
HE'S GOT ME CORNERED.
JUST AS I PLANNED IT.
CRACK!
HEY!
TOO SLOW, HAMMER!
PREPARING AVENJET FOR TAKEOFF.

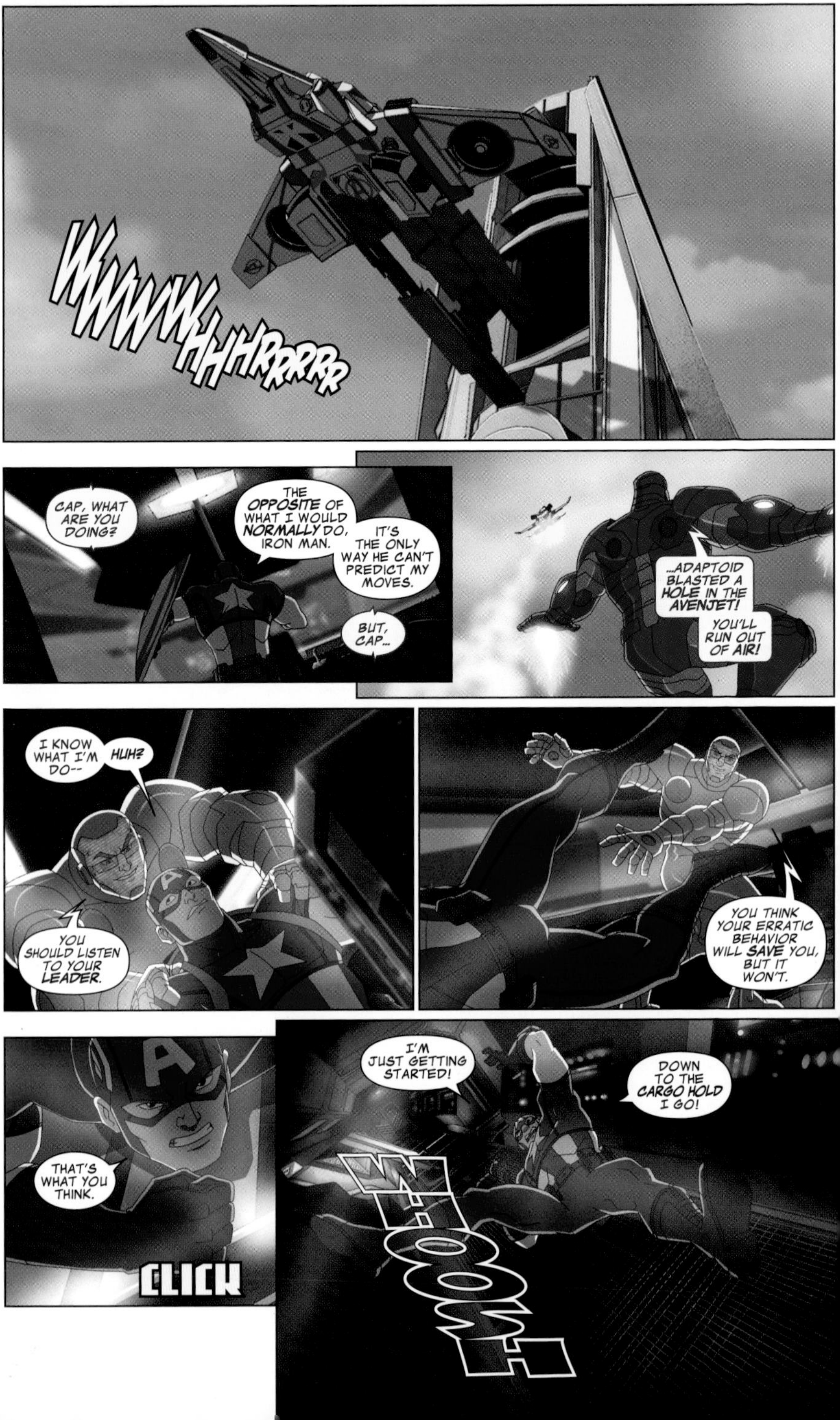
WWWWWHHHRRRRR
CAP, WHAT ARE YOU DOING?
THE OPPOSITE OF WHAT I WOULD NORMALLY DO, IRON MAN.
IT'S THE ONLY WAY HE CAN'T PREDICT MY MOVES.
BUT, CAP...
...ADAPTOID BLASTED A HOLE IN THE AVENJET!
YOU'LL RUN OUT OF AIR!
I KNOW WHAT I'M DO--
HUH?
YOU SHOULD LISTEN TO YOUR LEADER.
YOU THINK YOUR ERRATIC BEHAVIOR WILL SAVE YOU, BUT IT WON'T.
THAT'S WHAT YOU THINK.
CLICK
I'M JUST GETTING STARTED!
DOWN TO THE CARGO HOLD I GO!
WHOOOM!

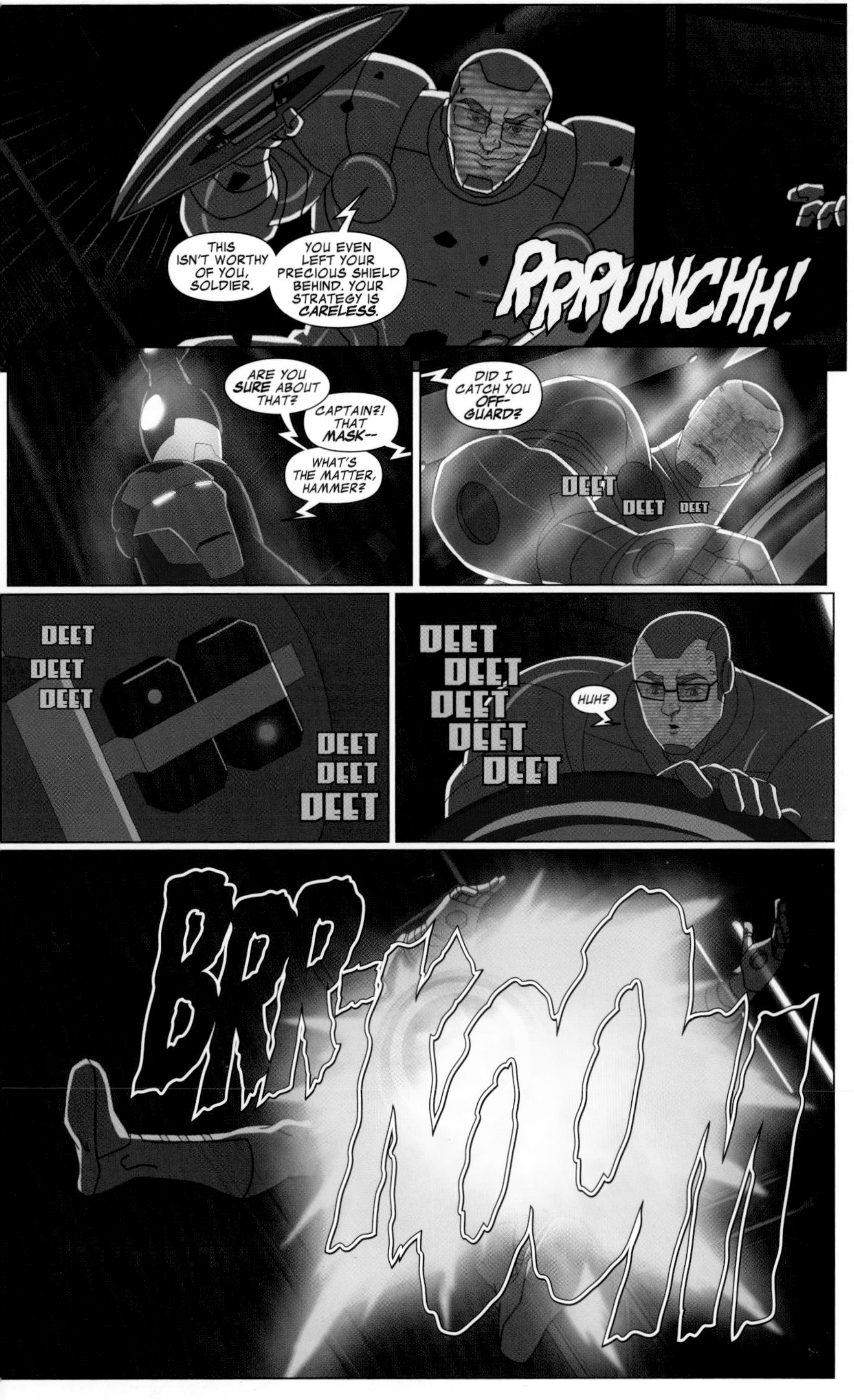
THIS ISN'T WORTHY OF YOU, SOLDIER.
YOU EVEN LEFT YOUR PRECIOUS SHIELD BEHIND. YOUR STRATEGY IS CARELESS.
RRRUNCHH!
ARE YOU SURE ABOUT THAT?
CAPTAIN?! THAT MASK--
WHAT'S THE MATTER, HAMMER?
DID I CATCH YOU OFF-GUARD?
DEET DEET DEET
DEET DEET DEET
DEET DEET DEET
DEET DEET DEET DEET DEET
HUH?
BRR-KOOM

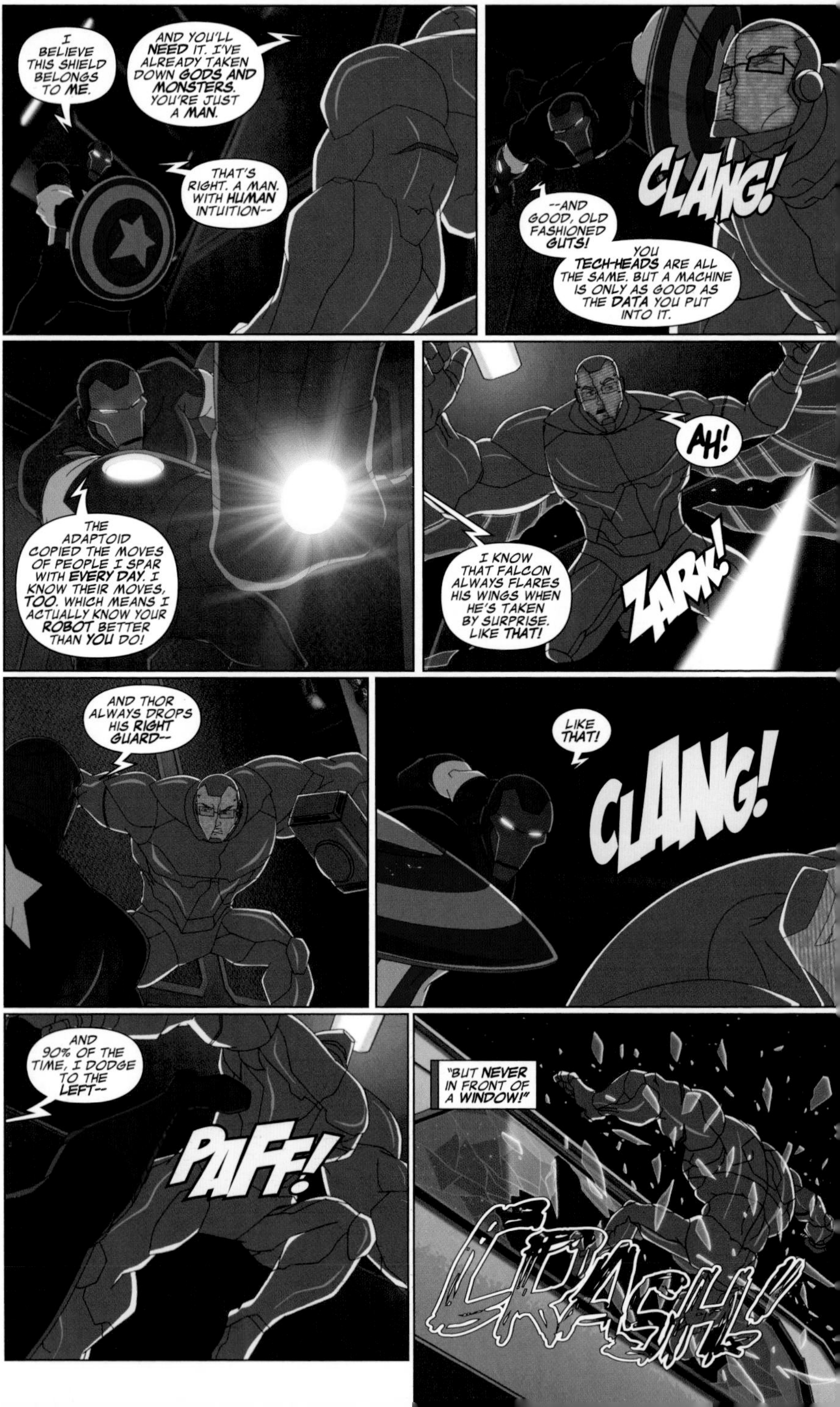

I BELIEVE THIS SHIELD BELONGS TO ME.
AND YOU'LL NEED IT. I'VE ALREADY TAKEN DOWN GODS AND MONSTERS. YOU'RE JUST A MAN.
THAT'S RIGHT. A MAN. WITH HUMAN INTUITION--
CLANG!
--AND GOOD, OLD FASHIONED GUTS!
YOU TECH-HEADS ARE ALL THE SAME. BUT A MACHINE IS ONLY AS GOOD AS THE DATA YOU PUT INTO IT.
THE ADAPTOID COPIED THE MOVES OF PEOPLE I SPAR WITH EVERY DAY. I KNOW THEIR MOVES, TOO. WHICH MEANS I ACTUALLY KNOW YOUR ROBOT BETTER THAN YOU DO!
AH!
I KNOW THAT FALCON ALWAYS FLARES HIS WINGS WHEN HE'S TAKEN BY SURPRISE. LIKE THAT!
ZARK!
AND THOR ALWAYS DROPS HIS RIGHT GUARD--
LIKE THAT!
CLANG!
AND 90% OF THE TIME, I DODGE TO THE LEFT--
PAFF!
"BUT NEVER IN FRONT OF A WINDOW!"
CRASH!

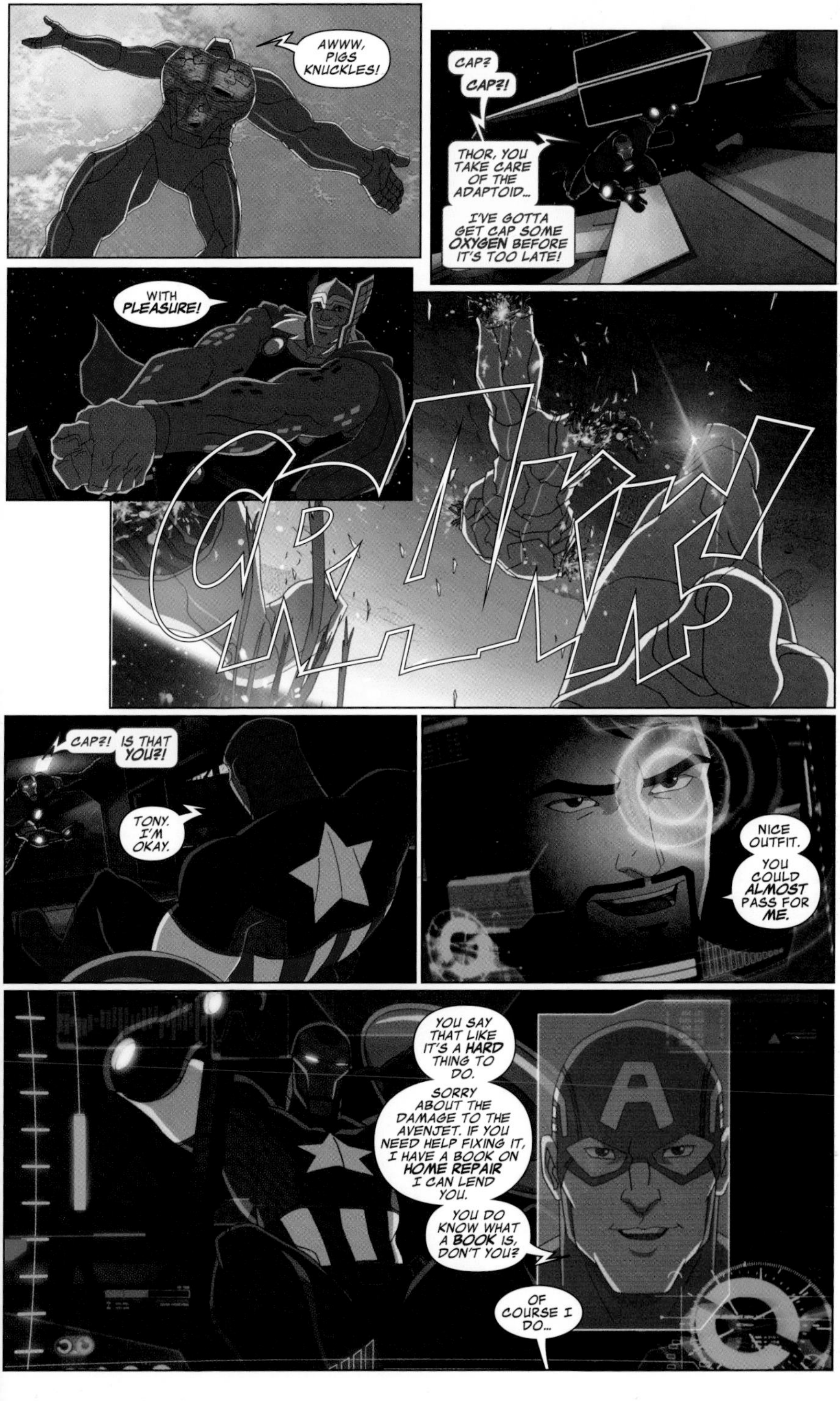
AWWW, PIGS KNUCKLES!
CAP? CAP?!
THOR, YOU TAKE CARE OF THE ADAPTOID...
I'VE GOTTA GET CAP SOME OXYGEN BEFORE IT'S TOO LATE!
WITH PLEASURE!
CAP?! IS THAT YOU?!
TONY. I'M OKAY.
NICE OUTFIT.
YOU COULD ALMOST PASS FOR ME.
YOU SAY THAT LIKE IT'S A HARD THING TO DO.
SORRY ABOUT THE DAMAGE TO THE AVENJET. IF YOU NEED HELP FIXING IT, I HAVE A BOOK ON HOME REPAIR I CAN LEND YOU.
YOU DO KNOW WHAT A BOOK IS, DON'T YOU?
OF COURSE I DO...

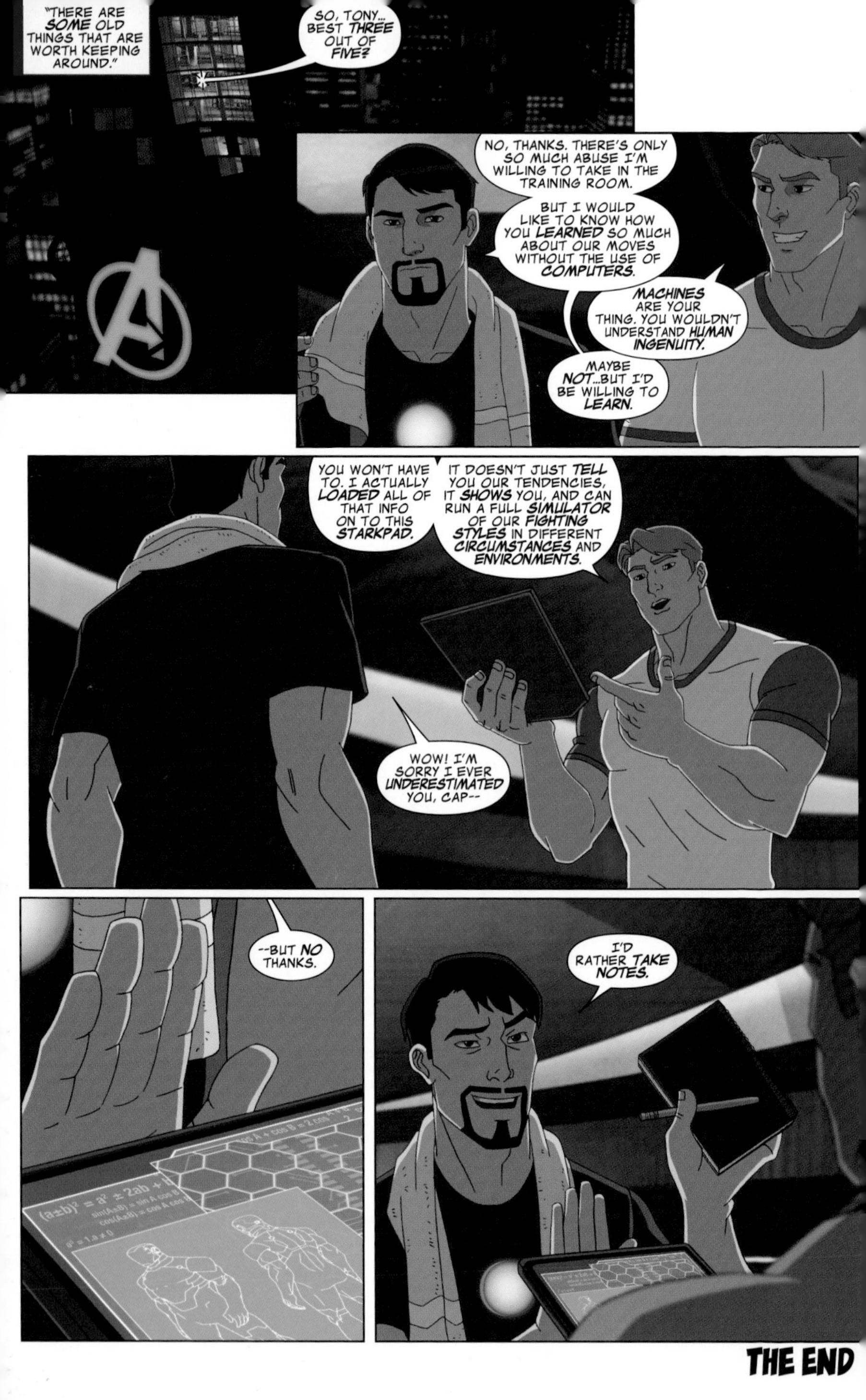
"THERE ARE SOME OLD THINGS THAT ARE WORTH KEEPING AROUND."
SO, TONY... BEST THREE OUT OF FIVE?
NO, THANKS. THERE'S ONLY SO MUCH ABUSE I'M WILLING TO TAKE IN THE TRAINING ROOM.
BUT I WOULD LIKE TO KNOW HOW YOU LEARNED SO MUCH ABOUT OUR MOVES WITHOUT THE USE OF COMPUTERS.
MACHINES ARE YOUR THING. YOU WOULDN'T UNDERSTAND HUMAN INGENUITY.
MAYBE NOT...BUT I'D BE WILLING TO LEARN.
YOU WON'T HAVE TO. I ACTUALLY LOADED ALL OF THAT INFO ON TO THIS STARKPAD.
IT DOESN'T JUST TELL YOU OUR TENDENCIES, IT SHOWS YOU, AND CAN RUN A FULL SIMULATOR OF OUR FIGHTING STYLES IN DIFFERENT CIRCUMSTANCES AND ENVIRONMENTS.
WOW! I'M SORRY I EVER UNDERESTIMATED YOU, CAP--
--BUT NO THANKS.
I'D RATHER TAKE NOTES.
THE END

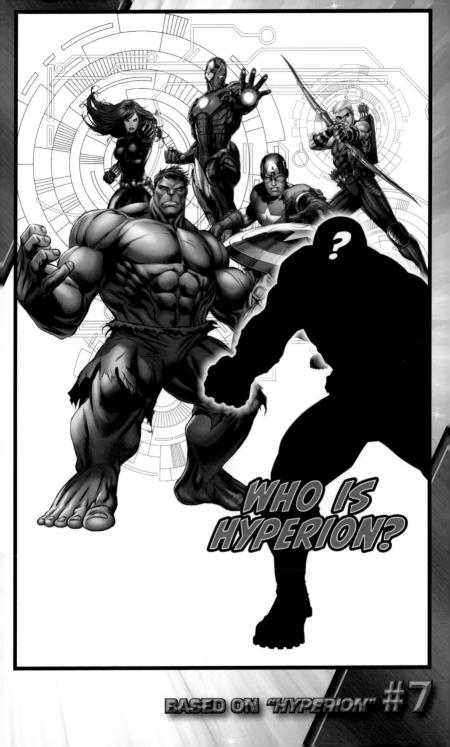

WHO IS HYPERION?

BASED ON "HYPERION" #7

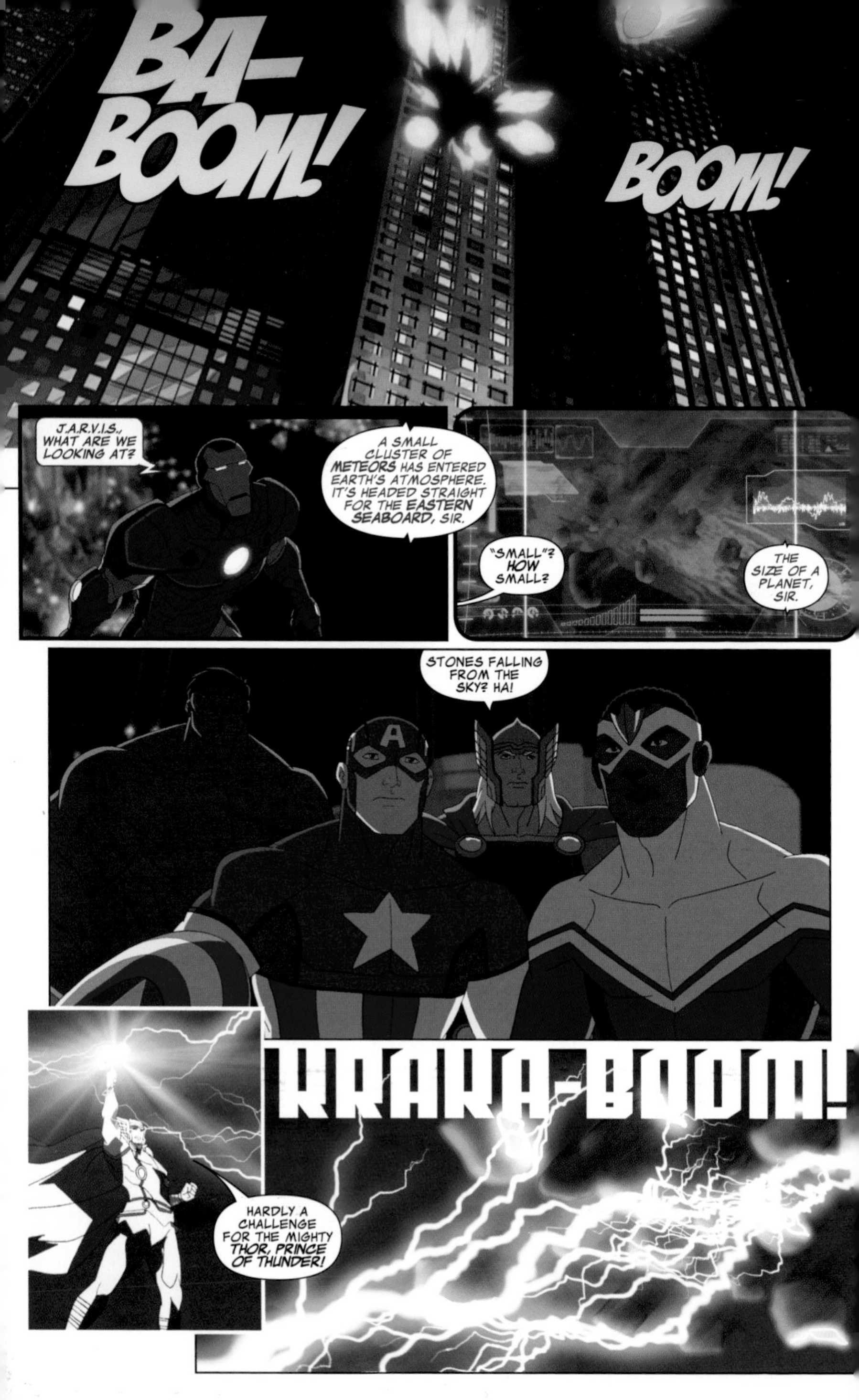

BA-BOOM!
BOOM!
J.A.R.V.I.S., WHAT ARE WE LOOKING AT?
A SMALL CLUSTER OF METEORS HAS ENTERED EARTH'S ATMOSPHERE. IT'S HEADED STRAIGHT FOR THE EASTERN SEABOARD, SIR.
"SMALL"? HOW SMALL?
THE SIZE OF A PLANET, SIR.
STONES FALLING FROM THE SKY? HA!
KRAKA-BOOM!
HARDLY A CHALLENGE FOR THE MIGHTY THOR, PRINCE OF THUNDER!

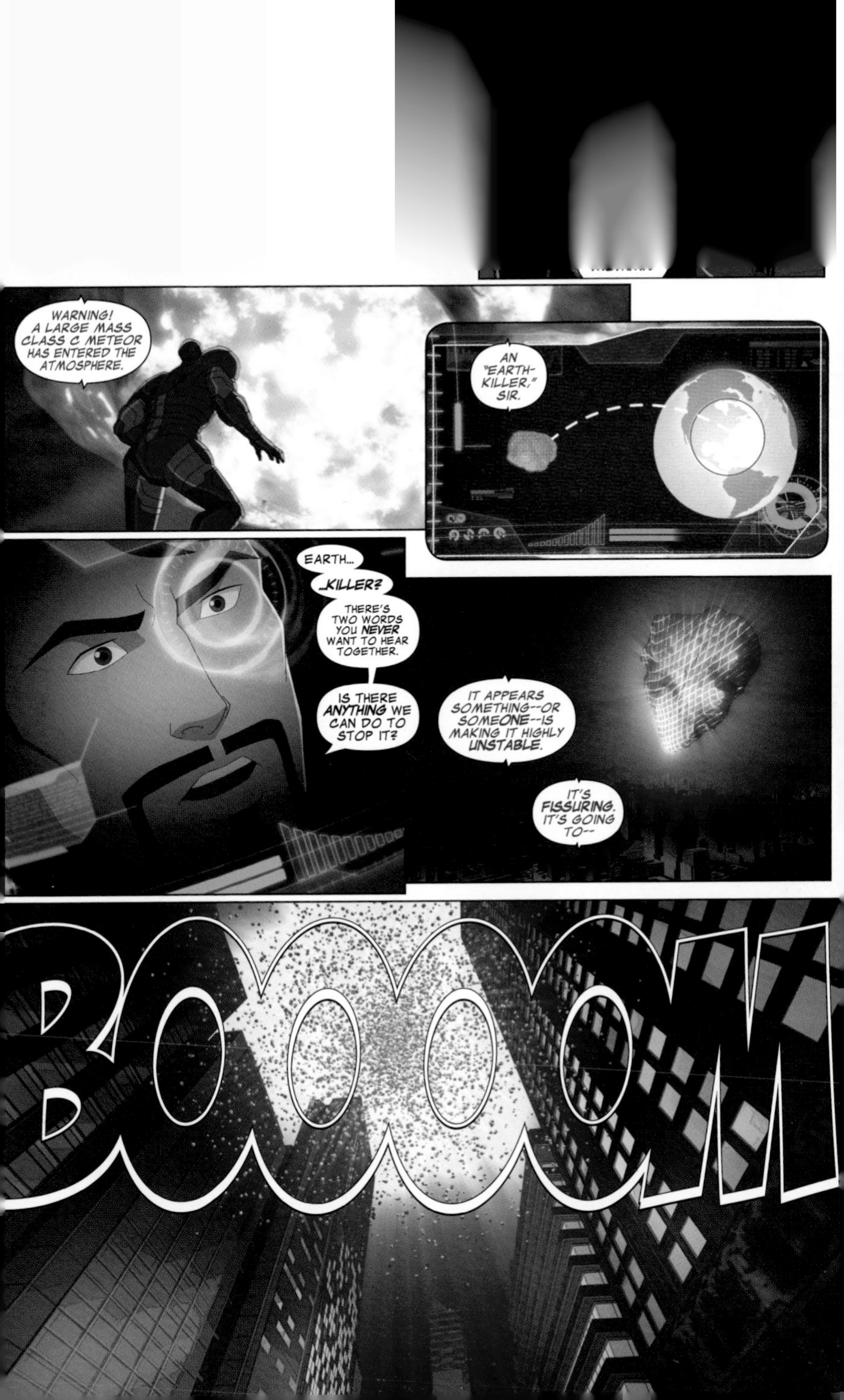
WARNING! A LARGE MASS CLASS C METEOR HAS ENTERED THE ATMOSPHERE.
AN "EARTH-KILLER," SIR.
EARTH...
...KILLER?
THERE'S TWO WORDS YOU NEVER WANT TO HEAR TOGETHER.
IS THERE ANYTHING WE CAN DO TO STOP IT?
IT APPEARS SOMETHING--OR SOMEONE--IS MAKING IT HIGHLY UNSTABLE.
IT'S FISSURING. IT'S GOING TO--
BOOOOM

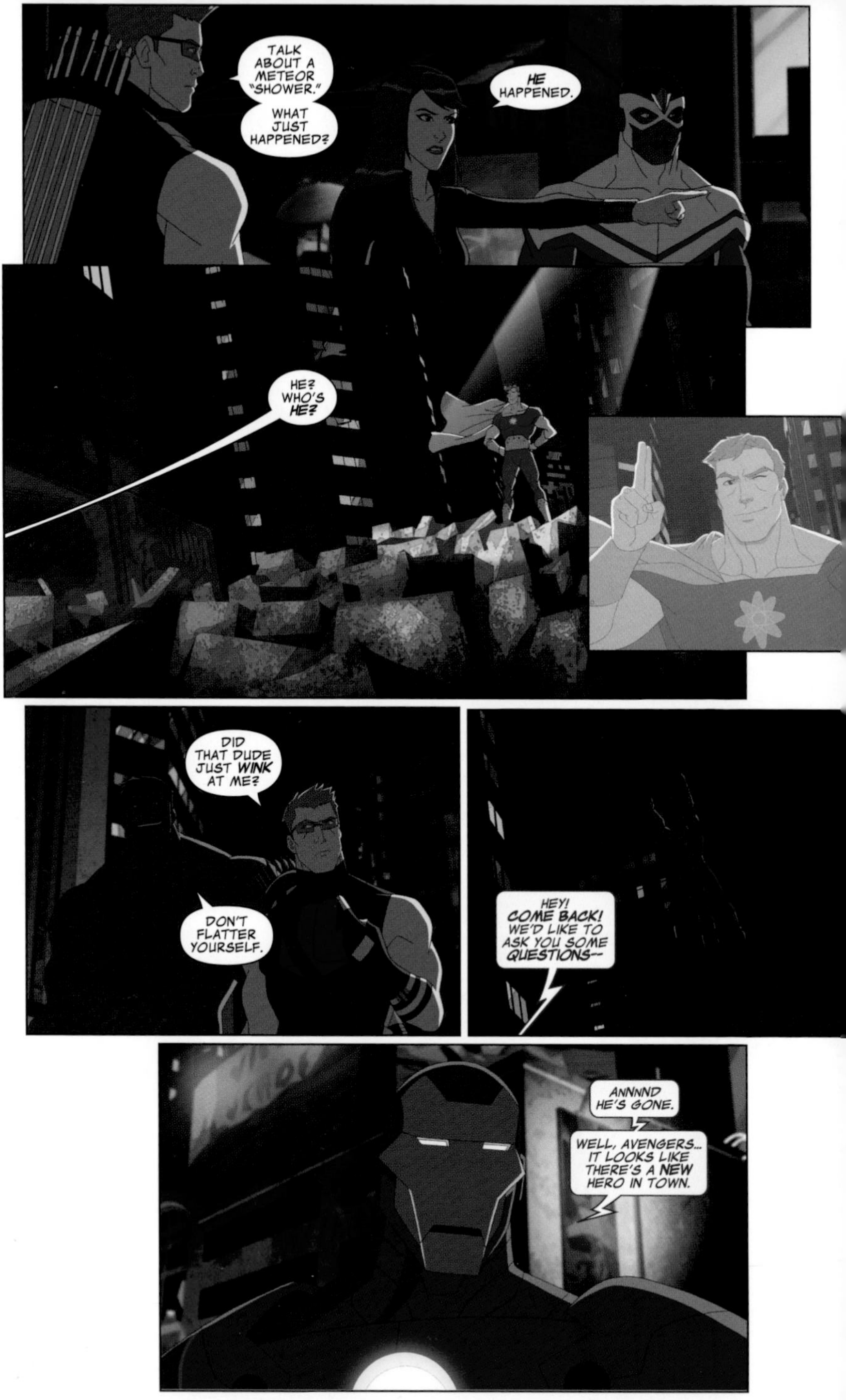
TALK ABOUT A METEOR "SHOWER."
WHAT JUST HAPPENED?
HE HAPPENED.
HE? WHO'S HE?
DID THAT DUDE JUST WINK AT ME?
DON'T FLATTER YOURSELF.
HEY! COME BACK! WE'D LIKE TO ASK YOU SOME QUESTIONS--
ANNNND HE'S GONE.
WELL, AVENGERS... IT LOOKS LIKE THERE'S A NEW HERO IN TOWN.

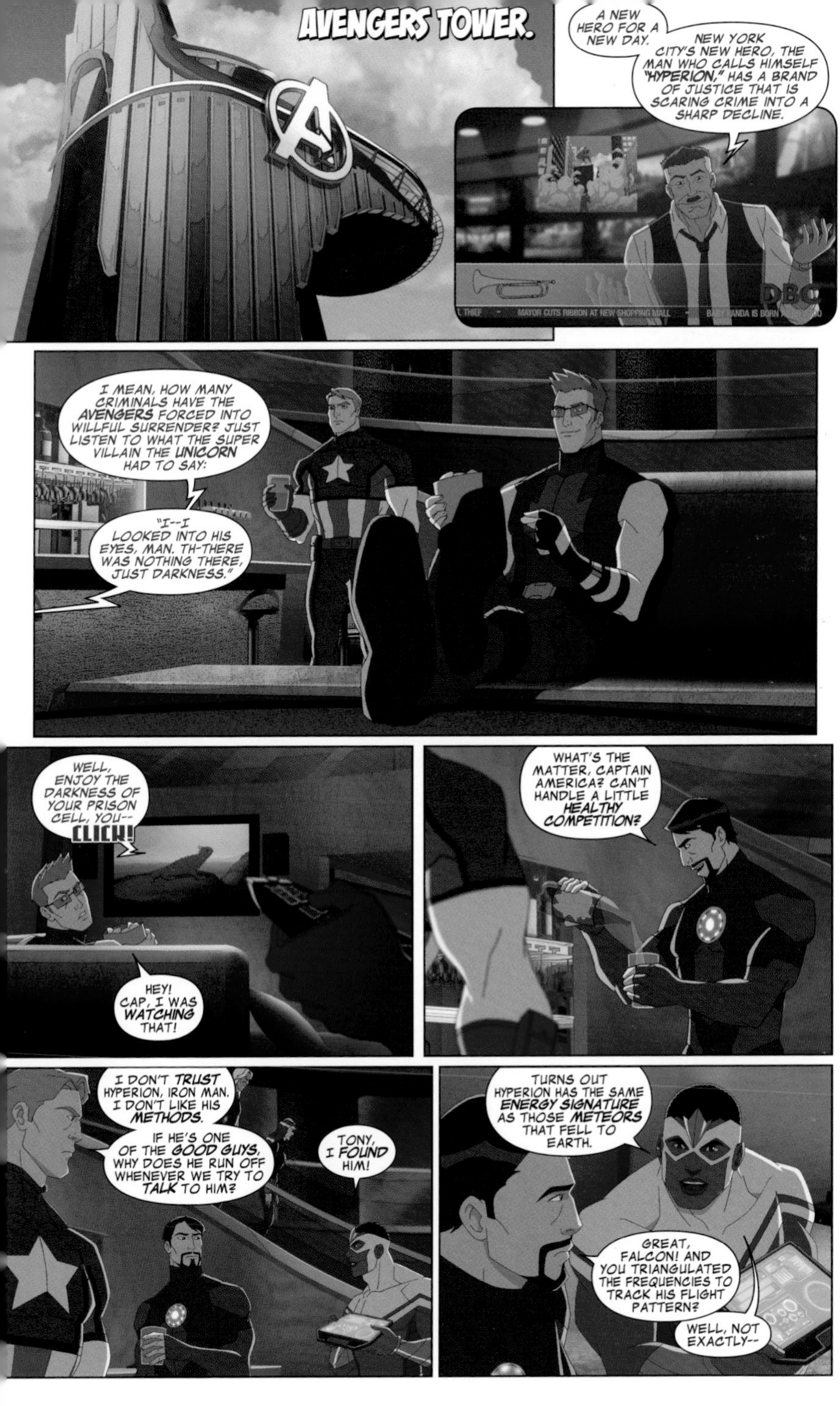
AVENGERS TOWER.
A NEW HERO FOR A NEW DAY.
NEW YORK CITY'S NEW HERO, THE MAN WHO CALLS HIMSELF "HYPERION," HAS A BRAND OF JUSTICE THAT IS SCARING CRIME INTO A SHARP DECLINE.
MAYOR CUTS RIBBON AT NEW SHOPPING MALL
I MEAN, HOW MANY CRIMINALS HAVE THE AVENGERS FORCED INTO WILLFUL SURRENDER? JUST LISTEN TO WHAT THE SUPER VILLAIN THE UNICORN HAD TO SAY:
"I--I LOOKED INTO HIS EYES, MAN. TH-THERE WAS NOTHING THERE, JUST DARKNESS."
WELL, ENJOY THE DARKNESS OF YOUR PRISON CELL, YOU--
CLICK!
HEY! CAP, I WAS WATCHING THAT!
WHAT'S THE MATTER, CAPTAIN AMERICA? CAN'T HANDLE A LITTLE HEALTHY COMPETITION?
I DON'T TRUST HYPERION, IRON MAN. I DON'T LIKE HIS METHODS.
IF HE'S ONE OF THE GOOD GUYS, WHY DOES HE RUN OFF WHENEVER WE TRY TO TALK TO HIM?
TONY, I FOUND HIM!
TURNS OUT HYPERION HAS THE SAME ENERGY SIGNATURE AS THOSE METEORS THAT FELL TO EARTH.
GREAT, FALCON! AND YOU TRIANGULATED THE FREQUENCIES TO TRACK HIS FLIGHT PATTERN?
WELL, NOT EXACTLY--

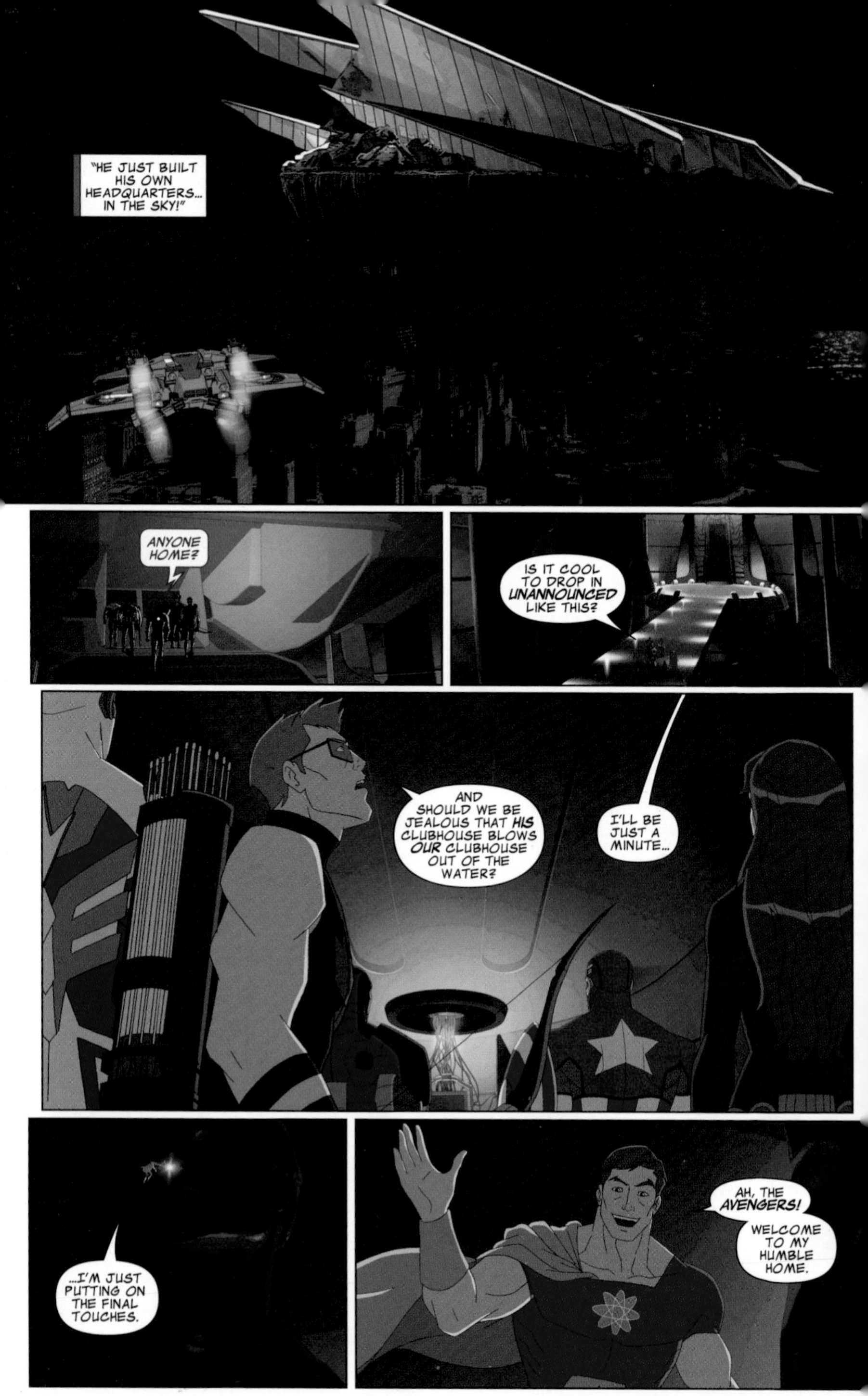
"HE JUST BUILT HIS OWN HEADQUARTERS... IN THE SKY!"
ANYONE HOME?
IS IT COOL TO DROP IN UNANNOUNCED LIKE THIS?
AND SHOULD WE BE JEALOUS THAT HIS CLUBHOUSE BLOWS OUR CLUBHOUSE OUT OF THE WATER?
I'LL BE JUST A MINUTE...
...I'M JUST PUTTING ON THE FINAL TOUCHES.
AH, THE AVENGERS!
WELCOME TO MY HUMBLE HOME.

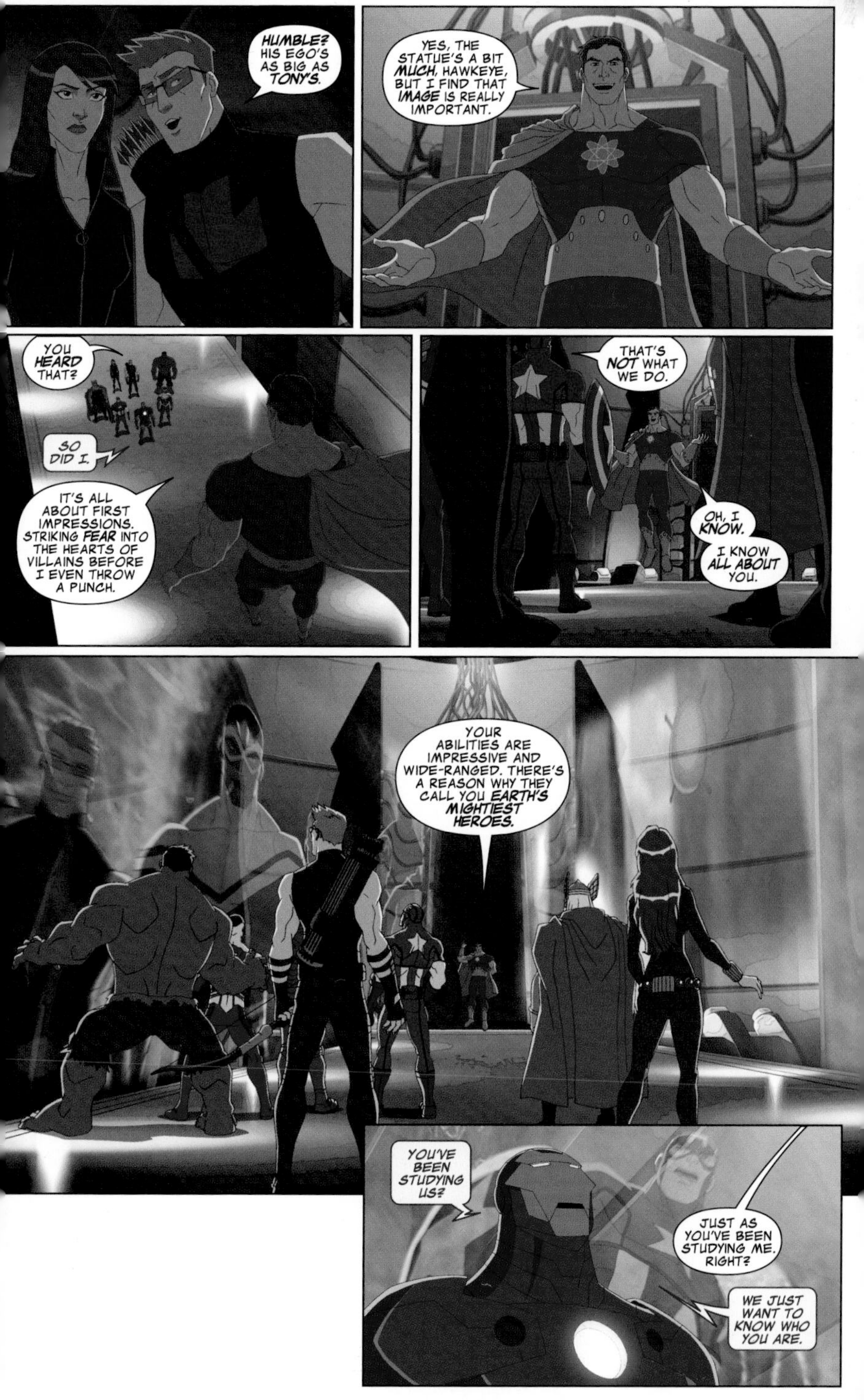

HUMBLE? HIS EGO'S AS BIG AS TONY'S.
YES, THE STATUE'S A BIT MUCH, HAWKEYE, BUT I FIND THAT IMAGE IS REALLY IMPORTANT.
YOU HEARD THAT?
SO DID I.
IT'S ALL ABOUT FIRST IMPRESSIONS. STRIKING FEAR INTO THE HEARTS OF VILLAINS BEFORE I EVEN THROW A PUNCH.
THAT'S NOT WHAT WE DO.
OH, I KNOW.
I KNOW ALL ABOUT YOU.
YOUR ABILITIES ARE IMPRESSIVE AND WIDE-RANGED. THERE'S A REASON WHY THEY CALL YOU EARTH'S MIGHTIEST HEROES.
YOU'VE BEEN STUDYING US?
JUST AS YOU'VE BEEN STUDYING ME. RIGHT?
WE JUST WANT TO KNOW WHO YOU ARE.

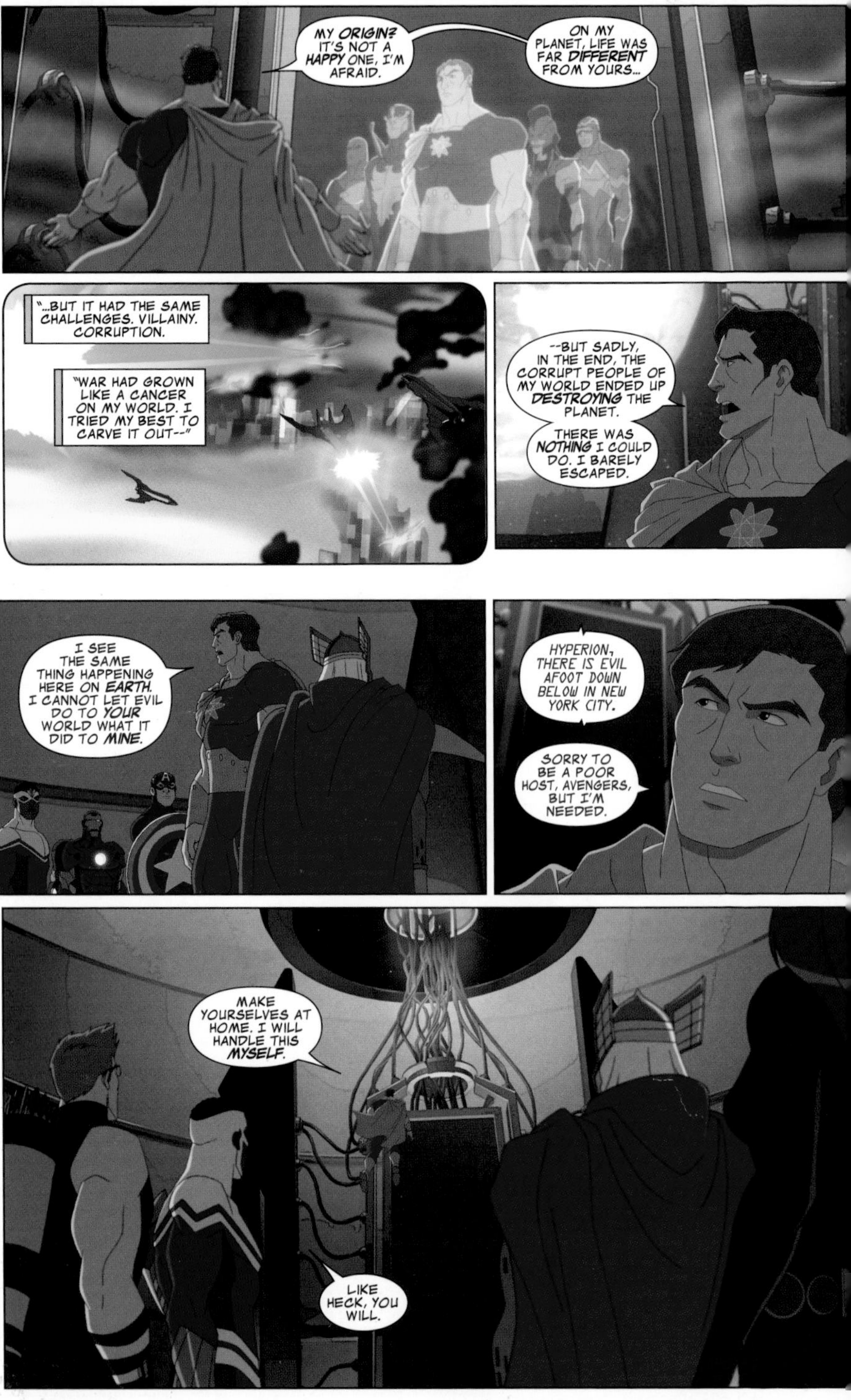

MY ORIGIN? IT'S NOT A HAPPY ONE, I'M AFRAID.
ON MY PLANET, LIFE WAS FAR DIFFERENT FROM YOURS...
"...BUT IT HAD THE SAME CHALLENGES. VILLAINY. CORRUPTION.
"WAR HAD GROWN LIKE A CANCER ON MY WORLD. I TRIED MY BEST TO CARVE IT OUT--"
--BUT SADLY, IN THE END, THE CORRUPT PEOPLE OF MY WORLD ENDED UP DESTROYING THE PLANET.
THERE WAS NOTHING I COULD DO. I BARELY ESCAPED.
I SEE THE SAME THING HAPPENING HERE ON EARTH. I CANNOT LET EVIL DO TO YOUR WORLD WHAT IT DID TO MINE.
HYPERION, THERE IS EVIL AFOOT DOWN BELOW IN NEW YORK CITY.
SORRY TO BE A POOR HOST, AVENGERS, BUT I'M NEEDED.
MAKE YOURSELVES AT HOME. I WILL HANDLE THIS MYSELF.
LIKE HECK, YOU WILL.

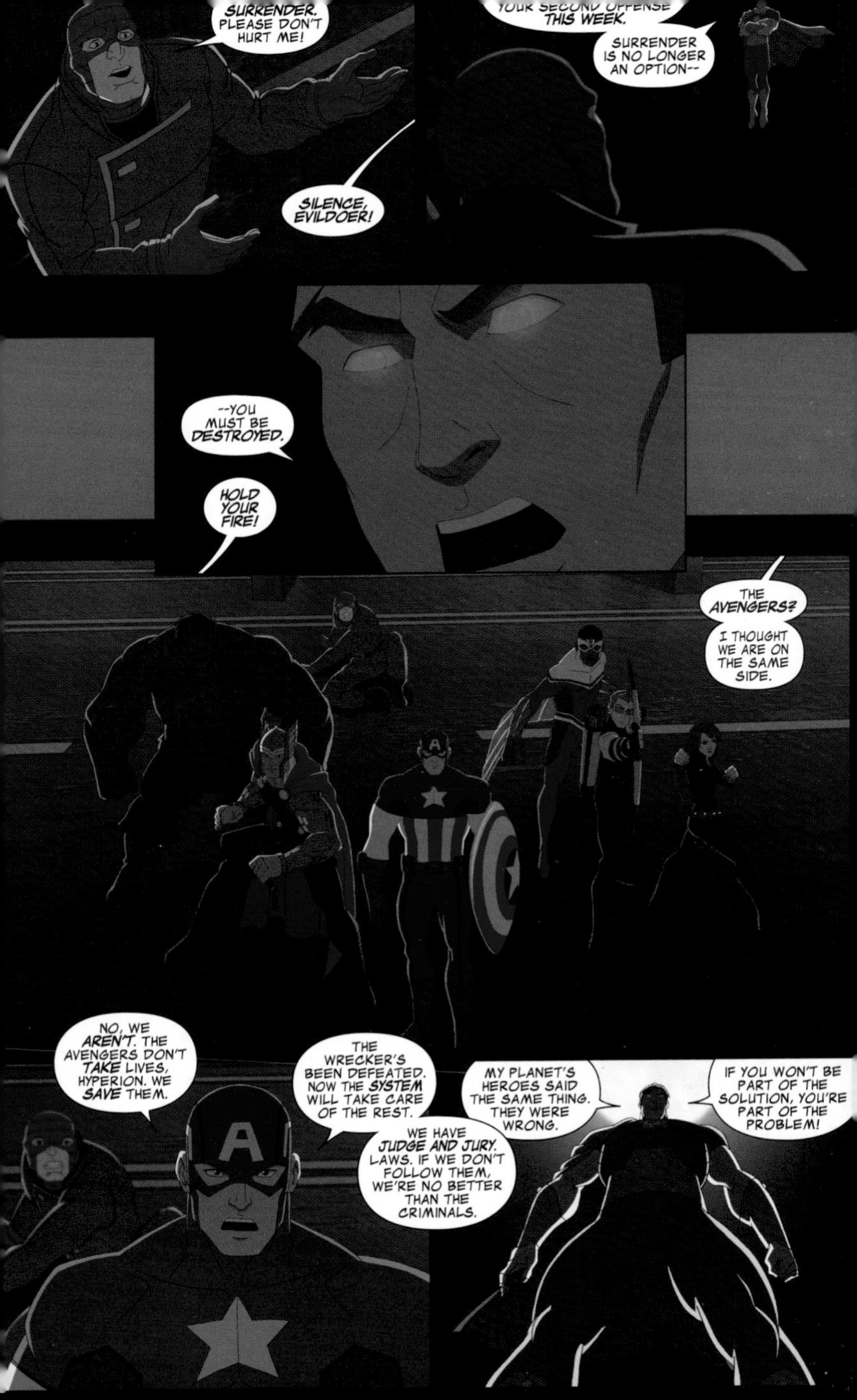
SURRENDER. PLEASE DON'T HURT ME!
SILENCE, EVILDOER!
YOUR SECOND OFFENSE THIS WEEK.
SURRENDER IS NO LONGER AN OPTION--
--YOU MUST BE DESTROYED.
HOLD YOUR FIRE!
THE AVENGERS?
I THOUGHT WE ARE ON THE SAME SIDE.
NO, WE AREN'T. THE AVENGERS DON'T TAKE LIVES, HYPERION. WE SAVE THEM.
THE WRECKER'S BEEN DEFEATED. NOW THE SYSTEM WILL TAKE CARE OF THE REST.
WE HAVE JUDGE AND JURY. LAWS. IF WE DON'T FOLLOW THEM, WE'RE NO BETTER THAN THE CRIMINALS.
MY PLANET'S HEROES SAID THE SAME THING. THEY WERE WRONG.
IF YOU WON'T BE PART OF THE SOLUTION, YOU'RE PART OF THE PROBLEM!

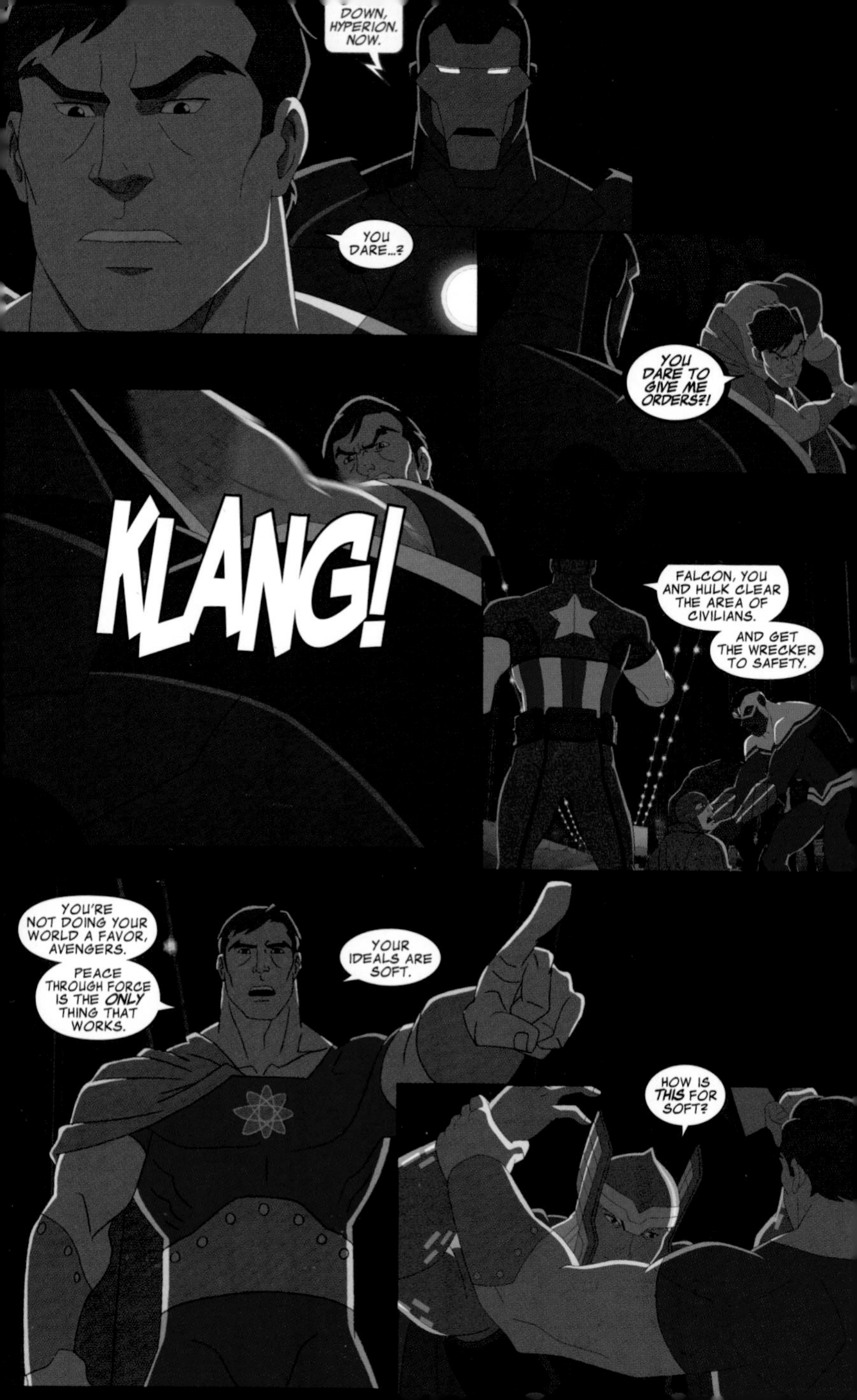
DOWN, HYPERION. NOW.
YOU DARE...?
YOU DARE TO GIVE ME ORDERS?!
KLANG!
FALCON, YOU AND HULK CLEAR THE AREA OF CIVILIANS.
AND GET THE WRECKER TO SAFETY.
YOU'RE NOT DOING YOUR WORLD A FAVOR, AVENGERS.
PEACE THROUGH FORCE IS THE ONLY THING THAT WORKS.
YOUR IDEALS ARE SOFT.
HOW IS THIS FOR SOFT?

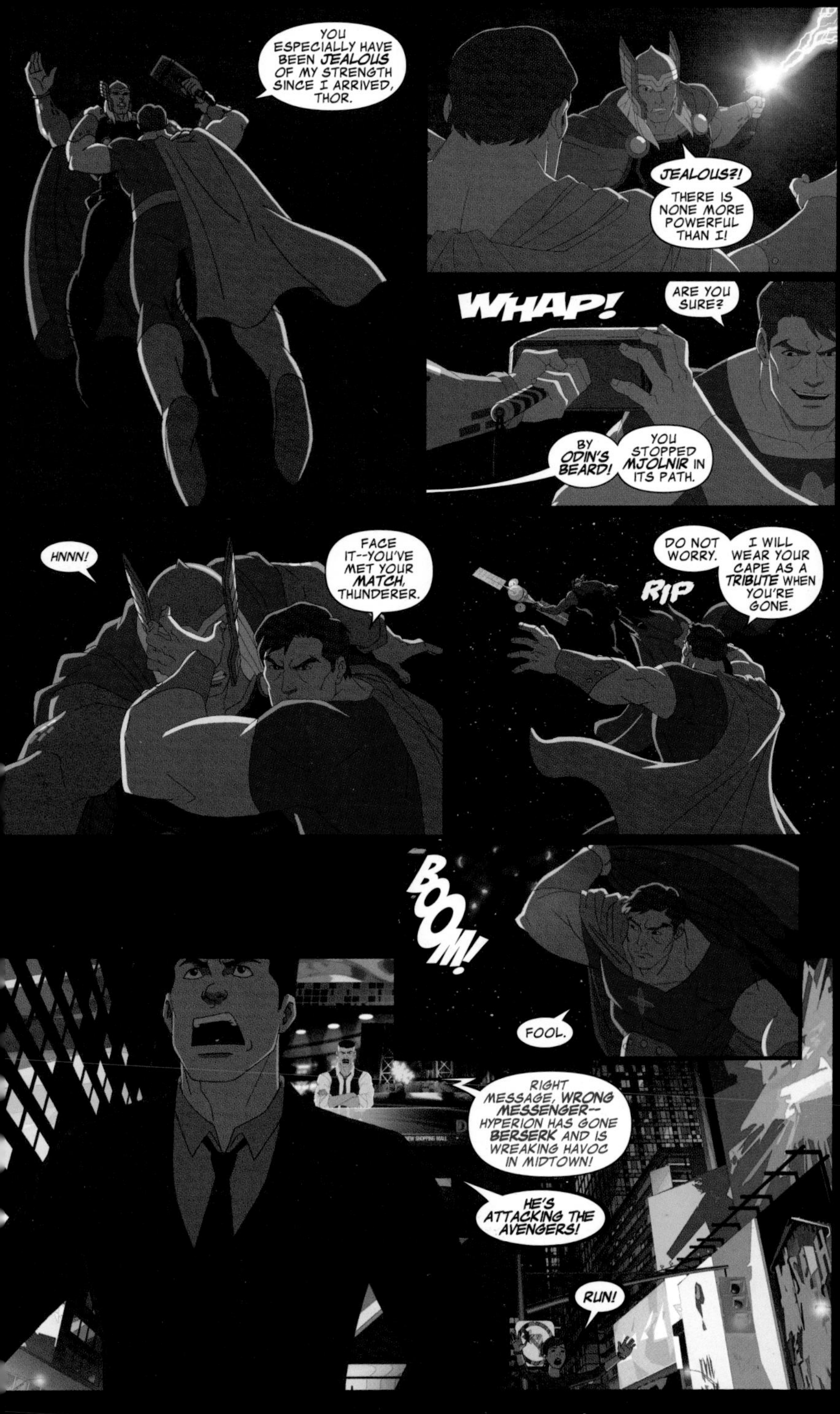
YOU ESPECIALLY HAVE BEEN JEALOUS OF MY STRENGTH SINCE I ARRIVED, THOR.
JEALOUS?! THERE IS NONE MORE POWERFUL THAN I!
WHAP!
ARE YOU SURE?
BY ODIN'S BEARD!
YOU STOPPED MJOLNIR IN ITS PATH.
HNNN!
FACE IT--YOU'VE MET YOUR MATCH, THUNDERER.
DO NOT WORRY.
I WILL WEAR YOUR CAPE AS A TRIBUTE WHEN YOU'RE GONE.
RIP
BOOM!
FOOL.
RIGHT MESSAGE, WRONG MESSENGER-- HYPERION HAS GONE BERSERK AND IS WREAKING HAVOC IN MIDTOWN!
HE'S ATTACKING THE AVENGERS!
RUN!

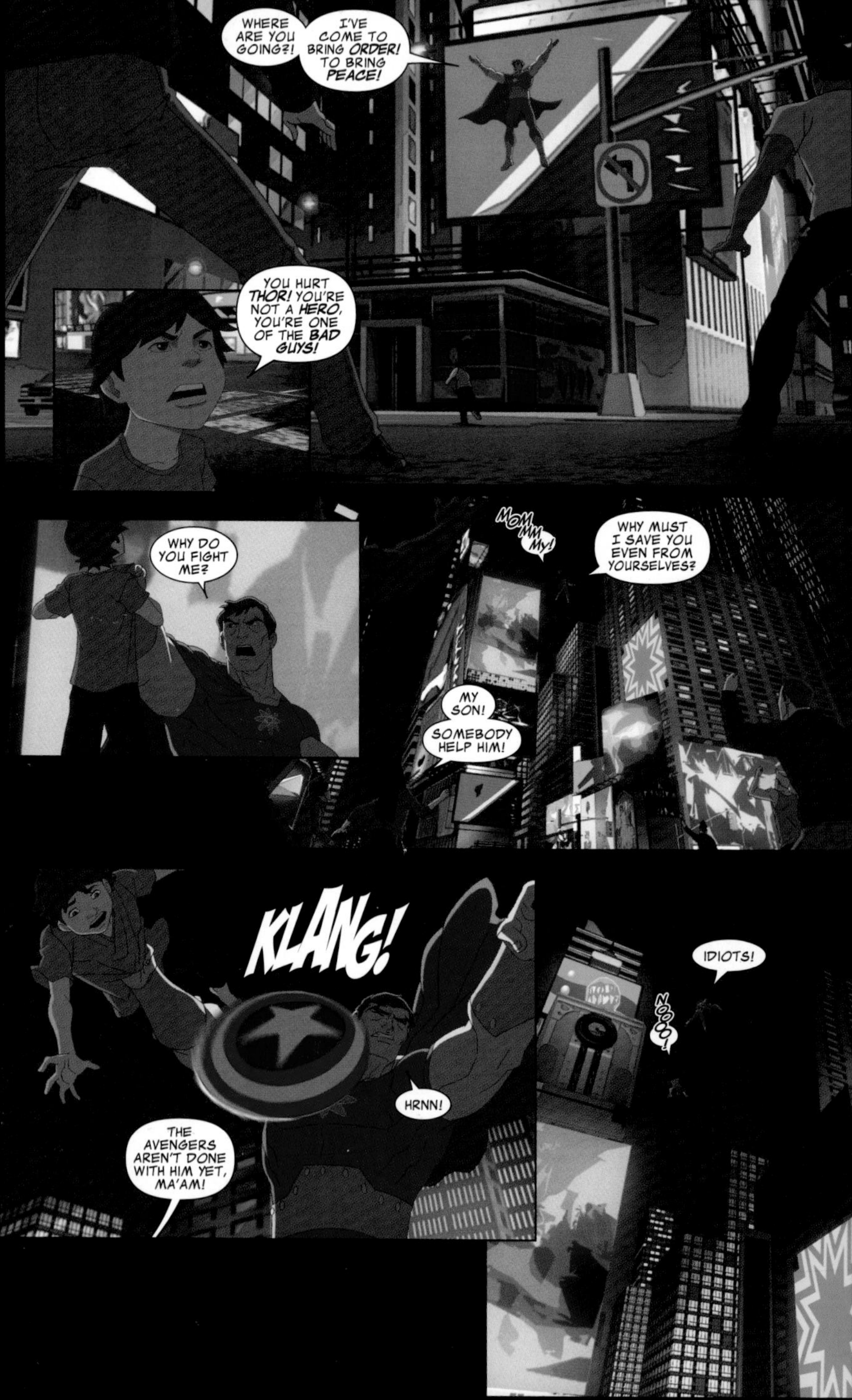
WHERE ARE YOU GOING?!
I'VE COME TO BRING ORDER! TO BRING PEACE!
YOU HURT THOR! YOU'RE NOT A HERO, YOU'RE ONE OF THE BAD GUYS!
WHY DO YOU FIGHT ME?
MOMMMMY!
WHY MUST I SAVE YOU EVEN FROM YOURSELVES?
MY SON!
SOMEBODY HELP HIM!
KLANG!
HRNN!
THE AVENGERS AREN'T DONE WITH HIM YET, MA'AM!
IDIOTS!
NOOOO!

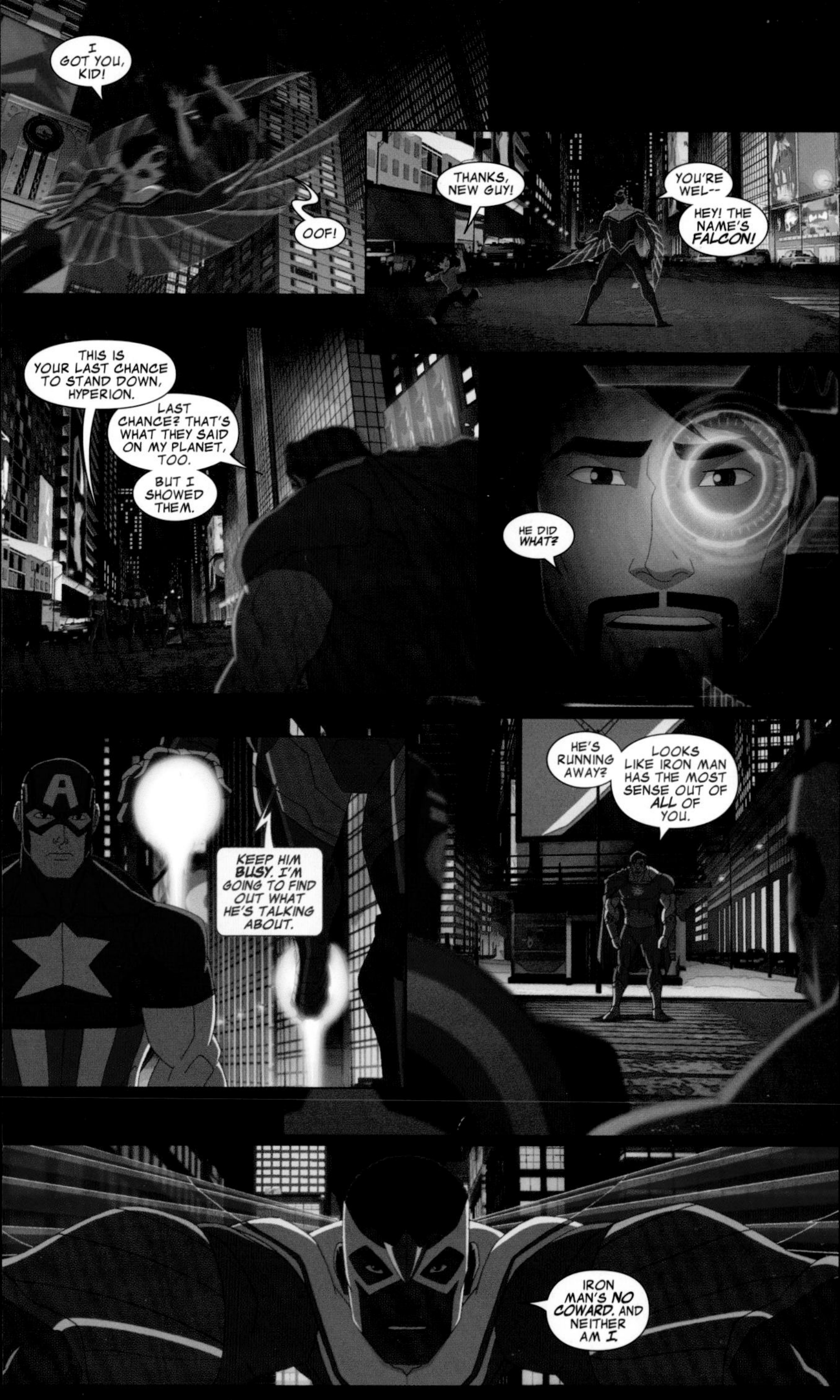

I GOT YOU, KID!
OOF!
THANKS, NEW GUY!
YOU'RE WEL--
HEY! THE NAME'S FALCON!
THIS IS YOUR LAST CHANCE TO STAND DOWN, HYPERION.
LAST CHANCE? THAT'S WHAT THEY SAID ON MY PLANET, TOO.
BUT I SHOWED THEM.
HE DID WHAT?
KEEP HIM BUSY. I'M GOING TO FIND OUT WHAT HE'S TALKING ABOUT.
HE'S RUNNING AWAY?
LOOKS LIKE IRON MAN HAS THE MOST SENSE OUT OF ALL OF YOU.
IRON MAN'S NO COWARD. AND NEITHER AM I.

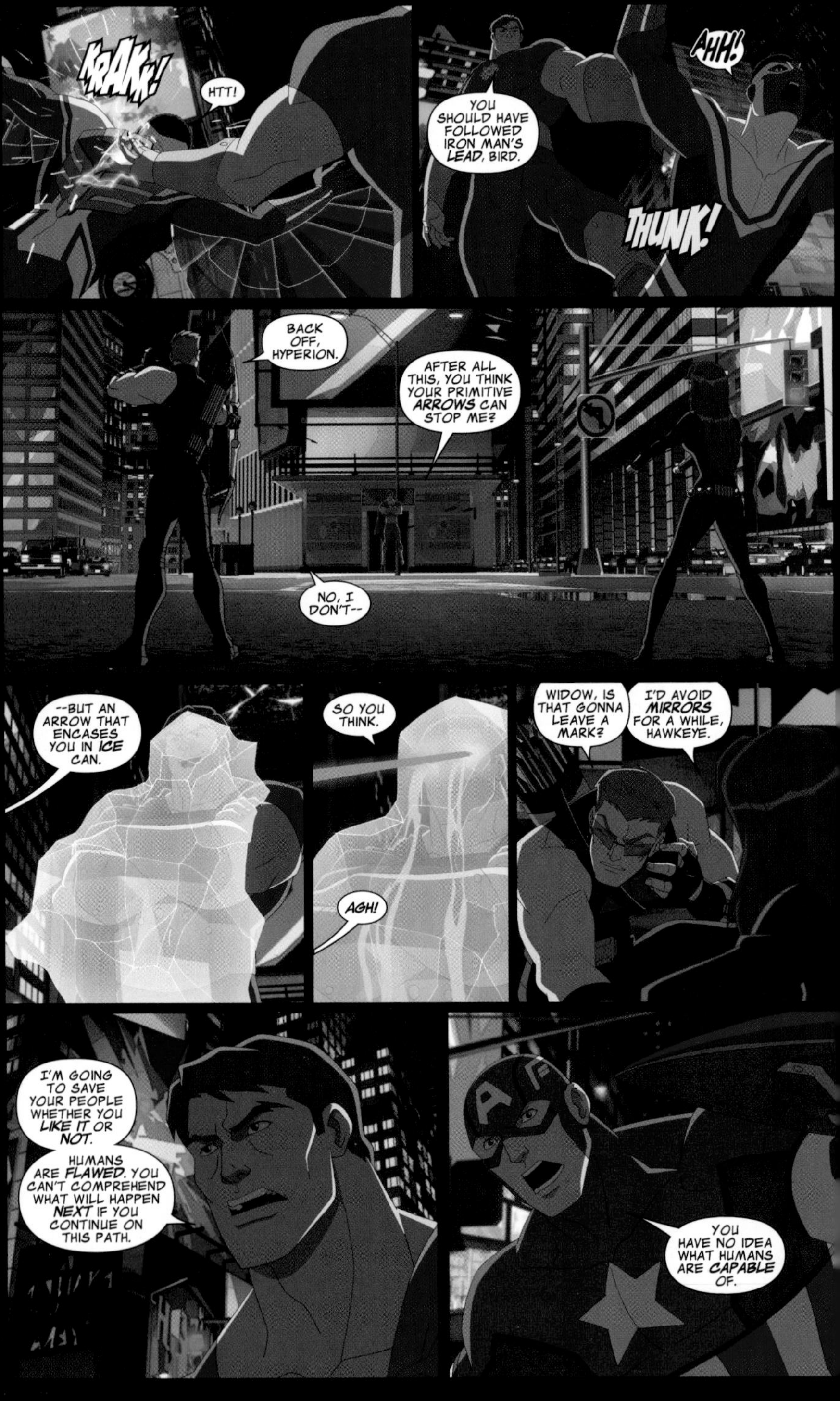
KRAKK!
HTT!
YOU SHOULD HAVE FOLLOWED IRON MAN'S LEAD, BIRD.
AHH!
THUNK!
BACK OFF, HYPERION.
AFTER ALL THIS, YOU THINK YOUR PRIMITIVE ARROWS CAN STOP ME?
NO, I DON'T--
--BUT AN ARROW THAT ENCASES YOU IN ICE CAN.
SO YOU THINK.
AGH!
WIDOW, IS THAT GONNA LEAVE A MARK?
I'D AVOID MIRRORS FOR A WHILE, HAWKEYE.
I'M GOING TO SAVE YOUR PEOPLE WHETHER YOU LIKE IT OR NOT.
HUMANS ARE FLAWED. YOU CAN'T COMPREHEND WHAT WILL HAPPEN NEXT IF YOU CONTINUE ON THIS PATH.
YOU HAVE NO IDEA WHAT HUMANS ARE CAPABLE OF.

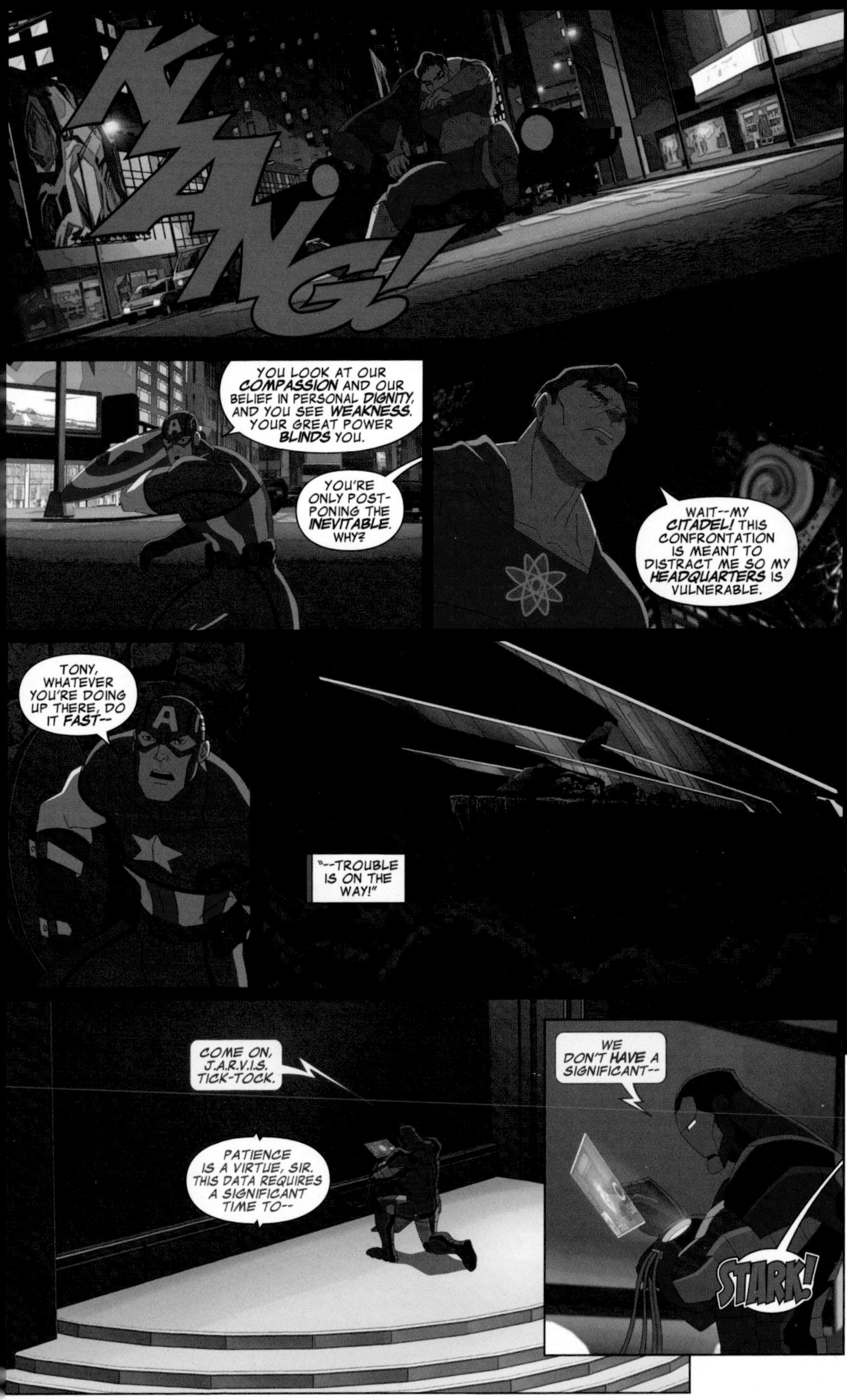
KRANG!
YOU LOOK AT OUR COMPASSION AND OUR BELIEF IN PERSONAL DIGNITY, AND YOU SEE WEAKNESS. YOUR GREAT POWER BLINDS YOU.
YOU'RE ONLY POST-PONING THE INEVITABLE. WHY?
WAIT--MY CITADEL! THIS CONFRONTATION IS MEANT TO DISTRACT ME SO MY HEADQUARTERS IS VULNERABLE.
TONY, WHATEVER YOU'RE DOING UP THERE, DO IT FAST--
"--TROUBLE IS ON THE WAY!"
COME ON, J.A.R.V.I.S. TICK-TOCK.
PATIENCE IS A VIRTUE, SIR. THIS DATA REQUIRES A SIGNIFICANT TIME TO--
WE DON'T HAVE A SIGNIFICANT--
STARK!

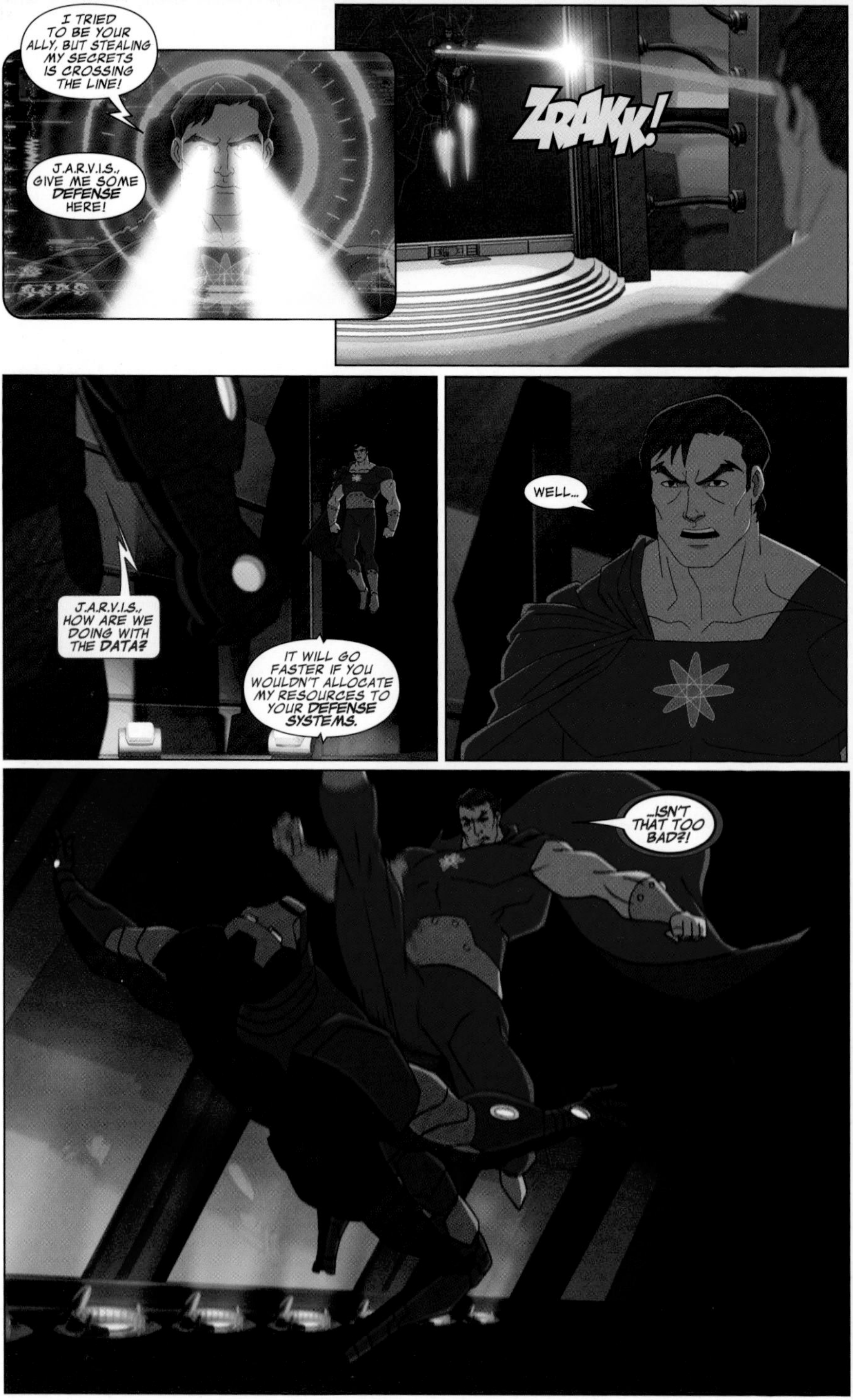
I TRIED TO BE YOUR ALLY, BUT STEALING MY SECRETS IS CROSSING THE LINE!
J.A.R.V.I.S., GIVE ME SOME DEFENSE HERE!
ZRAKK!
J.A.R.V.I.S., HOW ARE WE DOING WITH THE DATA?
IT WILL GO FASTER IF YOU WOULDN'T ALLOCATE MY RESOURCES TO YOUR DEFENSE SYSTEMS.
WELL...
...ISN'T THAT TOO BAD?!

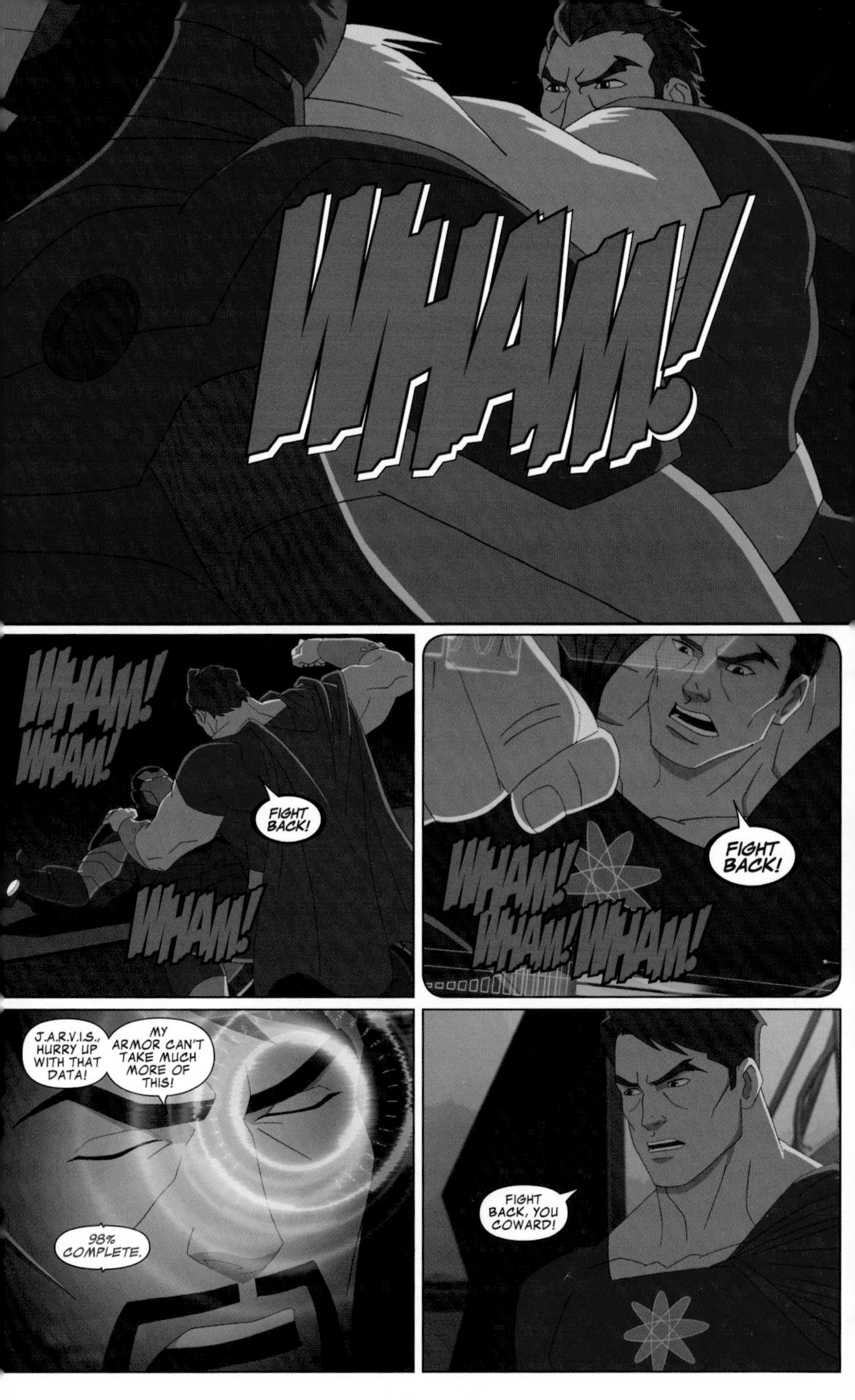
WHAM!
WHAM!
WHAM!
FIGHT BACK!
WHAM!
FIGHT BACK!
WHAM!
WHAM!
WHAM!
J.A.R.V.I.S., HURRY UP WITH THAT DATA!
MY ARMOR CAN'T TAKE MUCH MORE OF THIS!
98% COMPLETE.
FIGHT BACK, YOU COWARD!

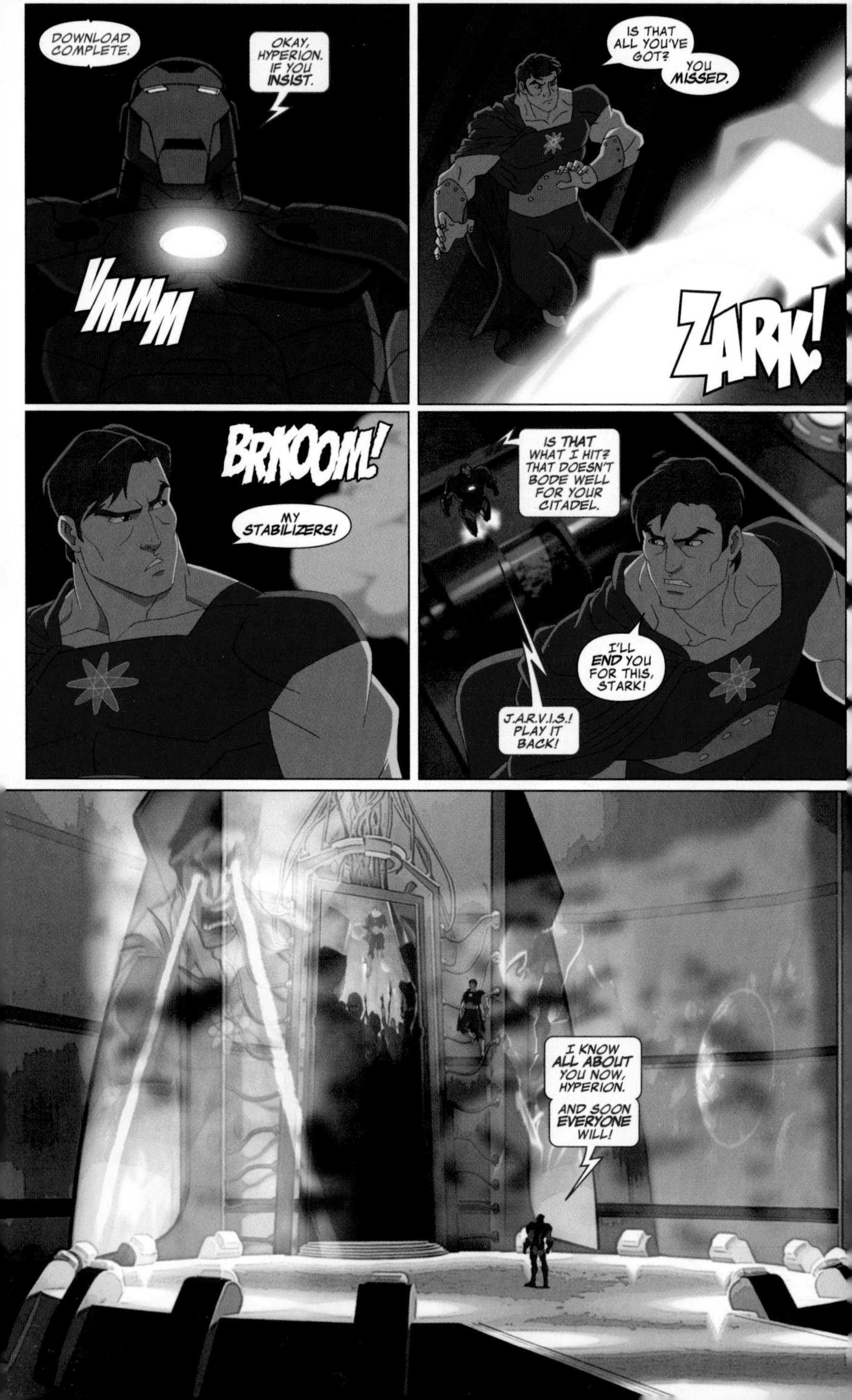
DOWNLOAD COMPLETE.
OKAY, HYPERION. IF YOU INSIST.
VMMMM
IS THAT ALL YOU'VE GOT?
YOU MISSED.
ZARK!
BRKOOM!
MY STABILIZERS!
IS THAT WHAT I HIT? THAT DOESN'T BODE WELL FOR YOUR CITADEL.
I'LL END YOU FOR THIS, STARK!
J.A.R.V.I.S.! PLAY IT BACK!
I KNOW ALL ABOUT YOU NOW, HYPERION.
AND SOON EVERYONE WILL!

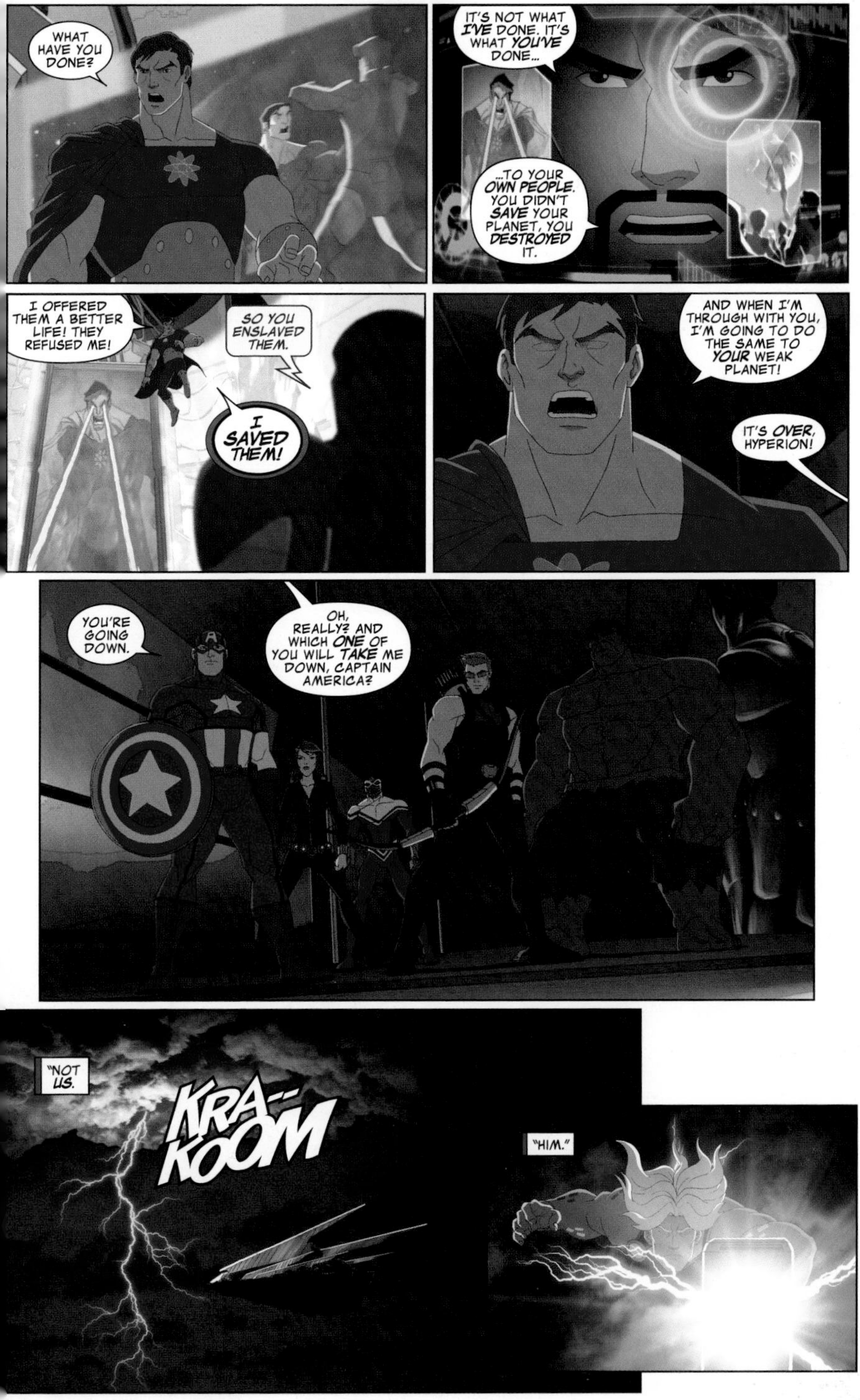
WHAT HAVE YOU DONE?
IT'S NOT WHAT I'VE DONE. IT'S WHAT YOU'VE DONE...
...TO YOUR OWN PEOPLE. YOU DIDN'T SAVE YOUR PLANET, YOU DESTROYED IT.
I OFFERED THEM A BETTER LIFE! THEY REFUSED ME!
SO YOU ENSLAVED THEM.
I SAVED THEM!
AND WHEN I'M THROUGH WITH YOU, I'M GOING TO DO THE SAME TO YOUR WEAK PLANET!
IT'S OVER, HYPERION!
YOU'RE GOING DOWN.
OH, REALLY? AND WHICH ONE OF YOU WILL TAKE ME DOWN, CAPTAIN AMERICA?
"NOT US.
KRA-KOOM
"HIM."

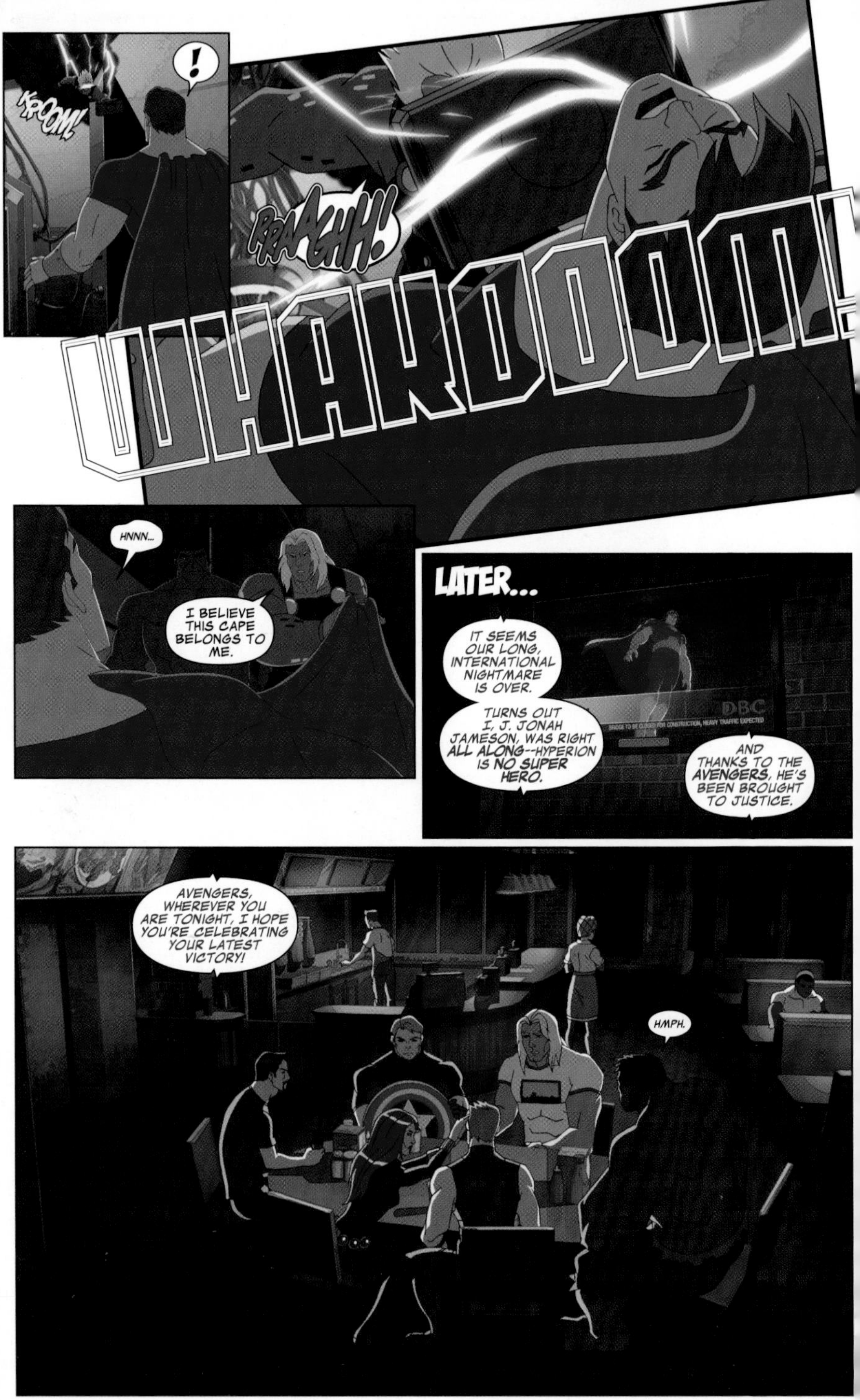
KRAOOM!
!
RRAAGHH!
WHARDOOM!
HNNN...
I BELIEVE THIS CAPE BELONGS TO ME.
LATER...
IT SEEMS OUR LONG, INTERNATIONAL NIGHTMARE IS OVER.
TURNS OUT I, J. JONAH JAMESON, WAS RIGHT ALL ALONG--HYPERION IS NO SUPER HERO.
DBC
AND THANKS TO THE AVENGERS, HE'S BEEN BROUGHT TO JUSTICE.
AVENGERS, WHEREVER YOU ARE TONIGHT, I HOPE YOU'RE CELEBRATING YOUR LATEST VICTORY!
HMPH.

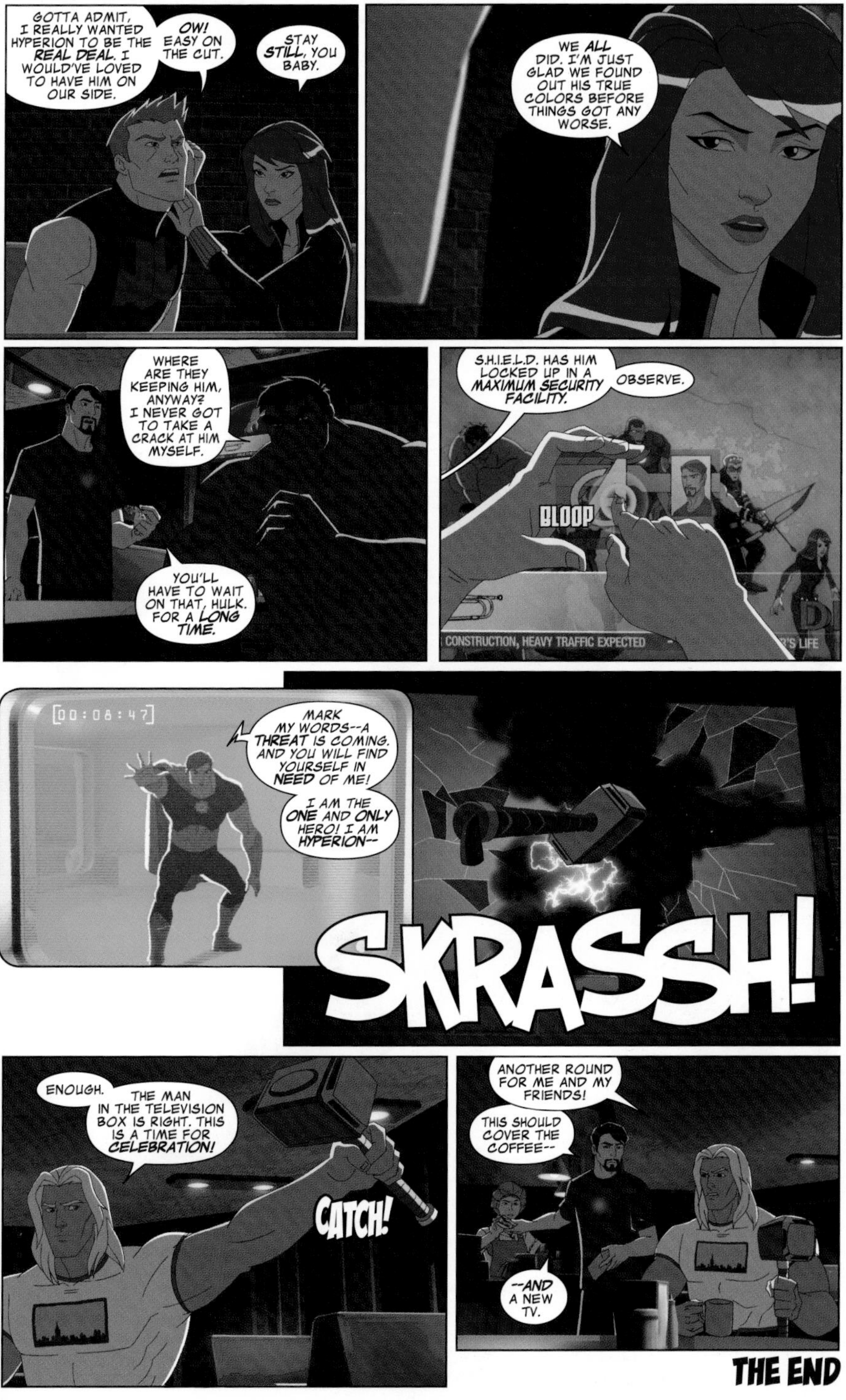
GOTTA ADMIT, I REALLY WANTED HYPERION TO BE THE REAL DEAL. I WOULD'VE LOVED TO HAVE HIM ON OUR SIDE.
OW! EASY ON THE CUT.
STAY STILL, YOU BABY.
WE ALL DID. I'M JUST GLAD WE FOUND OUT HIS TRUE COLORS BEFORE THINGS GOT ANY WORSE.
WHERE ARE THEY KEEPING HIM, ANYWAY? I NEVER GOT TO TAKE A CRACK AT HIM MYSELF.
YOU'LL HAVE TO WAIT ON THAT, HULK. FOR A LONG TIME.
S.H.I.E.L.D. HAS HIM LOCKED UP IN A MAXIMUM SECURITY FACILITY.
OBSERVE.
BLOOP
CONSTRUCTION, HEAVY TRAFFIC EXPECTED
R'S LIFE
[00:08:47]
MARK MY WORDS--A THREAT IS COMING. AND YOU WILL FIND YOURSELF IN NEED OF ME!
I AM THE ONE AND ONLY HERO! I AM HYPERION--
SKRASSH!
ENOUGH.
THE MAN IN THE TELEVISION BOX IS RIGHT. THIS IS A TIME FOR CELEBRATION!
CATCH!
ANOTHER ROUND FOR ME AND MY FRIENDS!
THIS SHOULD COVER THE COFFEE--
--AND A NEW TV.

THE END

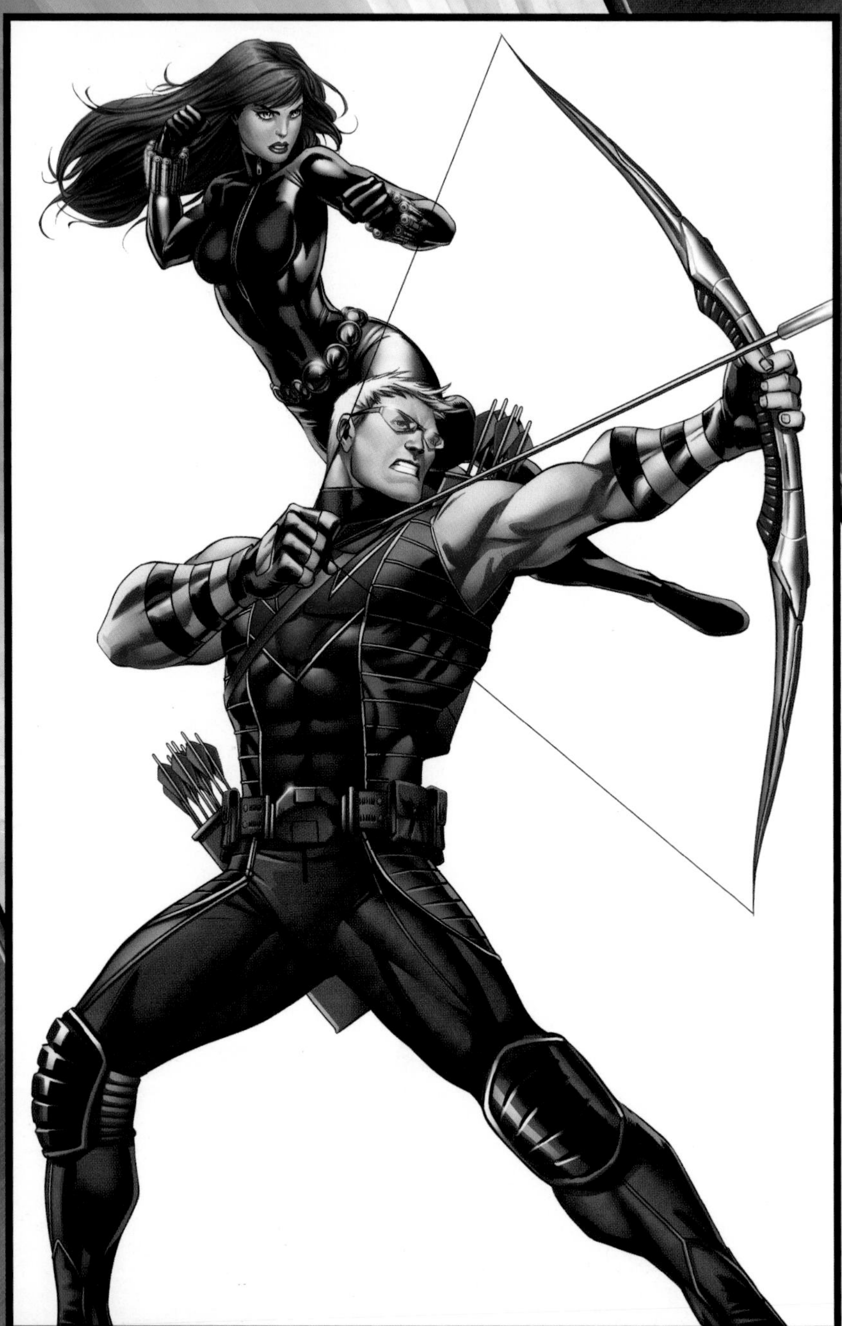

#8 BASED ON "MOLECULE KID"

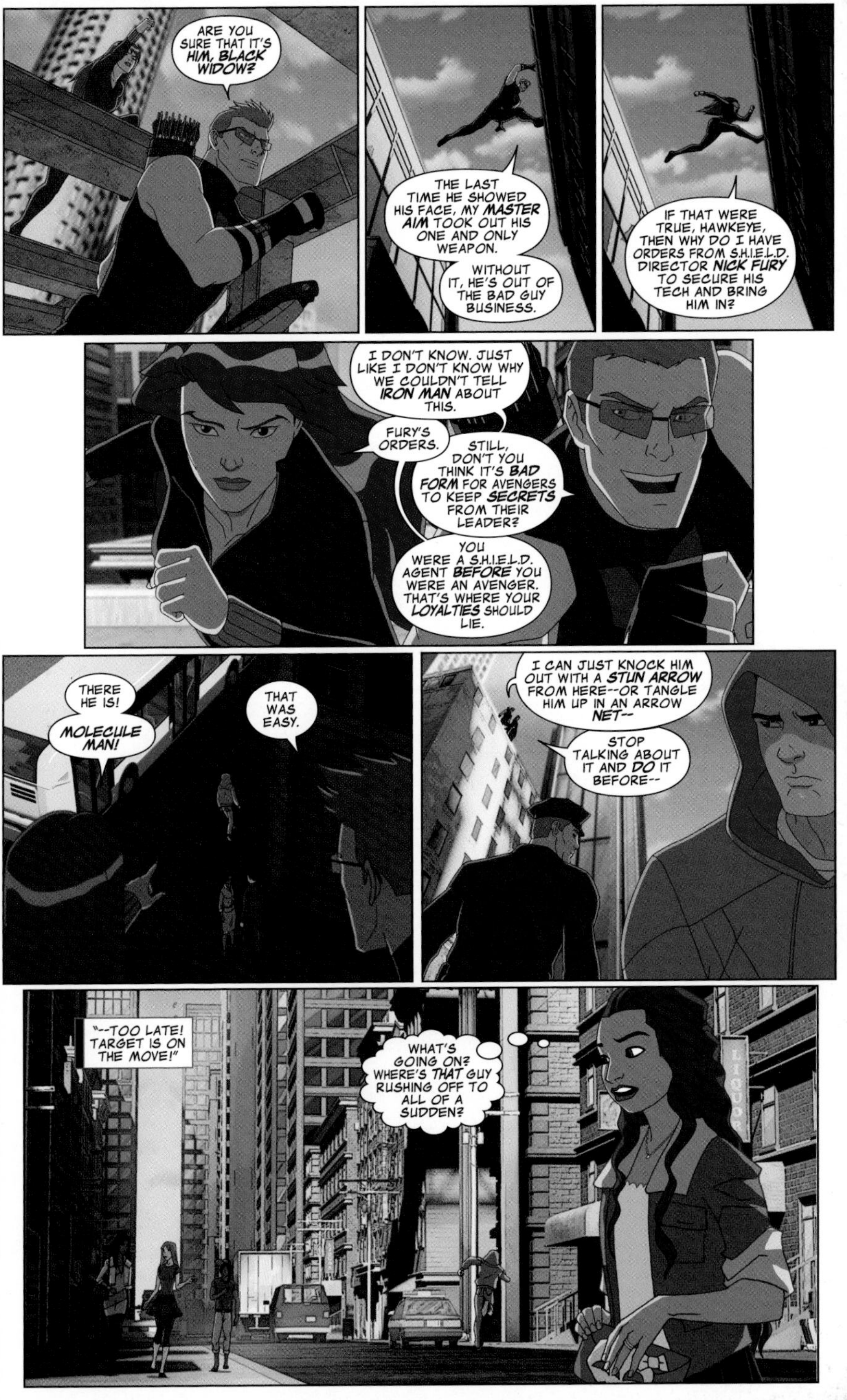
ARE YOU SURE THAT IT'S HIM, BLACK WIDOW?
THE LAST TIME HE SHOWED HIS FACE, MY MASTER AIM TOOK OUT HIS ONE AND ONLY WEAPON.
WITHOUT IT, HE'S OUT OF THE BAD GUY BUSINESS.
IF THAT WERE TRUE, HAWKEYE, THEN WHY DO I HAVE ORDERS FROM S.H.I.E.L.D. DIRECTOR NICK FURY TO SECURE HIS TECH AND BRING HIM IN?
I DON'T KNOW. JUST LIKE I DON'T KNOW WHY WE COULDN'T TELL IRON MAN ABOUT THIS.
FURY'S ORDERS.
STILL, DON'T YOU THINK IT'S BAD FORM FOR AVENGERS TO KEEP SECRETS FROM THEIR LEADER?
YOU WERE A S.H.I.E.L.D. AGENT BEFORE YOU WERE AN AVENGER. THAT'S WHERE YOUR LOYALTIES SHOULD LIE.
THERE HE IS!
MOLECULE MAN!
THAT WAS EASY.
I CAN JUST KNOCK HIM OUT WITH A STUN ARROW FROM HERE--OR TANGLE HIM UP IN AN ARROW NET--
STOP TALKING ABOUT IT AND DO IT BEFORE--
"--TOO LATE! TARGET IS ON THE MOVE!"
WHAT'S GOING ON? WHERE'S THAT GUY RUSHING OFF TO ALL OF A SUDDEN?
LIQUOR

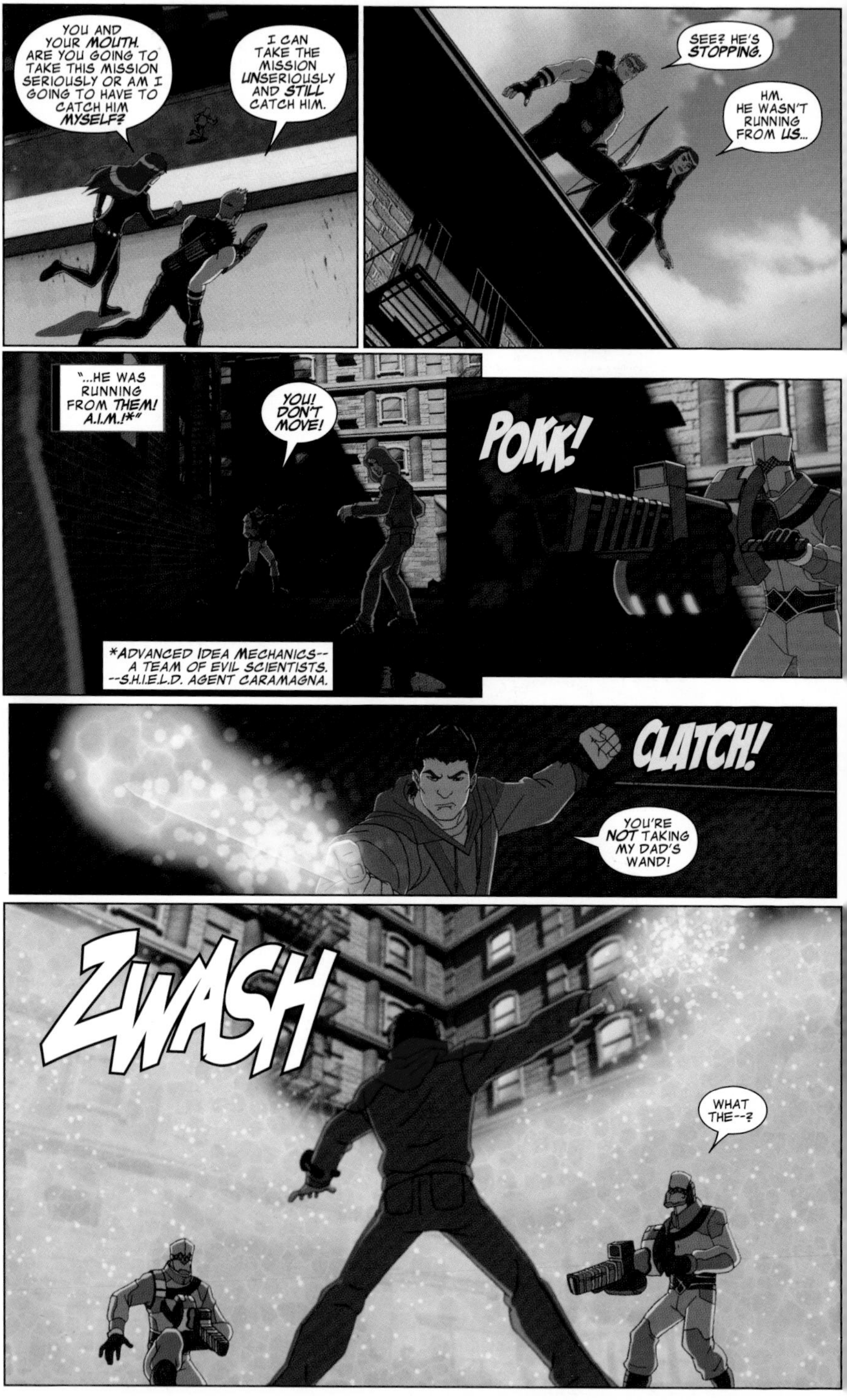

YOU AND YOUR MOUTH. ARE YOU GOING TO TAKE THIS MISSION SERIOUSLY OR AM I GOING TO HAVE TO CATCH HIM MYSELF?
I CAN TAKE THE MISSION UNSERIOUSLY AND STILL CATCH HIM.
SEE? HE'S STOPPING.
HM. HE WASN'T RUNNING FROM US...
"...HE WAS RUNNING FROM THEM! A.I.M.!*"
YOU! DON'T MOVE!
*ADVANCED IDEA MECHANICS-- A TEAM OF EVIL SCIENTISTS. --S.H.I.E.L.D. AGENT CARAMAGNA.
POKK!
CLATCH!
YOU'RE NOT TAKING MY DAD'S WAND!
ZWASH
WHAT THE--?

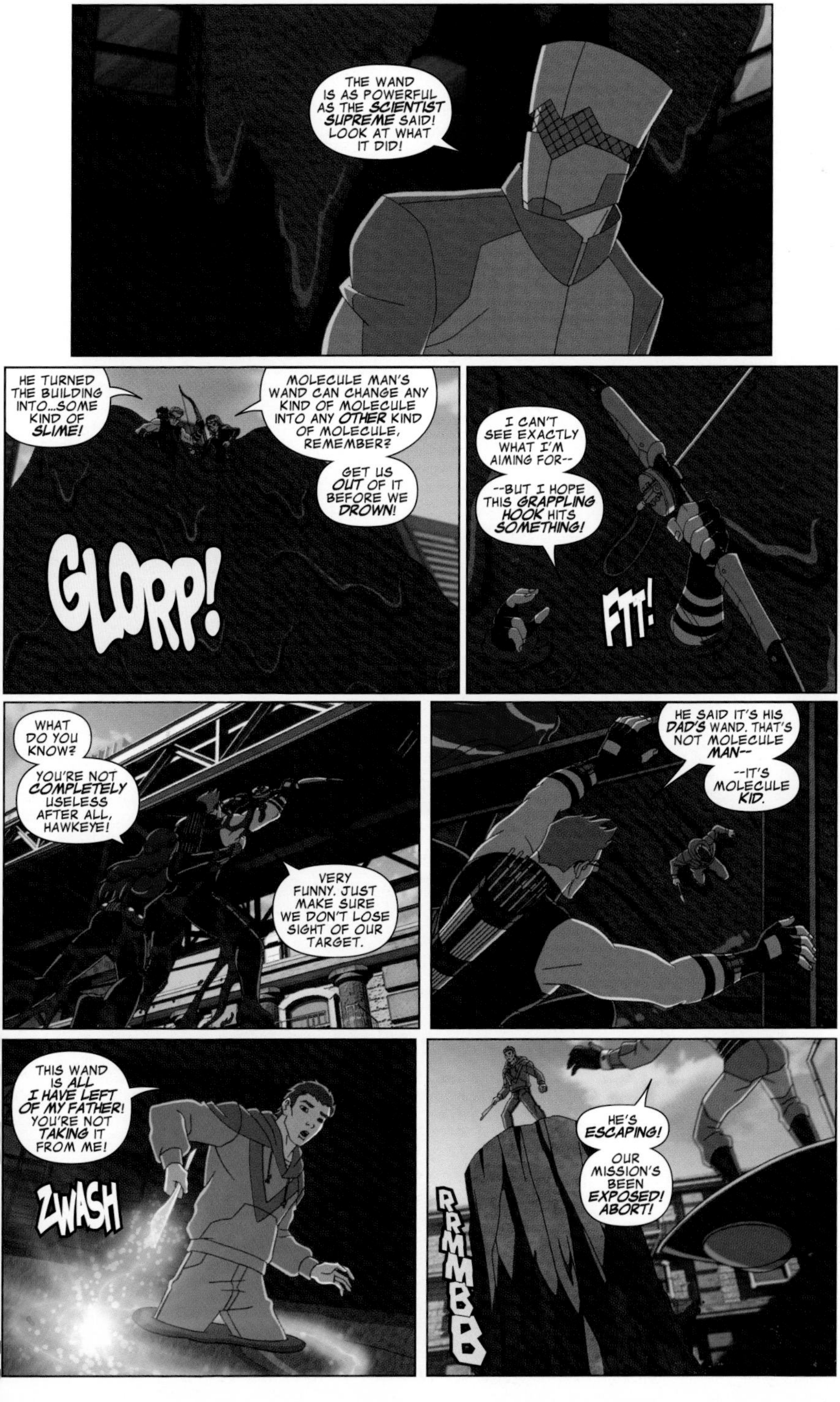
THE WAND IS AS POWERFUL AS THE SCIENTIST SUPREME SAID! LOOK AT WHAT IT DID!
HE TURNED THE BUILDING INTO...SOME KIND OF SLIME!
MOLECULE MAN'S WAND CAN CHANGE ANY KIND OF MOLECULE INTO ANY OTHER KIND OF MOLECULE, REMEMBER?
GET US OUT OF IT BEFORE WE DROWN!
GLORP!
I CAN'T SEE EXACTLY WHAT I'M AIMING FOR--
--BUT I HOPE THIS GRAPPLING HOOK HITS SOMETHING!
FTT!
WHAT DO YOU KNOW?
YOU'RE NOT COMPLETELY USELESS AFTER ALL, HAWKEYE!
VERY FUNNY. JUST MAKE SURE WE DON'T LOSE SIGHT OF OUR TARGET.
HE SAID IT'S HIS DAD'S WAND. THAT'S NOT MOLECULE MAN--
--IT'S MOLECULE KID.
THIS WAND IS ALL I HAVE LEFT OF MY FATHER! YOU'RE NOT TAKING IT FROM ME!
ZWASH
HE'S ESCAPING!
OUR MISSION'S BEEN EXPOSED! ABORT!
RRMMBB

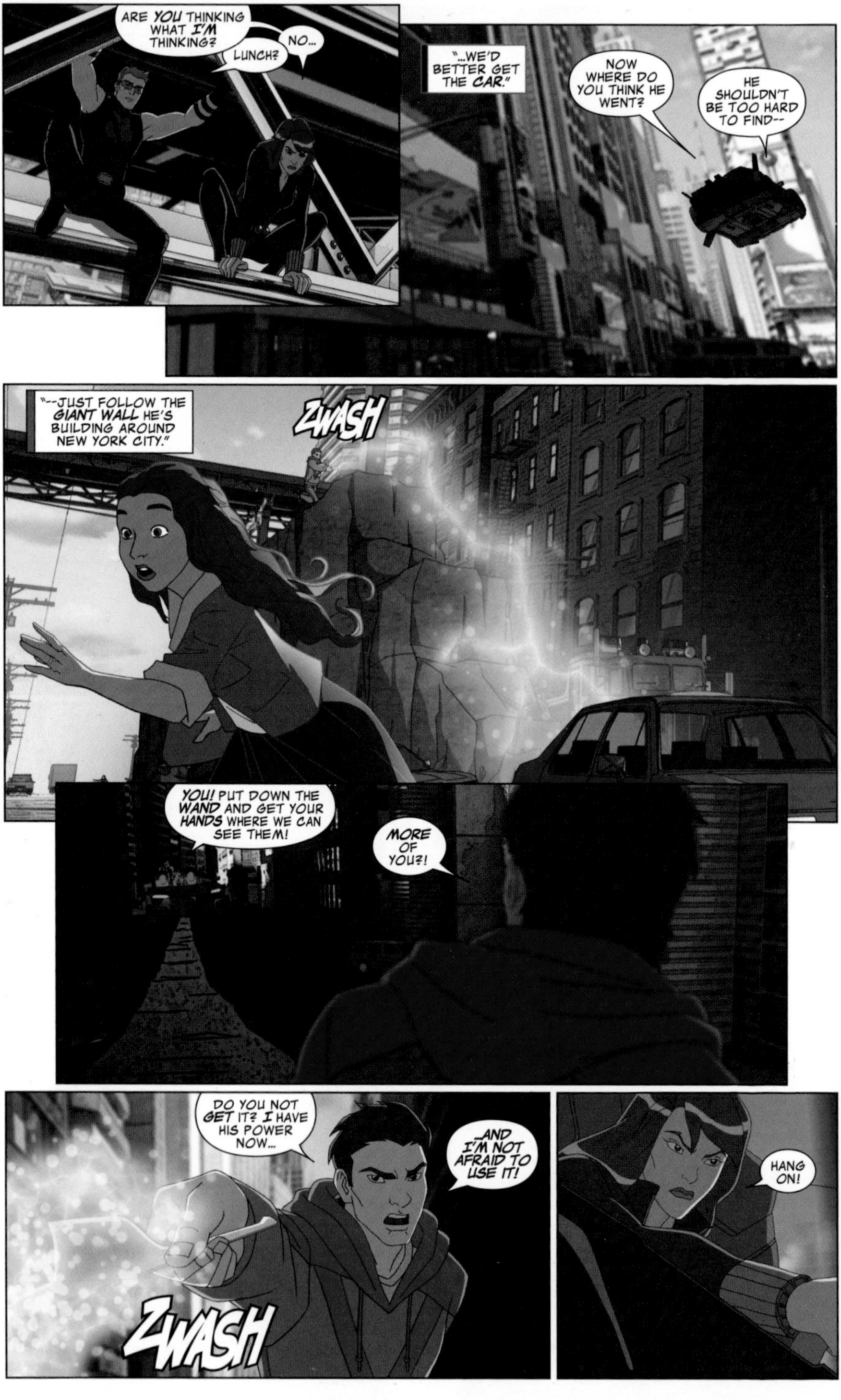
ARE YOU THINKING WHAT I'M THINKING?
LUNCH?
NO...
"...WE'D BETTER GET THE CAR."
NOW WHERE DO YOU THINK HE WENT?
HE SHOULDN'T BE TOO HARD TO FIND--
"--JUST FOLLOW THE GIANT WALL HE'S BUILDING AROUND NEW YORK CITY."
ZWASH
YOU! PUT DOWN THE WAND AND GET YOUR HANDS WHERE WE CAN SEE THEM!
MORE OF YOU?!
DO YOU NOT GET IT? I HAVE HIS POWER NOW...
...AND I'M NOT AFRAID TO USE IT!
ZWASH
HANG ON!

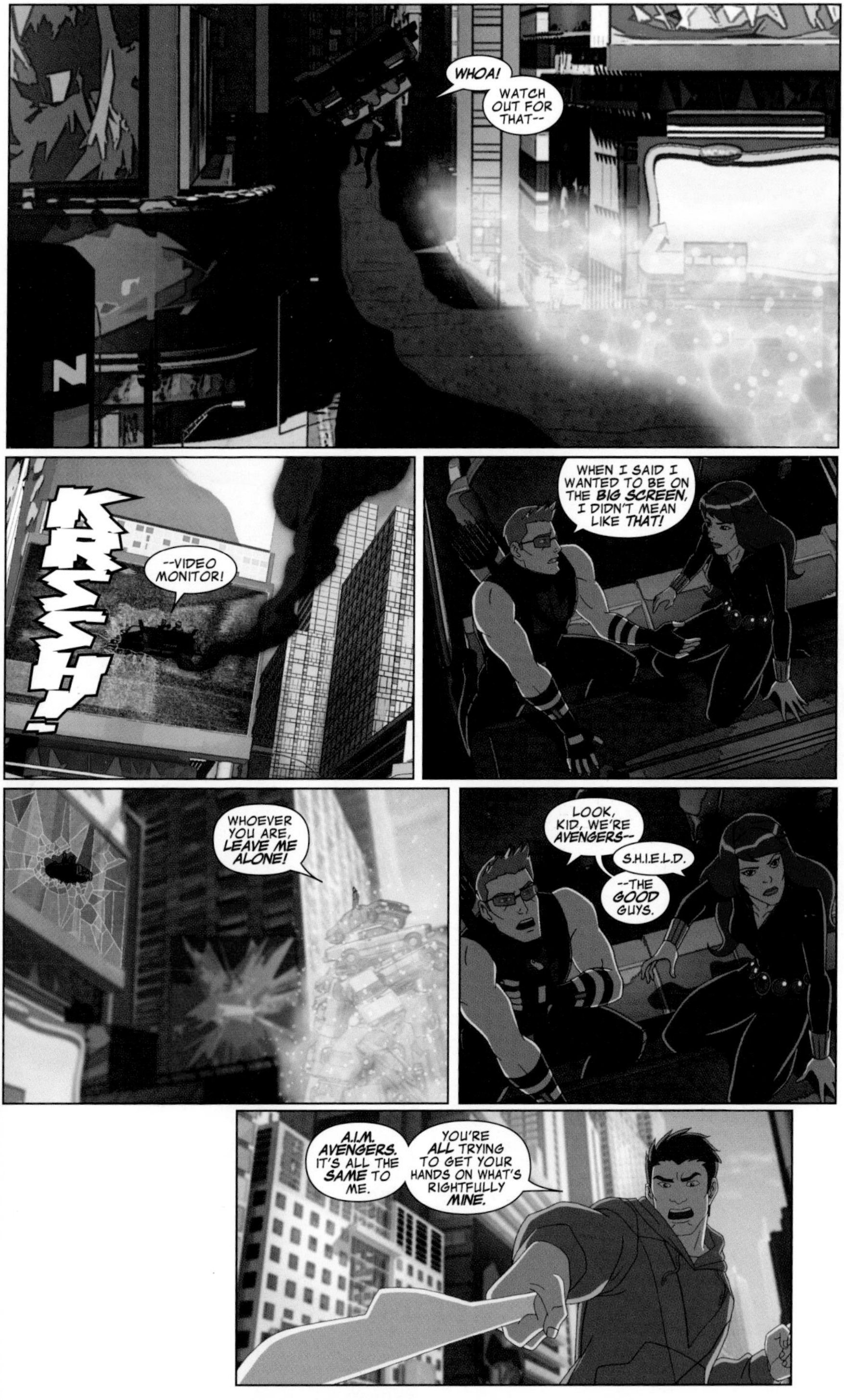
WHOA!
WATCH OUT FOR THAT--
KRSSH!
--VIDEO MONITOR!
WHEN I SAID I WANTED TO BE ON THE BIG SCREEN, I DIDN'T MEAN LIKE THAT!
WHOEVER YOU ARE, LEAVE ME ALONE!
LOOK, KID, WE'RE AVENGERS--
S.H.I.E.L.D.
--THE GOOD GUYS.
A.I.M. AVENGERS. IT'S ALL THE SAME TO ME.
YOU'RE ALL TRYING TO GET YOUR HANDS ON WHAT'S RIGHTFULLY MINE.

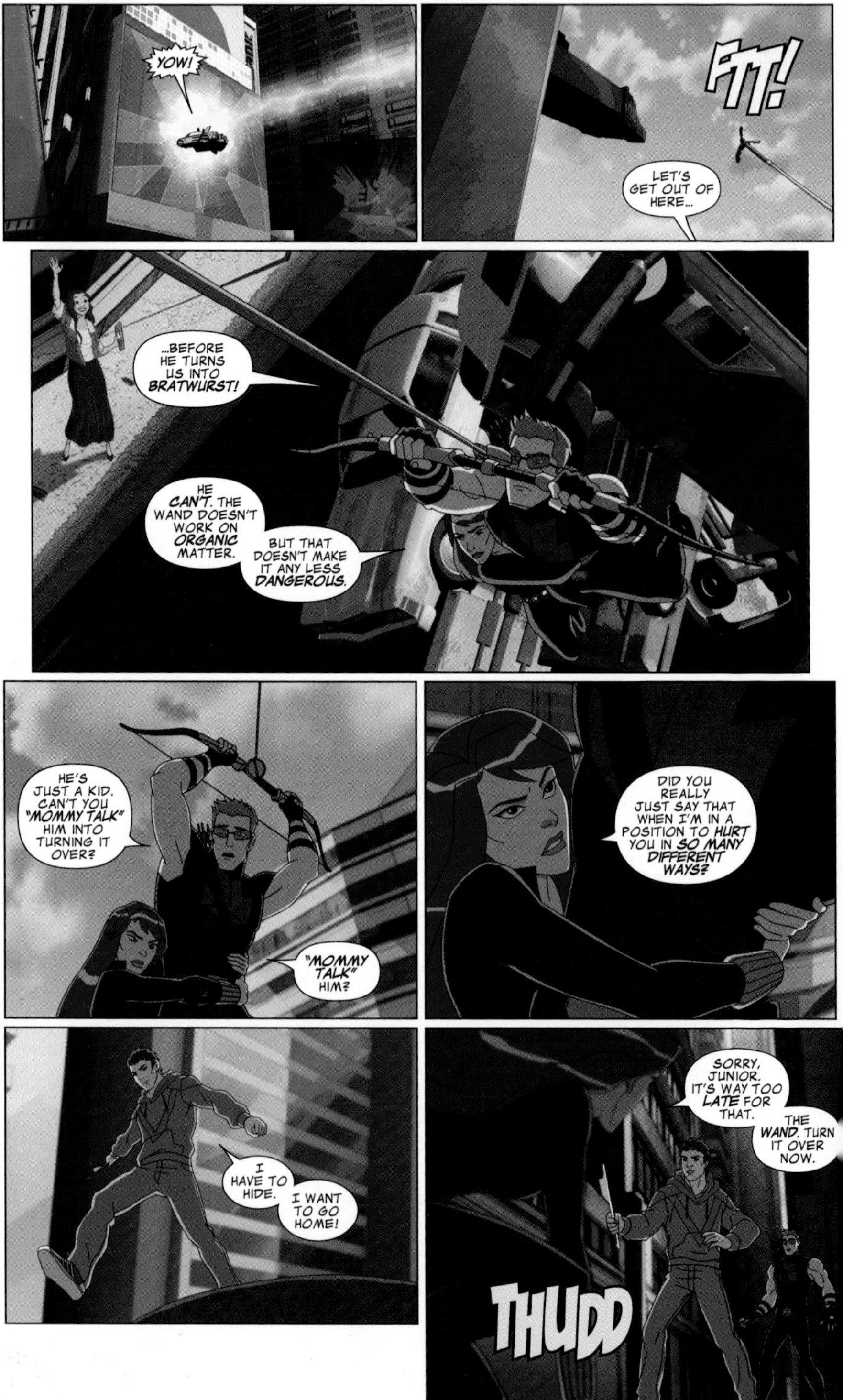
YOW!
FTT!
LET'S GET OUT OF HERE...
...BEFORE HE TURNS US INTO BRATWURST!
HE CAN'T. THE WAND DOESN'T WORK ON ORGANIC MATTER.
BUT THAT DOESN'T MAKE IT ANY LESS DANGEROUS.
HE'S JUST A KID. CAN'T YOU "MOMMY TALK" HIM INTO TURNING IT OVER?
"MOMMY TALK" HIM?
DID YOU REALLY JUST SAY THAT WHEN I'M IN A POSITION TO HURT YOU IN SO MANY DIFFERENT WAYS?
I HAVE TO HIDE.
I WANT TO GO HOME!
SORRY, JUNIOR. IT'S WAY TOO LATE FOR THAT.
THE WAND. TURN IT OVER NOW.
THUDD

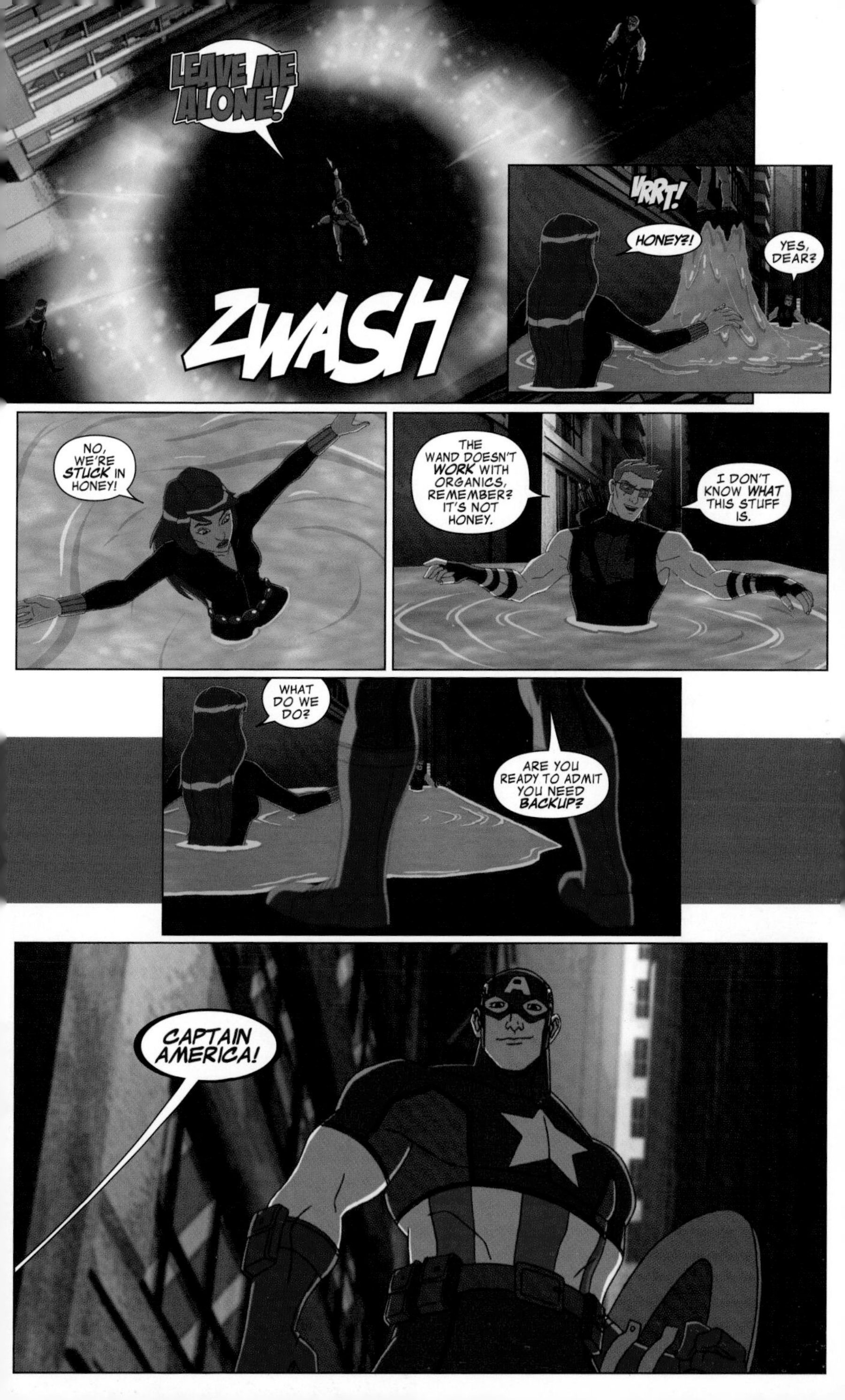
LEAVE ME ALONE!
ZWASH
VRRT!
HONEY?!
YES, DEAR?
NO, WE'RE STUCK IN HONEY!
THE WAND DOESN'T WORK WITH ORGANICS, REMEMBER? IT'S NOT HONEY.
I DON'T KNOW WHAT THIS STUFF IS.
WHAT DO WE DO?
ARE YOU READY TO ADMIT YOU NEED BACKUP?
CAPTAIN AMERICA!

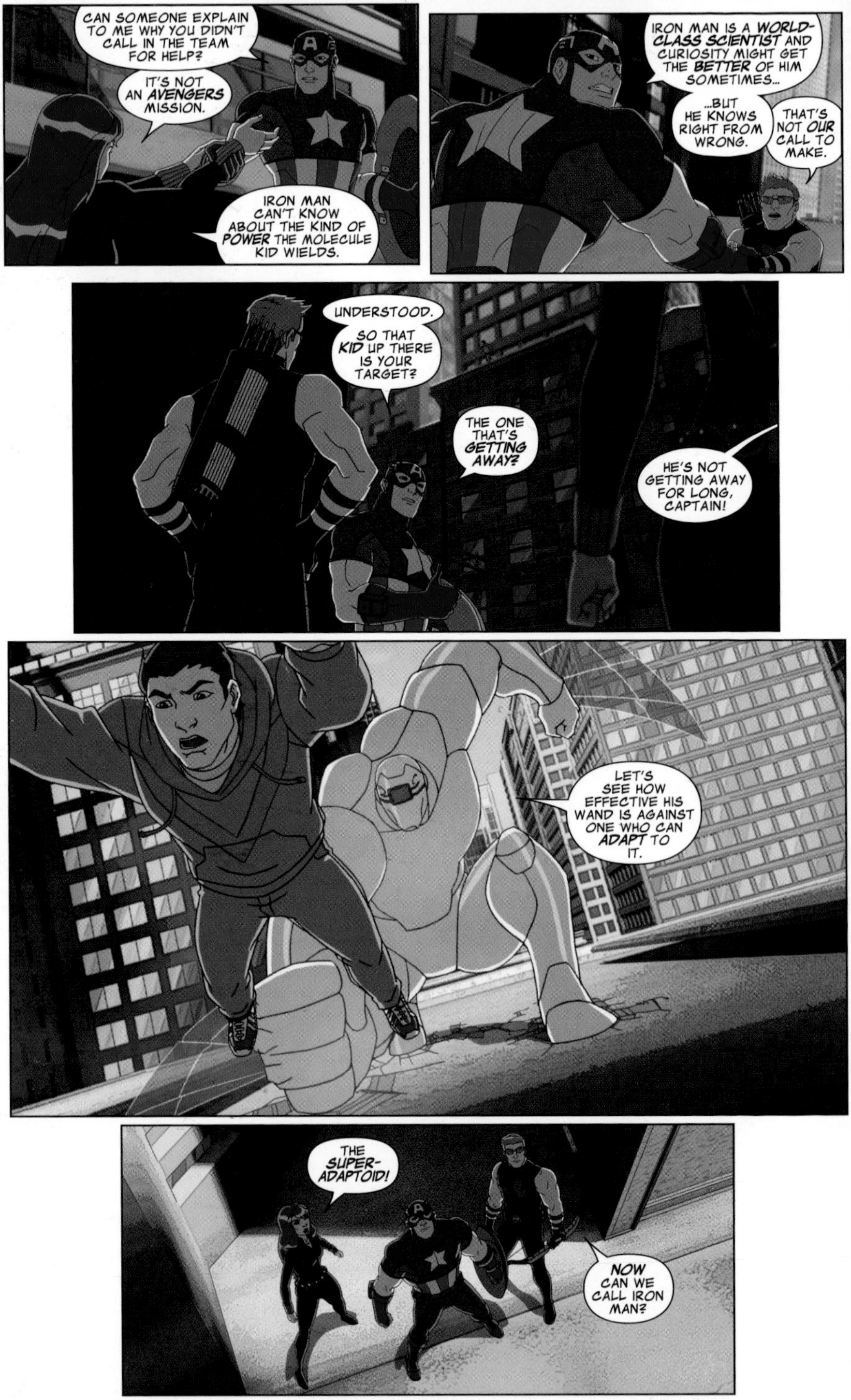
CAN SOMEONE EXPLAIN TO ME WHY YOU DIDN'T CALL IN THE TEAM FOR HELP?
IT'S NOT AN AVENGERS MISSION.
IRON MAN CAN'T KNOW ABOUT THE KIND OF POWER THE MOLECULE KID WIELDS.
IRON MAN IS A WORLD-CLASS SCIENTIST AND CURIOSITY MIGHT GET THE BETTER OF HIM SOMETIMES...
...BUT HE KNOWS RIGHT FROM WRONG.
THAT'S NOT OUR CALL TO MAKE.
UNDERSTOOD. SO THAT KID UP THERE IS YOUR TARGET?
THE ONE THAT'S GETTING AWAY?
HE'S NOT GETTING AWAY FOR LONG, CAPTAIN!
LET'S SEE HOW EFFECTIVE HIS WAND IS AGAINST ONE WHO CAN ADAPT TO IT.
THE SUPER-ADAPTOID!
NOW CAN WE CALL IRON MAN?

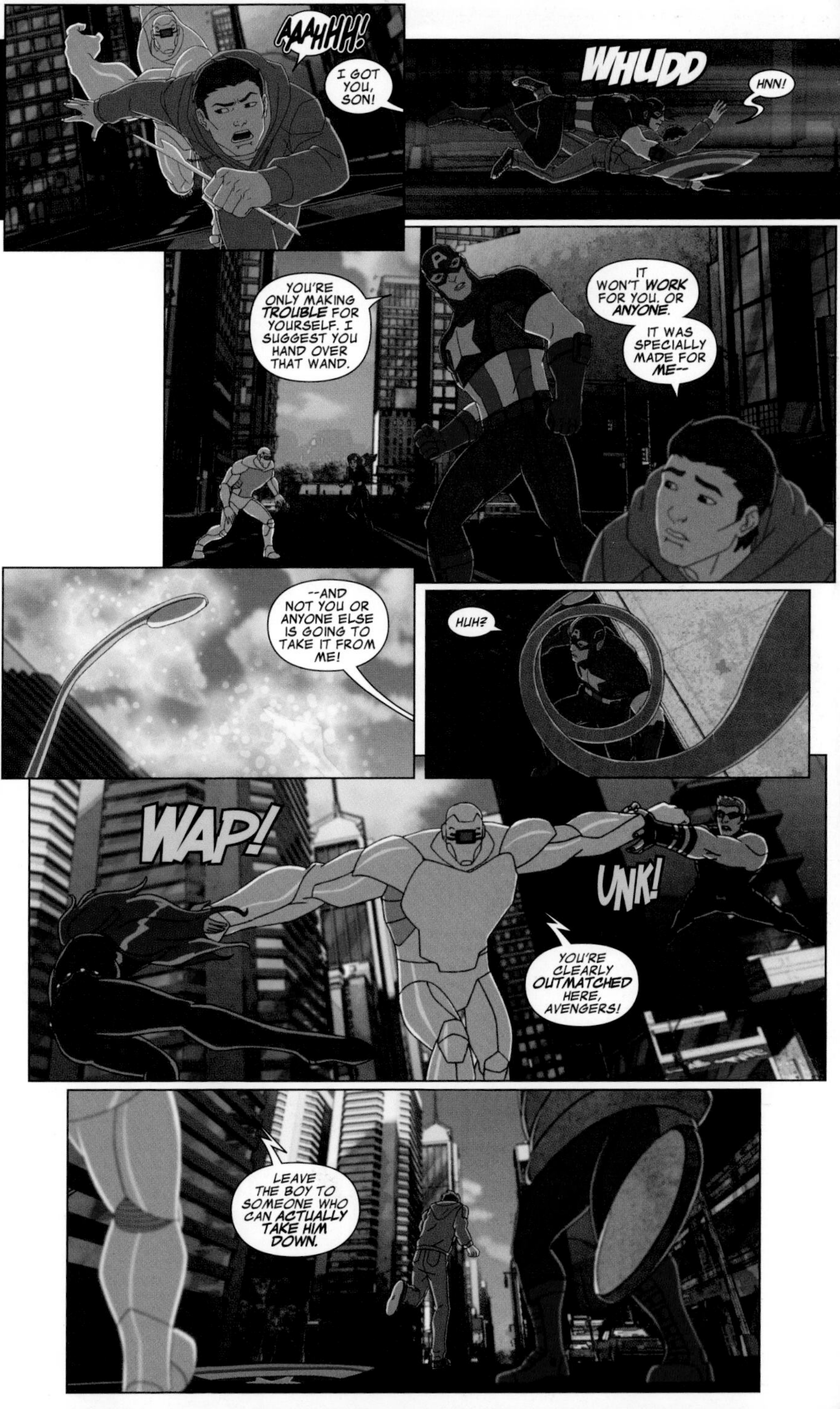
AAAHHH!
I GOT YOU, SON!
WHUDD
HNN!
YOU'RE ONLY MAKING TROUBLE FOR YOURSELF. I SUGGEST YOU HAND OVER THAT WAND.
IT WON'T WORK FOR YOU. OR ANYONE.
IT WAS SPECIALLY MADE FOR ME--
--AND NOT YOU OR ANYONE ELSE IS GOING TO TAKE IT FROM ME!
HUH?
WAP!
UNK!
YOU'RE CLEARLY OUTMATCHED HERE, AVENGERS!
LEAVE THE BOY TO SOMEONE WHO CAN ACTUALLY TAKE HIM DOWN.

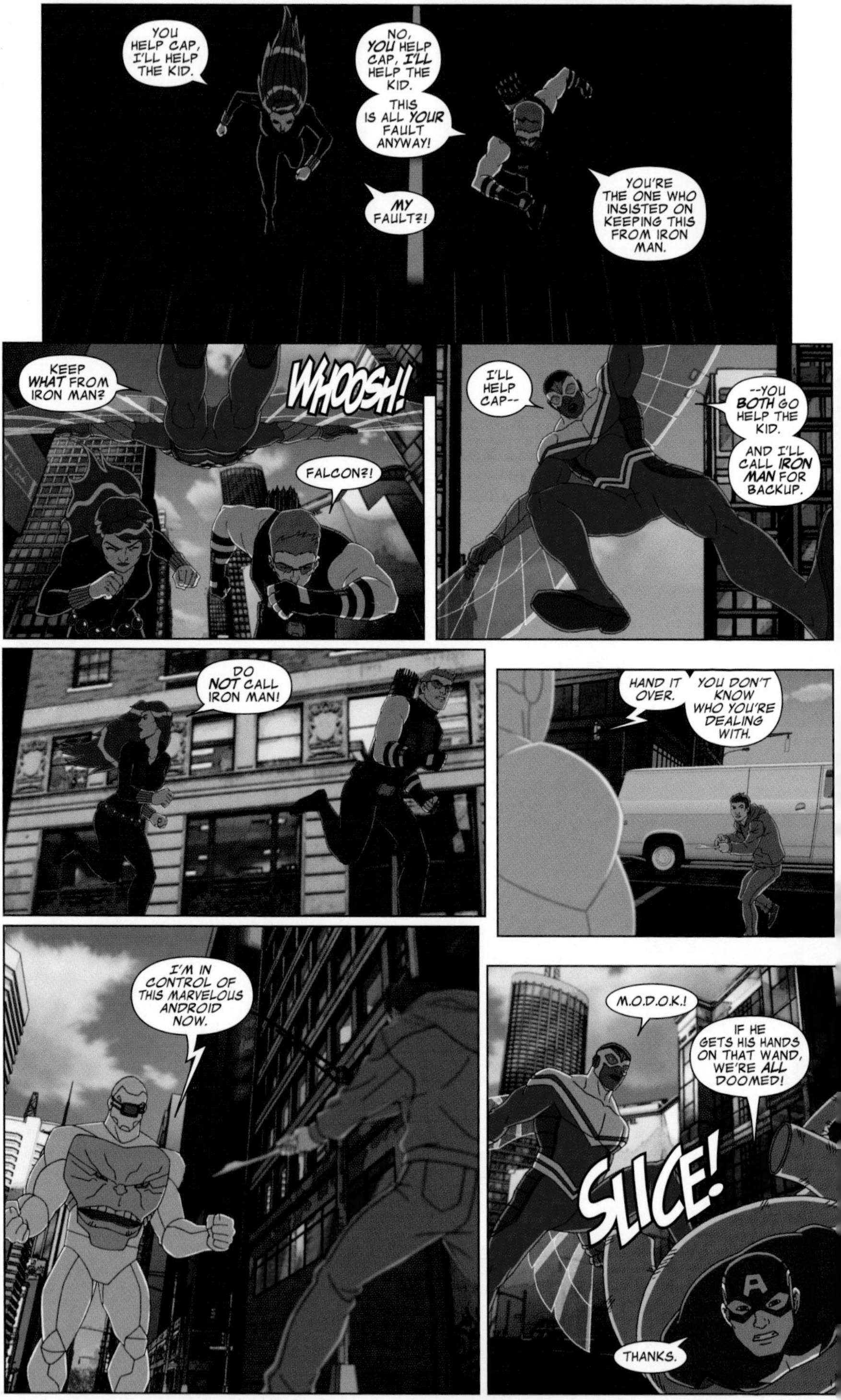
YOU HELP CAP, I'LL HELP THE KID.
NO, YOU HELP CAP, I'LL HELP THE KID.
THIS IS ALL YOUR FAULT ANYWAY!
MY FAULT?!
YOU'RE THE ONE WHO INSISTED ON KEEPING THIS FROM IRON MAN.
KEEP WHAT FROM IRON MAN?
WHOOSH!
FALCON?!
I'LL HELP CAP--
--YOU BOTH GO HELP THE KID.
AND I'LL CALL IRON MAN FOR BACKUP.
DO NOT CALL IRON MAN!
HAND IT OVER.
YOU DON'T KNOW WHO YOU'RE DEALING WITH.
I'M IN CONTROL OF THIS MARVELOUS ANDROID NOW.
M.O.D.O.K.!
IF HE GETS HIS HANDS ON THAT WAND, WE'RE ALL DOOMED!
SLICE!
THANKS.

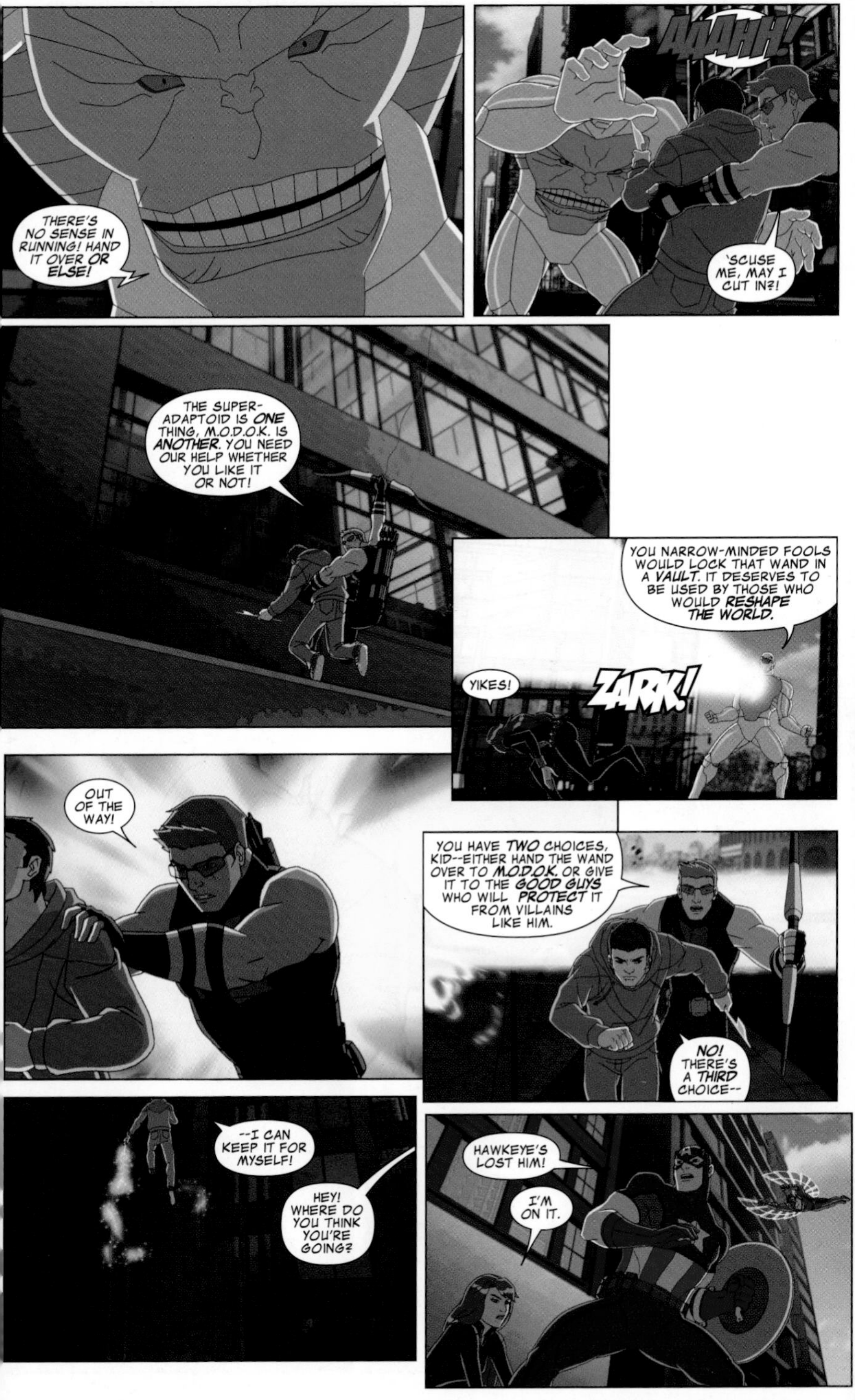
THERE'S NO SENSE IN RUNNING! HAND IT OVER OR ELSE!
AAAHH!
'SCUSE ME, MAY I CUT IN?!
THE SUPER-ADAPTOID IS ONE THING, M.O.D.O.K. IS ANOTHER. YOU NEED OUR HELP WHETHER YOU LIKE IT OR NOT!
YOU NARROW-MINDED FOOLS WOULD LOCK THAT WAND IN A VAULT. IT DESERVES TO BE USED BY THOSE WHO WOULD RESHAPE THE WORLD.
YIKES!
ZARK!
OUT OF THE WAY!
YOU HAVE TWO CHOICES, KID--EITHER HAND THE WAND OVER TO M.O.D.O.K. OR GIVE IT TO THE GOOD GUYS WHO WILL PROTECT IT FROM VILLAINS LIKE HIM.
NO! THERE'S A THIRD CHOICE--
--I CAN KEEP IT FOR MYSELF!
HEY! WHERE DO YOU THINK YOU'RE GOING?
HAWKEYE'S LOST HIM!
I'M ON IT.

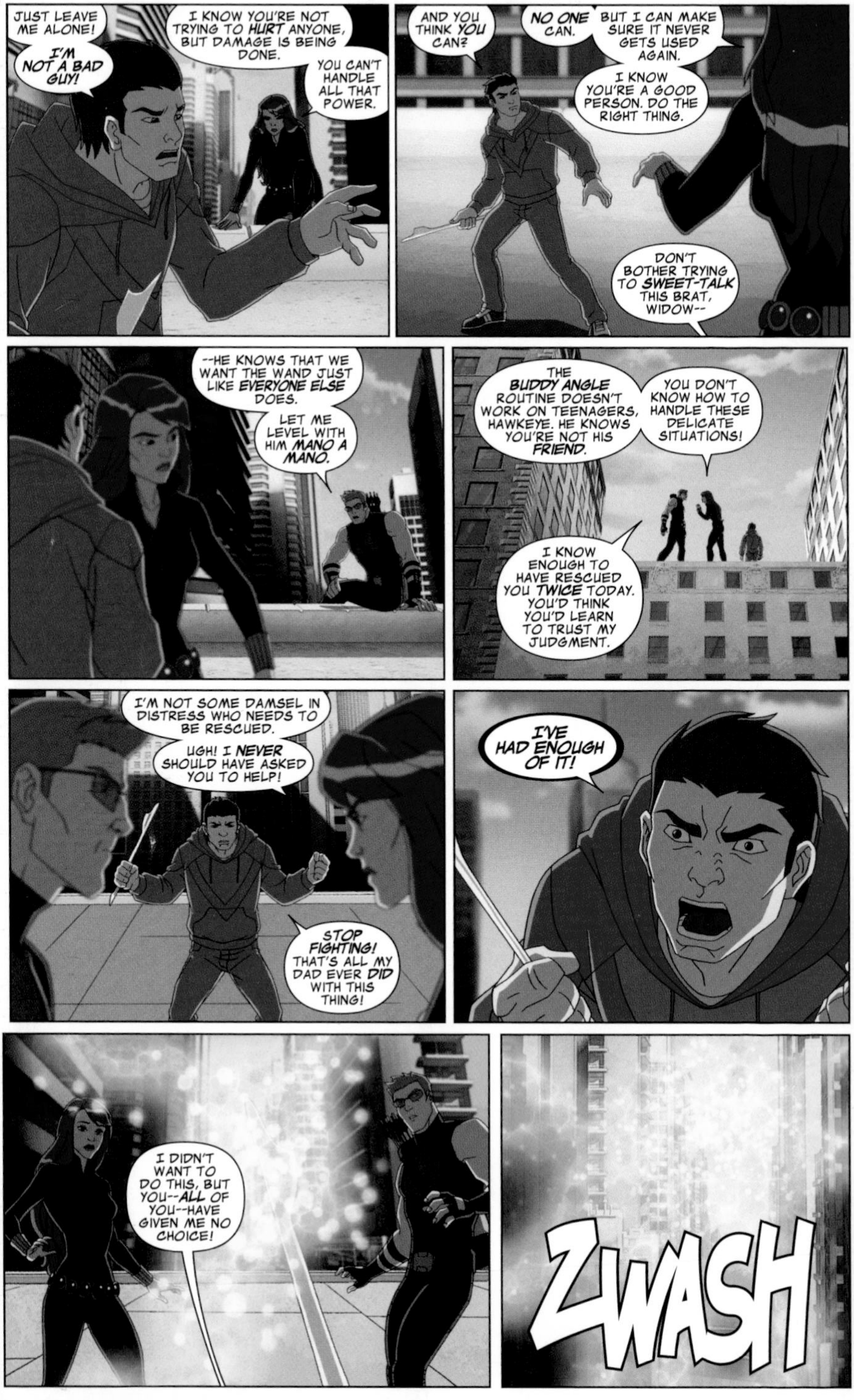
JUST LEAVE ME ALONE!
I'M NOT A BAD GUY!
I KNOW YOU'RE NOT TRYING TO HURT ANYONE, BUT DAMAGE IS BEING DONE.
YOU CAN'T HANDLE ALL THAT POWER.
AND YOU THINK YOU CAN?
NO ONE CAN.
BUT I CAN MAKE SURE IT NEVER GETS USED AGAIN.
I KNOW YOU'RE A GOOD PERSON. DO THE RIGHT THING.
DON'T BOTHER TRYING TO SWEET-TALK THIS BRAT, WIDOW--
--HE KNOWS THAT WE WANT THE WAND JUST LIKE EVERYONE ELSE DOES.
LET ME LEVEL WITH HIM MANO A MANO.
THE BUDDY ANGLE ROUTINE DOESN'T WORK ON TEENAGERS, HAWKEYE. HE KNOWS YOU'RE NOT HIS FRIEND.
YOU DON'T KNOW HOW TO HANDLE THESE DELICATE SITUATIONS!
I KNOW ENOUGH TO HAVE RESCUED YOU TWICE TODAY. YOU'D THINK YOU'D LEARN TO TRUST MY JUDGMENT.
I'M NOT SOME DAMSEL IN DISTRESS WHO NEEDS TO BE RESCUED.
UGH! I NEVER SHOULD HAVE ASKED YOU TO HELP!
STOP FIGHTING! THAT'S ALL MY DAD EVER DID WITH THIS THING!
I'VE HAD ENOUGH OF IT!
I DIDN'T WANT TO DO THIS, BUT YOU--ALL OF YOU--HAVE GIVEN ME NO CHOICE!
ZWASH

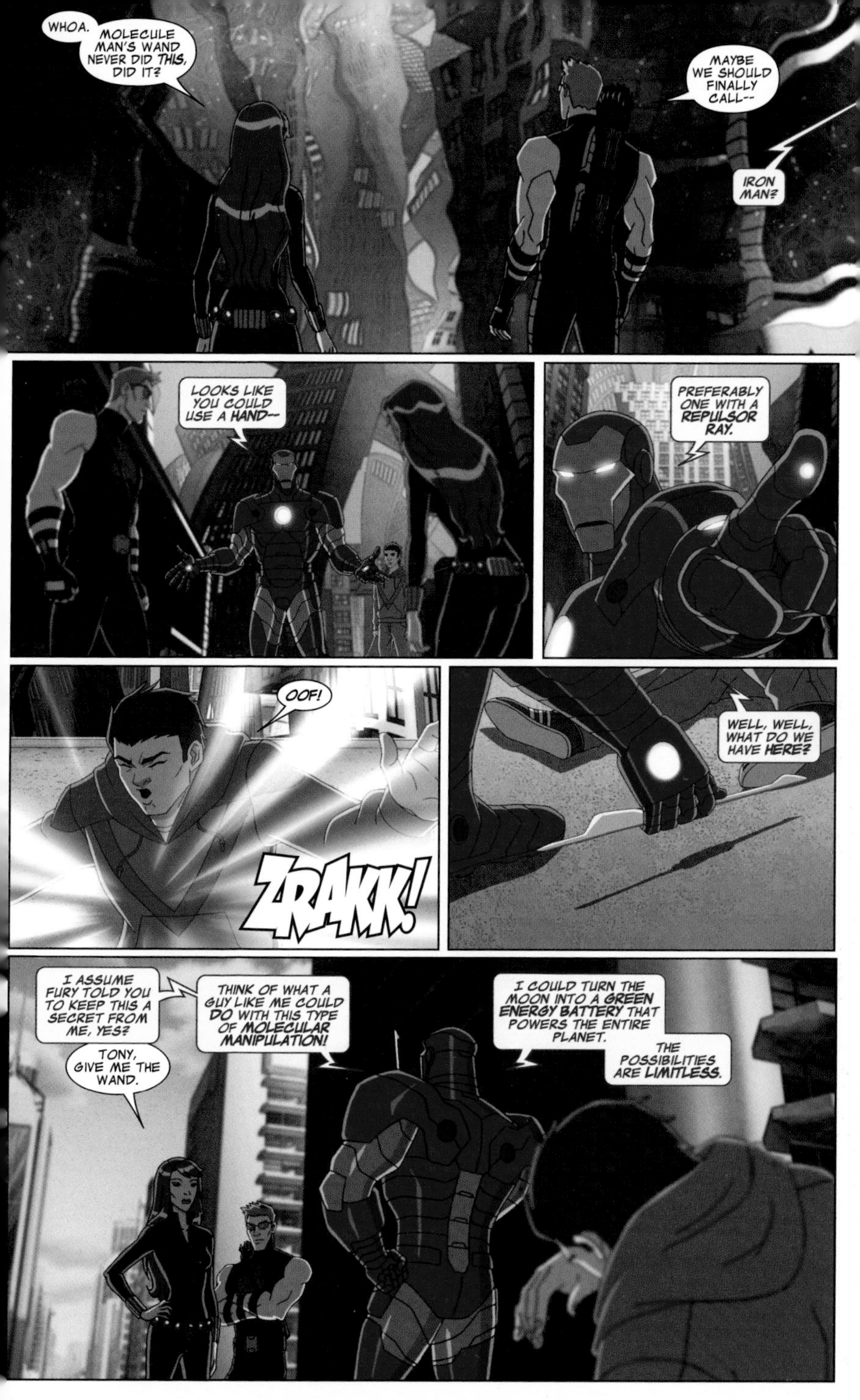
WHOA.
MOLECULE MAN'S WAND NEVER DID THIS, DID IT?
MAYBE WE SHOULD FINALLY CALL--
IRON MAN?
LOOKS LIKE YOU COULD USE A HAND--
PREFERABLY ONE WITH A REPULSOR RAY.
OOF!
ZRAKK!
WELL, WELL, WHAT DO WE HAVE HERE?
I ASSUME FURY TOLD YOU TO KEEP THIS A SECRET FROM ME, YES?
TONY, GIVE ME THE WAND.
THINK OF WHAT A GUY LIKE ME COULD DO WITH THIS TYPE OF MOLECULAR MANIPULATION!
I COULD TURN THE MOON INTO A GREEN ENERGY BATTERY THAT POWERS THE ENTIRE PLANET.
THE POSSIBILITIES ARE LIMITLESS.

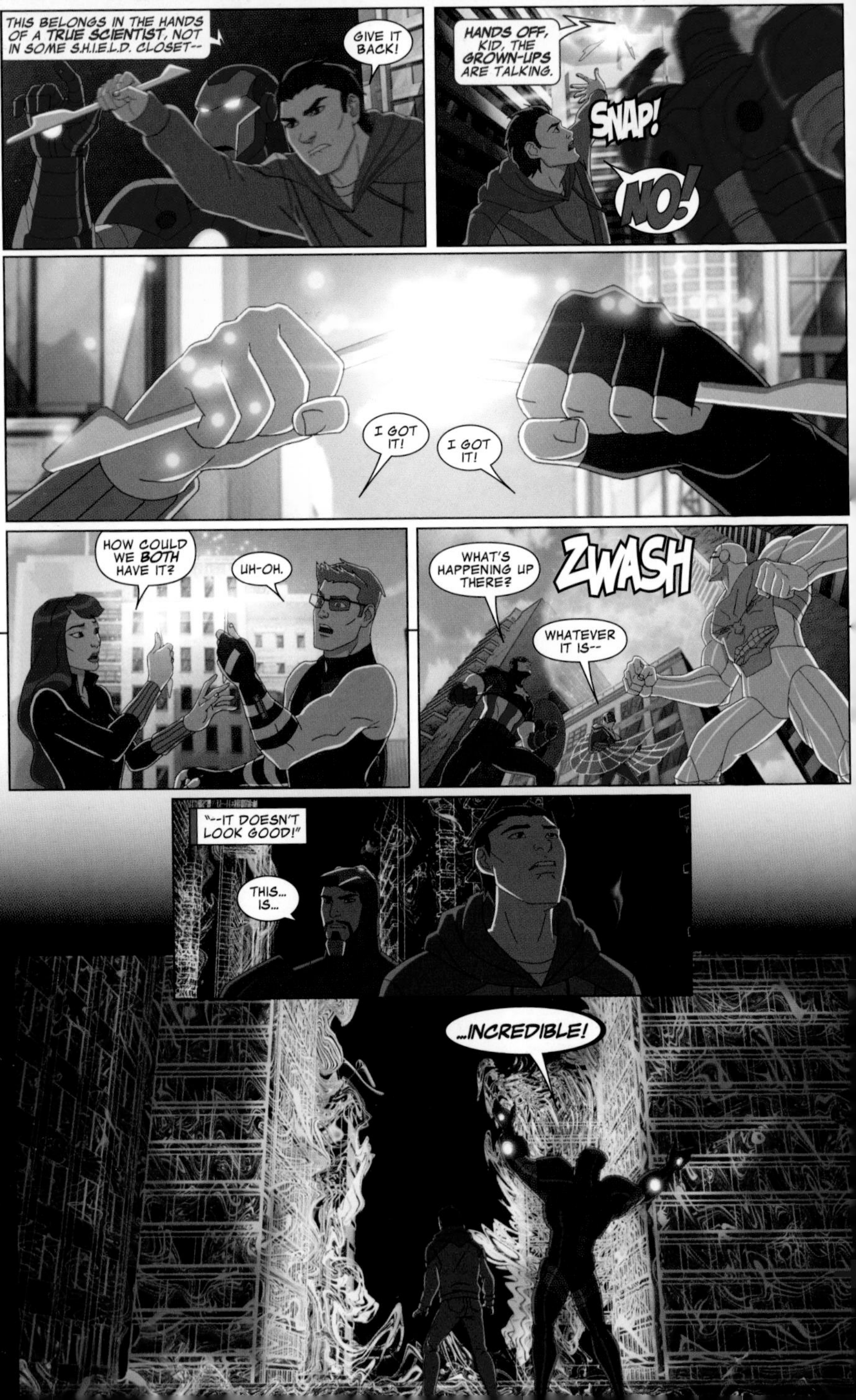
THIS BELONGS IN THE HANDS OF A **TRUE SCIENTIST**, NOT IN SOME S.H.I.E.L.D. CLOSET--
GIVE IT BACK!
HANDS OFF, KID, THE GROWN-UPS ARE TALKING.
SNAP!
NO!
I GOT IT!
I GOT IT!
HOW COULD WE **BOTH** HAVE IT?
UH-OH.
WHAT'S HAPPENING UP THERE?
ZWASH
WHATEVER IT IS--
"--IT DOESN'T LOOK GOOD!"
THIS... IS...
...INCREDIBLE!

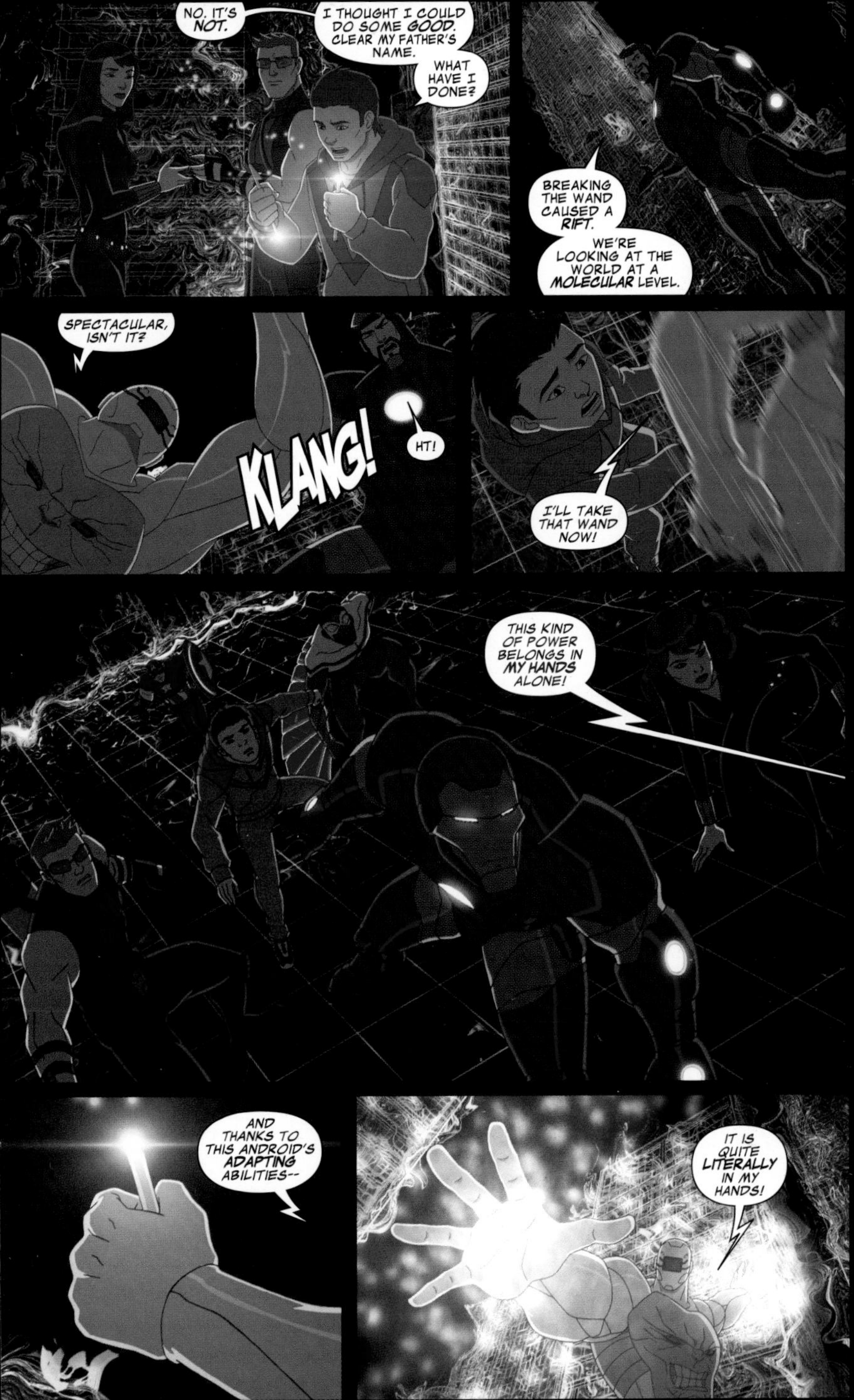
NO. IT'S NOT.
I THOUGHT I COULD DO SOME GOOD. CLEAR MY FATHER'S NAME.
WHAT HAVE I DONE?
BREAKING THE WAND CAUSED A RIFT.
WE'RE LOOKING AT THE WORLD AT A MOLECULAR LEVEL.
SPECTACULAR, ISN'T IT?
KLANG!
HT!
I'LL TAKE THAT WAND NOW!
THIS KIND OF POWER BELONGS IN MY HANDS ALONE!
AND THANKS TO THIS ANDROID'S ADAPTING ABILITIES--
IT IS QUITE LITERALLY IN MY HANDS!

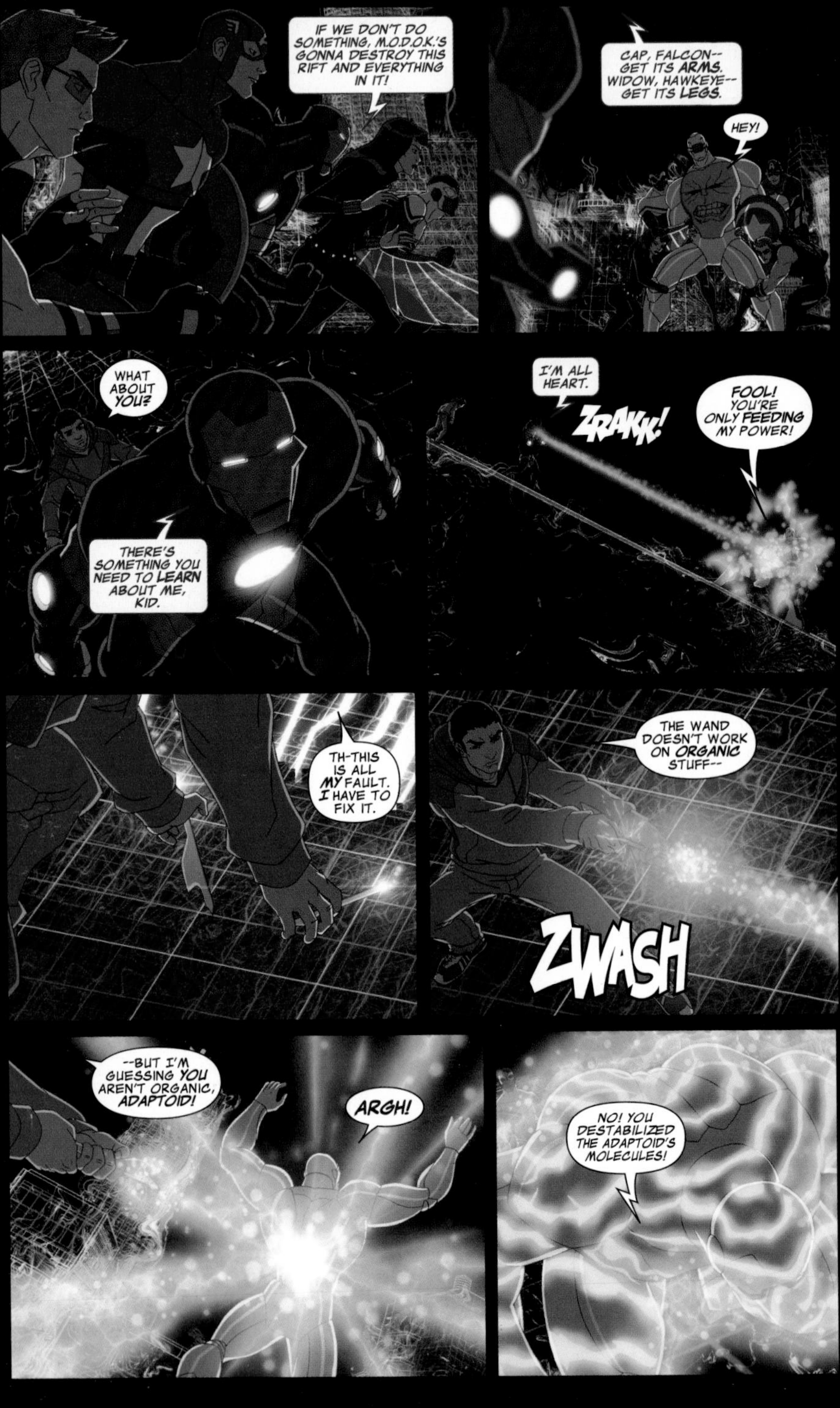
IF WE DON'T DO SOMETHING, M.O.D.O.K.'S GONNA DESTROY THIS RIFT AND EVERYTHING IN IT!
CAP, FALCON-- GET ITS ARMS. WIDOW, HAWKEYE-- GET ITS LEGS.
HEY!
WHAT ABOUT YOU?
THERE'S SOMETHING YOU NEED TO LEARN ABOUT ME, KID.
I'M ALL HEART.
ZRAKK!
FOOL! YOU'RE ONLY FEEDING MY POWER!
TH-THIS IS ALL MY FAULT. I HAVE TO FIX IT.
THE WAND DOESN'T WORK ON ORGANIC STUFF--
ZWASH
--BUT I'M GUESSING YOU AREN'T ORGANIC, ADAPTOID!
ARGH!
NO! YOU DESTABILIZED THE ADAPTOID'S MOLECULES!

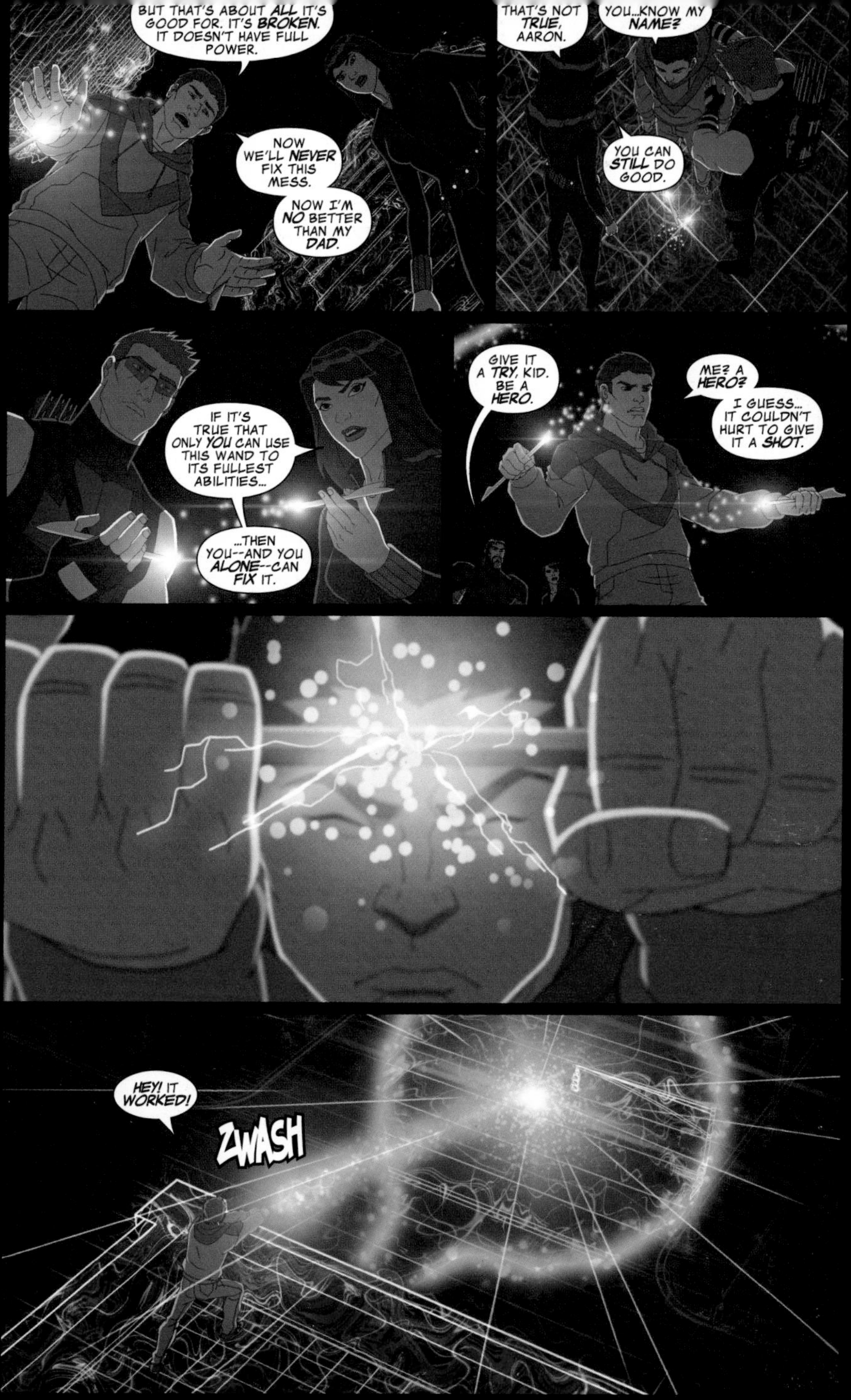
BUT THAT'S ABOUT ALL IT'S GOOD FOR. IT'S BROKEN. IT DOESN'T HAVE FULL POWER.
NOW WE'LL NEVER FIX THIS MESS.
NOW I'M NO BETTER THAN MY DAD.
THAT'S NOT TRUE, AARON.
YOU...KNOW MY NAME?
YOU CAN STILL DO GOOD.
IF IT'S TRUE THAT ONLY YOU CAN USE THIS WAND TO ITS FULLEST ABILITIES...
...THEN YOU--AND YOU ALONE--CAN FIX IT.
GIVE IT A TRY, KID. BE A HERO.
ME? A HERO?
I GUESS... IT COULDN'T HURT TO GIVE IT A SHOT.
HEY! IT WORKED!
ZWASH

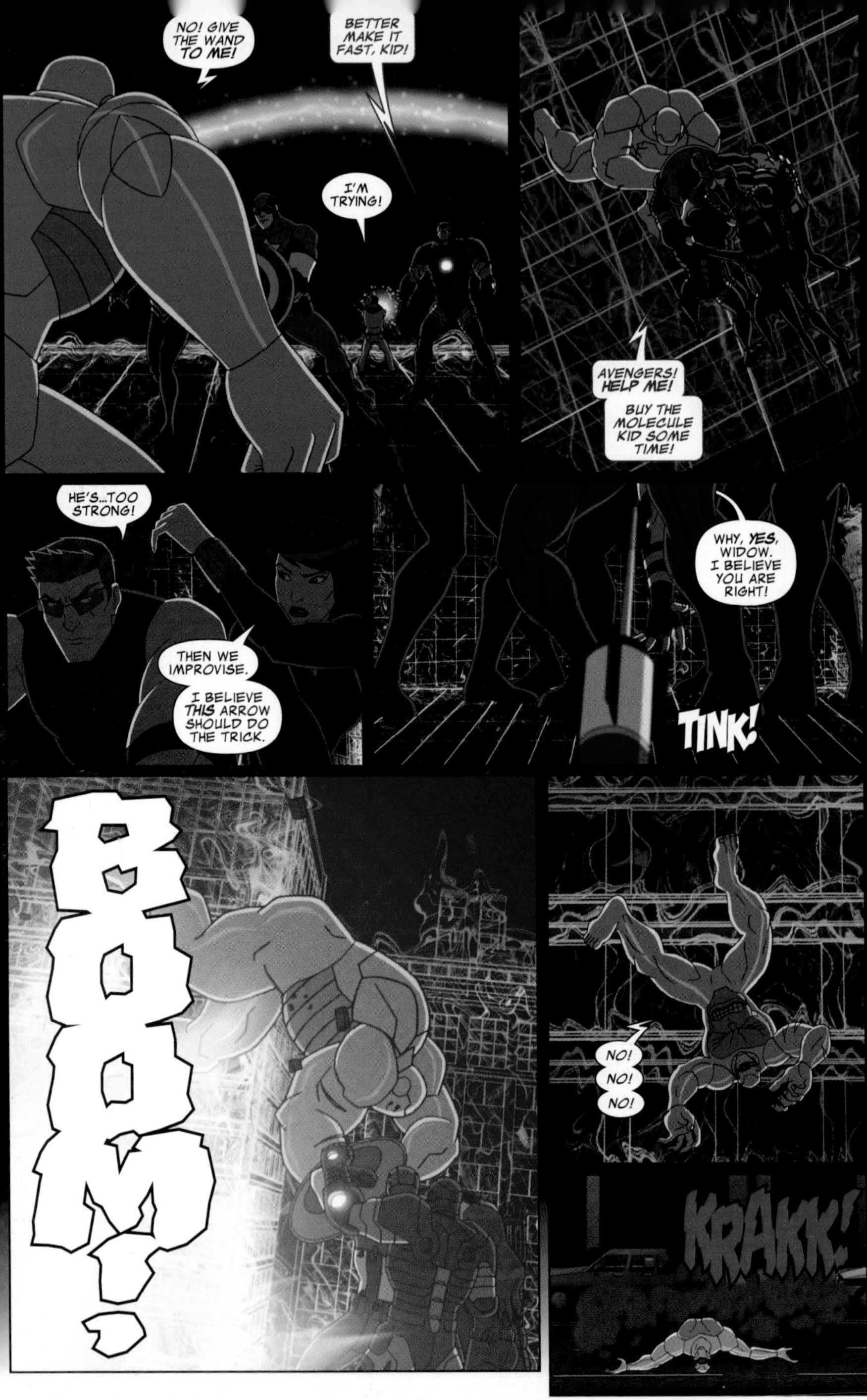
NO! GIVE THE WAND TO ME!
BETTER MAKE IT FAST, KID!
I'M TRYING!
AVENGERS! HELP ME!
BUY THE MOLECULE KID SOME TIME!
HE'S...TOO STRONG!
THEN WE IMPROVISE.
I BELIEVE THIS ARROW SHOULD DO THE TRICK.
WHY, YES, WIDOW. I BELIEVE YOU ARE RIGHT!
TINK!
BOOM!
NO! NO! NO!
KRAKK!

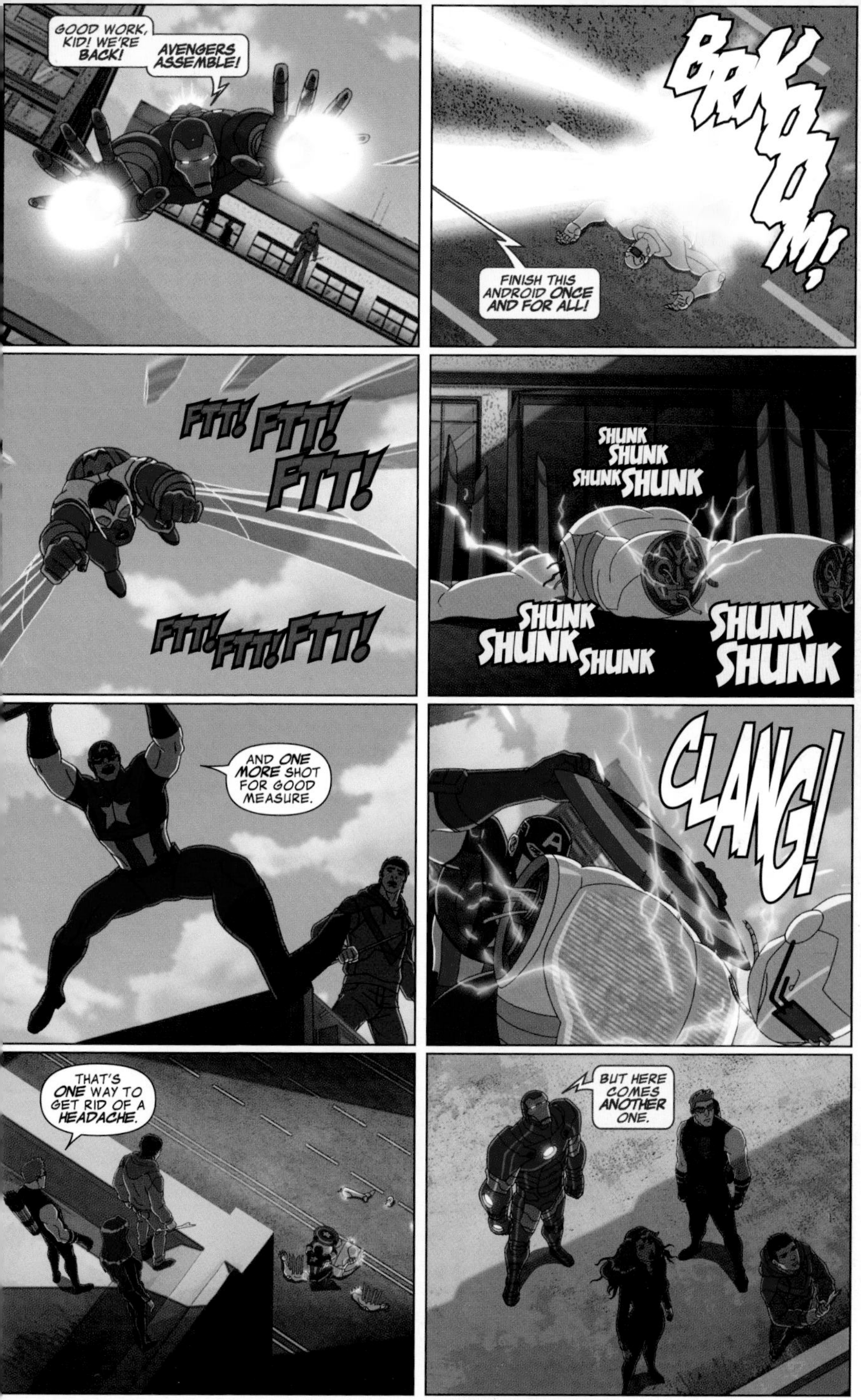
GOOD WORK, KID! WE'RE BACK!
AVENGERS ASSEMBLE!
BRKOOOM!
FINISH THIS ANDROID ONCE AND FOR ALL!
FTT! FTT! FTT!
FTT! FTT! FTT!
SHUNK SHUNK SHUNK SHUNK
SHUNK SHUNK SHUNK
SHUNK SHUNK
AND ONE MORE SHOT FOR GOOD MEASURE.
CLANG!
THAT'S ONE WAY TO GET RID OF A HEADACHE.
BUT HERE COMES ANOTHER ONE.

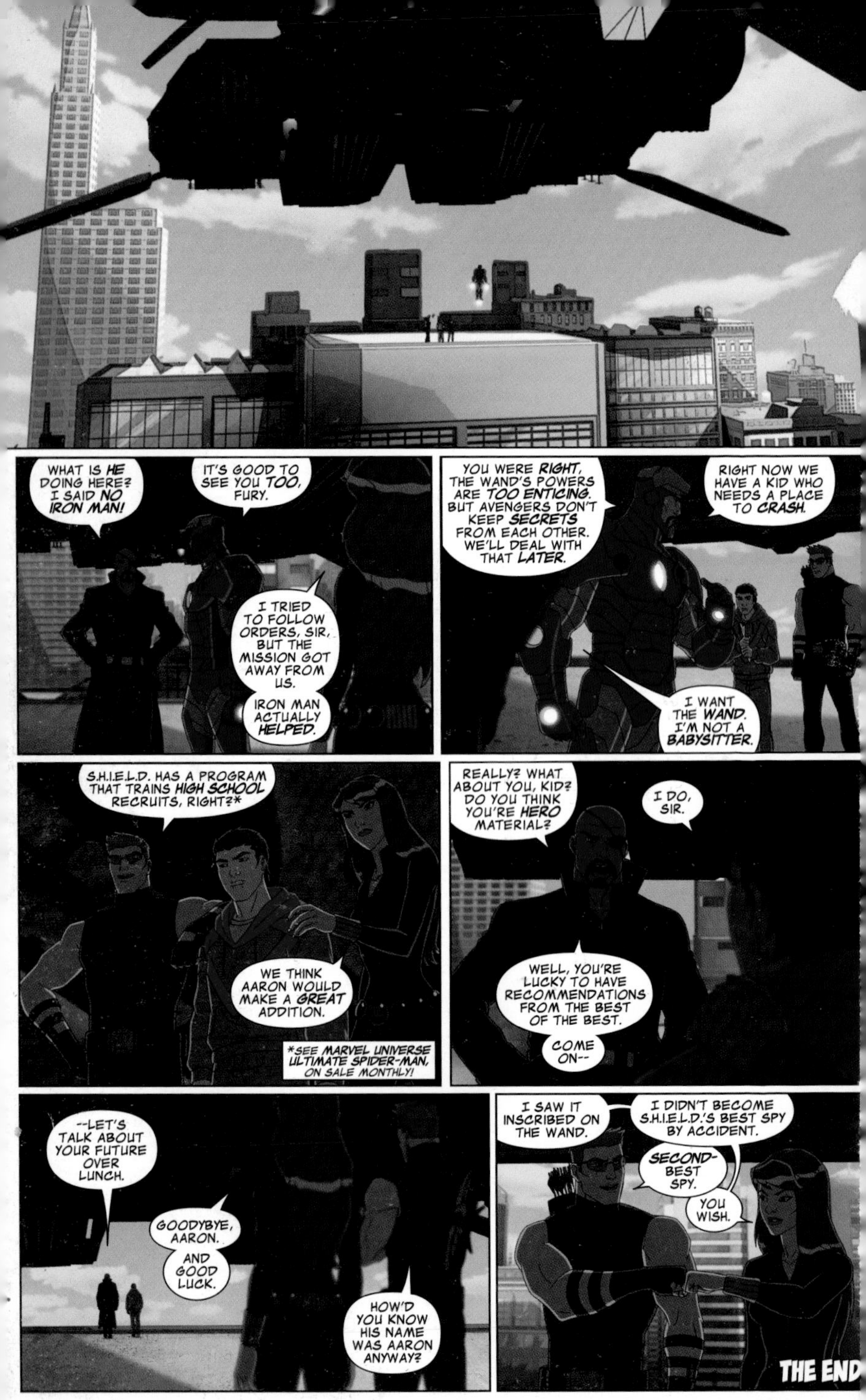
WHAT IS HE DOING HERE? I SAID NO IRON MAN!
IT'S GOOD TO SEE YOU TOO, FURY.
I TRIED TO FOLLOW ORDERS, SIR, BUT THE MISSION GOT AWAY FROM US.
IRON MAN ACTUALLY HELPED.
YOU WERE RIGHT, THE WAND'S POWERS ARE TOO ENTICING. BUT AVENGERS DON'T KEEP SECRETS FROM EACH OTHER. WE'LL DEAL WITH THAT LATER.
RIGHT NOW WE HAVE A KID WHO NEEDS A PLACE TO CRASH.
I WANT THE WAND. I'M NOT A BABYSITTER.
S.H.I.E.L.D. HAS A PROGRAM THAT TRAINS HIGH SCHOOL RECRUITS, RIGHT?*
WE THINK AARON WOULD MAKE A GREAT ADDITION.
*SEE MARVEL UNIVERSE ULTIMATE SPIDER-MAN, ON SALE MONTHLY!
REALLY? WHAT ABOUT YOU, KID? DO YOU THINK YOU'RE HERO MATERIAL?
I DO, SIR.
WELL, YOU'RE LUCKY TO HAVE RECOMMENDATIONS FROM THE BEST OF THE BEST.
COME ON--
--LET'S TALK ABOUT YOUR FUTURE OVER LUNCH.
GOODYBYE, AARON.
AND GOOD LUCK.
HOW'D YOU KNOW HIS NAME WAS AARON ANYWAY?
I SAW IT INSCRIBED ON THE WAND.
I DIDN'T BECOME S.H.I.E.L.D.'S BEST SPY BY ACCIDENT.
SECOND-BEST SPY.
YOU WISH.
THE END